W9-BFU-345

A S Q C
LIBRARY

JF
1525
.T 67
C 37
1990
c. 1

EXCELLENCE IN GOVERNMENT

Total Quality Management In The 1990s

by:
David K. Carr
Ian D. Littman

Coopers
&Lybrand

Copyright 1990 by Coopers & Lybrand

Bulk quantities of this book may be obtained from Federal TQM Services, Coopers & Lybrand, 1525 Wilson Blvd., Arlington, VA 22209. Phone (703) 875-2000.

All rights reserved. No part of this book may be reproduced or transmitted in any form or by any means, electronic or mechanical, including photocopying, recording, or by any information storage and retrieval system, without the written permission of Coopers & Lybrand.

Second printing, June 1991

Carr, David K. and Ian D. Littman

Excellence in Government: Total Quality Management in the 1990s

Library of Congress Catalog Number 90-084020

ISBN 0-944533-01-9

This book is dedicated to
all those in government who are
taking the risks needed to improve
the quality of public service

Table of Contents

Section 3: Making the Transformation

Acknowledgements

We express our appreciation to the organizations that contributed the time, information, and examples that made this book possible. These include:

U.S. Department of Agriculture

    Forest Service
    Ochoco National Forest

U.S. Air Force

    Aeronautical Systems Division
    Air Force Development Test Center
    Air Force Systems Command
    Ballistics Systems Division
    Electronic Systems Division
    Rome, N.Y., Air Development Center

U.S. Army

    Sacramento, Calif., Army Depot
    U.S. Army Accounting and Finance Center
    Watervliet, N.Y., Army Arsenal

AT&T

    Atlanta, Ga., Works
    Network Systems, Morristown, N.J.
    Shreveport, La., Works

U.S. Bureau of Indian Affairs
Navajo Area Office, Window Rock, Ariz.

State of California

Central Intelligence Agency

U.S. Coast Guard

Headquarters Division

U.S. Department of Commerce

Patent and Trademark Office

U.S. Department of Defense

Defense Commercial Communications Office
Defense Industrial Supply Center
Defense Logistics Agency
Office of Industrial Production and Quality

U.S. Department of Education

Division of Quality Assurance

U.S. Department of Energy

U.S. Environmental Protection Agency

U.S. Equal Employment Opportunity Commission

Federal Aviation Administration

Federal Quality Institute

Florida Department of Transportation, District 1,
Deland, Fla.

U.S. General Services Administration

Office of Physical Security and Law Enforcement

Internal Revenue Service

Cincinnati, Ohio, Fresno, Calif., and Ogden, Utah,
Service Centers

State of Michigan

Department of Commerce

National Aeronautics and Space Administration

Lewis Research Center, Cleveland, Ohio
Johnson Space Center, Houston, Tex.

U.S. Navy

Cherry Point, N.C. , Jacksonville, Fla., and Pensacola
Fla., Naval Aviation Depots
Combat Systems, Field Operations, and Ordnance
Support Group (NAVSEA 06G)
Crane, Ind., Naval Weapons Support Center
Naval Air Systems Command
Naval Avionics Center
Naval Facilities Engineering Command
Naval Industrial Improvement Program
Naval Publications and Forms Center
Navy Personnel Research and Development Center
Norfolk, Va., Public Works Center
Philadelphia, Pa., and Norfolk, Va., Naval Shipyards
Yorktown, Va., Naval Weapons Station

Northeast Wisconsin Quality Improvement
Network, Green Bay, Wis.

U.S. Social Security Administration, Dallas Regional Office

U.S. Department of Veterans Affairs

Veterans Affairs Medical Center, Kansas City, Mo.
Veterans Affairs Regional Office and Insurance
Center, Philadelphia, Pa.

County of Volusia, Fla.

City of Wilmington, N.C.

State of Wisconsin
  Department of Employment Relations, Employment
    and Training Office
  Department of Motor Vehicles, Bureau of
    Vehicle Services

We especially wish to thank the following people for sharing with us their quality journeys: George Allen, Ernst Becker, Michael Beha, J.T.Benn III, Ken Biddle, Theresa Brelsford, Carolyn Burstein, Dennis Cronin, Gregory Conway, Patrick Cummings, Martha Curry, Jodi Davenport, Patsy Davis, Scott Dillion, Richard Engel, Kenneth Fletcher, Jim Hamilton, Richard Hankinson, L.J. Hatala, Maureen Hlavacek, Charles Hooper, Janice Hopkins, Tom Kelly, Richard Kesteven, Ken Kittridge, Kai-Peter Koenig, Paul Koons, Edward Kubasiewicz, Betty Ledewitz, William Lindahl, John Loh, Merline Lovelace, Jeffrey Manthos, Paul Michaels, John Scott McAllister, Marilyn Mozingo, Lee Pollock, Everett Pyatt, Ken Staten, Barbara Shatto, David Steigman, Michele Steinhauer, James Stevens, Dan Stewart, Leslie Sullivan, the UNITY team, Noel Wall, James Wright, and Marilyn Zuckerman.

We appreciate the fine technical insights of our Coopers & Lybrand advisors Phil Odeen, Joe Kehoe, Cliff Cooksey, Sam Feinberg, John Condon, Gene Ganassi, Mike Schutta, Jim Dillard, Jeff Kellogg, and Donnee Ramelli.

Finally, this book would not have been possible without the work of its editors Steve Clyburn and Joy Mara, and graphic artists Aleta Hargett and Rob Bartolo, cartoonist Keith Braxton, production chief Terri Custer, and typists Gwendolyn Denny and Patricia Whalen.

Introduction

For the past five years government and industry organizations have been experimenting with or implementing a new way of managing operations called Total Quality Management (TQM). Some have achieved remarkable successes; others suffered dismal failures. *Excellence in Government* shows why.

Why We Wrote This Book

Government agencies have challenges today that are more difficult and complex than any faced by our nation in peacetime. They must cope with seemingly intractable deficits, steady growth in demand for traditional services, new and unusual requirements brought on by a drug epidemic and a highly competitive world economy, and increasing disillusionment with government's ability to serve the needs of its citizens. We can no longer "throw money" at these issues. The only realistic solution is to improve performance, providing more and better services for each tax dollar spent. We believe TQM is the best, and perhaps the only, method government can use to meet these challenges.

We hope this book will help promote TQM in government, because we see it as the best way to improve public services and national security and get more output for the dollar. To this end, we are giving copies of *Excellence in Government* to Members of Congress, the President, federal cabinet secretaries, the heads of major independent agencies, and the governors of all states, commonwealths, and territories. We address the last chapter of the book to them: they must lead the way to government excellence.

Coopers & Lybrand is the nation's largest provider of TQM implementation services to business and government. We want to share our experiences, and those of government organizations that have tried TQM. By doing this, we hope all will profit from the lessons learned by those who have "been there." The chief lesson is this: if you take a comprehensive approach to TQM, you will succeed. If you do not, you will fail.

Who Should Read This Book?

We wrote this book for three groups: elected and appointed officials, top administrators, and people charged with planning and coordinating TQM initiatives. It also will be useful to middle managers, who are essential to the success of TQM. Finally, we believe vendors and contractors will benefit from the book, particularly Chapter 7.

How To Use This Book

Our comprehensive approach to introducing TQM is laid out in Chapter 11, but please do not turn to those pages first, unless you are very familiar with TQM. Most readers need the background provided in the earlier chapters to understand the fundamental changes that make TQM succeed.

We divide the book into three major parts, plus appendices:

Part I - Background

The first three chapters introduce you to TQM, what it is and why and how governments use it, and its prime goal, which is to meet the expectations of people who use government products and services.

Part II - Improving Processes

The basic work of TQM is to improve processes, or the way work is done. Chapters 4 and 5 cover TQM's objectives, tools, and procedures for improving processes. Chapter 6 outlines the team approach through which TQM applies these tools and procedures. Chapter 7 explains why and how you must transfer these skills and procedures to groups outside your organization, including vendors and other government agencies and institutions.

Part III - Making the Transformation

If an organization is to adopt TQM fully, the involvement and cooperation of many different players are essential. Chapter 8 outlines the roles different personnel groups have in making TQM happen. Chapter 9 proposes strategies to manage the introduction of TQM. Chapter 10 describes the nature of the corporate culture needed for TQM and how to develop this culture. Chapter 11 explains our approach to implementing TQM in individual government organizations. Chapter 12 looks at government-wide efforts to promote quality management in the public service, education, and industry. Finally, Chapter 13 lays out a quality policy agenda for elected and appointed officials — changes in government policies and operations that must be made at the top.

Appendices

Appendix A lists a selection of readily available books, periodicals, and reports on TQM, with emphasis on the public sector. In addition, this appendix contains information on networks, groups, and organizations that can provide valuable information and assistance to an organization involved in TQM.

Appendix B summarizes the results of a TQM survey of senior government executives that we conducted in late 1989. This survey is frequently referred to in the book and is useful reading.

Our Sources

Almost all the material for *Excellence in Government* comes from the experiences of public sector organizations. We felt we could not simply lay out dry and academic prescriptions for TQM. Instead, we want to show, by example, how government officials at all levels have approached TQM and coped with the challenges of making major changes in management systems and corporate culture.

We gathered this information through interviews with our TQM clients, other government organizations that are introducing TQM, and consultants active in the field. We also reviewed the literature on TQM in government (a growing body of information). In addition, we used unpublished sources such as speeches, reports, and minutes of meetings.

Since TQM is new to the public sector, solid government examples of some aspects are not available. In a few cases we drew examples from the earlier experiences of government agencies that have employed selected TQM tools, but not as part of a TQM initiative. Each of these organizations, however, has now started to introduce TQM to its operations.

Some examples in the book are from "blue collar" government activities or defense organizations. These government sectors have more history and experience with TQM. "White collar" or civilian agencies should not ignore these examples, nor deem them irrelevant. Though some adjustments may be needed by other agencies to apply the lessons learned, the basic TQM approaches are the same for all government functions.

The Book's Limitations

Excellence in Government is not a substitute for the more detailed "how-to" resources listed in Appendix A. If you need to know in depth how to use the tools and procedures of TQM, you must read this material and get expert assistance. However, we believe this book will give you the background you need to initiate TQM or, as a senior government official, manage an organization that embraces TQM.

Our Vision Of Excellence In Government

In TQM, we talk much about having a "vision of excellence." Our vision of excellence in government is this:

Americans will take it for granted that governments' products and services are the best, and the quality of government is constantly improving. Government leaders and employees will be widely respected and admired. Teamed with industry and education, governments will make "Made in America" the world-wide symbol of excellence.

We hope you share this vision, and will help make it a reality.

David Carr
Ian Littman
Coopers & Lybrand
August 1990

Chapter
1

WHY EXCELLENCE?

■ What TQM means for elected officials and civil servants

■ TQM is a management philosophy of involving everyone in an organization in controlling and continuously improving how work is done, in order to meet customer expectations of quality

■ TQM has been applied to nearly every function of government

■ Four reasons governments need TQM:
   – Citizens are not satisfied with the quality of government services
   – Tight budgets and deficits
   – Competition for labor force
   – Survival

"Reasserting our leadership position will require a firm commitment to Total Quality Management and the principle of continuous improvement... Quality improvement principles apply...to the public sector as well as private enterprise."

— President George Bush, September 29, 1989

Budget deficits are forcing governments to cut, kill, and postpone needed programs, at a time when the country can ill afford their loss. Is there an alternative to the axe? Yes— improve how government work is done, to get real savings *and* better services. Right now, some forward-looking public organizations use *Total Quality Management* to:

- Save millions of dollars, while enhancing existing services;
- Win praise from citizens impressed with service quality; and
- Add new services citizens want and need.

You can achieve the same, or greater, levels of excellence. No matter where or how you serve the public, Total Quality Management (TQM) has much to offer:

Elected or appointed officials: TQM means increased performance by agencies, at lower cost. TQM gives you confidence that civil servants can carry out your policies as you intend. You will free up 10 to 20 percent of agency operations budget to add needed programs or reduce deficits. Constituent complaints about government services will drop to all-time lows, freeing you and your staff to concentrate on policy, not case work. At election time, voters will remember how you helped to improve government services.

Top career administrators: TQM will help to continuously improve how you accomplish your mission. Everyone in your organization will follow your vision of excellence in public service. TQM will reduce employee turnover and increase morale. It will show you how to cut waste from your program or agency without cutting productivity and efficiency. TQM will improve the quality of goods and services you purchase, while lowering their prices.

Middle managers: TQM will free you to concentrate on systems issues and improvement. No longer will you have to "ride herd" on your supervisors and employees, or "fire fight" problems that could have been prevented. You will gain power to control your budget and the way your unit does its work, and greater cooperation with other units in your organization. Your work will be more stimulating, and you will reap the greatest reward of a manager: watching your people grow.

Employees: TQM says that you, more than anyone else, know how to create excellence. TQM offers you the challenge, training, tools, and authority to self-manage your work. Your job will grow richer and more fulfilling as you make the changes needed for continuous improvement. You will gain greater job security, leadership training, and higher pay.

WHAT IS TQM?

Total Quality Management is a set of principles, tools, and procedures that provide guidance in the practical affairs of running an organization. Coopers & Lybrand defines it as:

Involving everyone in an organization in controlling and continuously improving how work is done, in order to meet customer expectations of quality.

In TQM, quality means everything of value to a public service organization and its customers (the end users of products and services). This includes the physical quality of the products and services, productivity, efficiency, ethics, morale, safety, and wise use of resources.

The TQM organization is dynamic, using strategic planning to align itself with the future. It is flexible, in order to respond to changes in demand and environment. In short, it is ideally suited for success in a world where the only constant is change.

Government organizations that use TQM agree that it is fundamentally different from traditional management. Some of these differences are shown in Figure 1-1, and are discussed in the chapters indicated.

Figure 1-1
Comparison of
Traditional
and TQM
Management
Principles

Traditional Management	Total Quality Management
Needs of users of products and services defined by specialists	**Customer focus**, where users of products and services define what they want (Chapter 3)
Errors and waste tolerated if they do not exceed set standards	**No tolerance** for errors, waste, and work that does not add value to products and services (Chapter 2)
Products and services inspected for problems, then "fixed"	**Prevention** of problems (Chapter 2)
Many decisions governed by assumptions and gut feelings	**Fact-based decisions** using hard data and scientific procedures (Chapter 5)
Short-term planning based around budget cycle	**Long-term planning** based on improving mission performance (Chapters 11 and 12)
Product or service designed sequentially by isolated departments	**Simultaneous design** of total product or service life cycle by teams from many functions (Chapter 4)
Control and improvement by individual managers and specialists	**Teamwork** among managers, specialists, employees, vendors, customers, and partner agencies (Chapters 6 and 7)
Improvement focused on one-time breakthroughs such as computers and automation	**Continuous improvement** of every aspect of how work is done (Chapter 2 and 4)
Vertical structure and centralization based on control	**Horizontal and decentralized structure** based on maximizing value added to products and services (Chapter 11)
Short-term contracts awarded based on price	**Vendor partnership** of long-term buyer/seller obligations, based on quality and continuous improvement (Chapter 7)

SOME EXAMPLES OF TQM IN GOVERNMENT

Do these management principles work in government? Throughout the book you will see examples from all types of public service functions:

Accounting	Library services
Building security	Loan processing
Communications	Medical care
Community development	Natural resource manage-
Contract and	ment
grant management	Patents and trademarks
Document distribution	Permit issuing
Economic development	Personnel
Entitlement programs	Procurement
Infrastructure maintenance	Public works
Information systems	Research and develop-
Inspection	ment
Intelligence	Ship and aircraft overhaul
Investigation	Supply management
Law enforcement	Tax collection

Let us start with four examples that show the basics of TQM: customer focus, teamwork, fact-based decisions, structure based on maximizing value added, and continuous improvement.

Customer Focus

The Philadelphia Veterans Affairs Regional Office and Insurance Center handles veterans' GI life insurance loan applications. A top executive there told Coopers & Lybrand, "We had a standard of processing 95 percent of the applications within five work days from the time we received them until the Treasury Department issued the check. We were proud we averaged 3.3 work days per loan.

"But when a TQM team asked veterans about our service, they heard complaints that it took up to two weeks to get a check. The team realized the veterans counted time from the calendar day they mailed an application to the day they got the check. So our standard did not meet our customers' expectations.

"The team added a special post box number, which saved time that the applications spent in the mail getting to us. We added a dedicated FAX machine for emergency requests. We worked internally and with Treasury to streamline the application approval and check mailing processes down to a 1.7 work day average.

"The immediate payoff was more satisfied customers. We also saved money by eliminating or reducing work that added little value to the application process — including time answering complaints, since our improvements have cut them by more than half.

"This taught us to tie what we do into customer expectations. We have to ask, have we aligned what we consider good service with what our customers really want?"

Teamwork And Fact-Based Decisions

Administrators at the Florida Department of Transportation (FDOT) estimate that TQM helped them save Florida taxpayers $28 million in 1989. Every branch of the department uses TQM, from the director to the lowest-paid employee; many FDOT contractors do, too. Most of the savings come from teamwork.

For example, a TQM team of managers and employees in FDOT District 5 found they were spending $21,940 per mowing season to manually service roadside grass-cutting equipment. They surveyed other mower operators to find out why.

They expected the big time wasters would be breakdowns, flat tires, and equipment repairs, but the greatest cause surprised them. Forty-five percent of the manual work was cleaning grass and dirt from mower decks with shovels and brooms, which took each crew 30 minutes at the end of each day.

The solution to the problem came in a structured brainstorming session: an $80, gasoline-powered leaf blower. "We gave one crew a blower and tracked their effectiveness," said a team member. "The trial crew was able to clean up in five minutes. They used the time saved to mow two more acres a day."

The increased productivity saves the district $2,600 a year per three-mower crew (this does not count the other six improvements the team developed). Sound insignificant? The FDOT has *hundreds* of mowers.

And the intangible benefits? Listen to what FDOT's employees have to say about TQM:

> *"It gives me and every other employee in the FDOT the opportunity to make a difference."*

> *"I like it because you can organize, clarify, and verify information."*

> *"We do the work; therefore, we must find the answers to doing it better."*

Decentralized Structure Based On Value Added To Services

How does a government organization get rid of unnecessary work and use the freed-up resources to create even greater savings? The Defense Industrial Supply Center (DISC) starts with the basics.

The DISC comptroller told Coopers & Lybrand, "Managers here used to have to get permission from my office to use employee overtime, sometimes for only one hour, which might cost $15. Now, who in my office is qualified to say whether a manager needs the extra hour? And the approval paperwork cost us another $15.

"So we stopped doing that — it's the managers' job now. Instead, we've decentralized our accountants and analysts into teams located in division offices, where they identify projects with savings potential and help the directors solve problems. Now, about all we do in the central office relates to specific appropriated and other accounts, and I need very few people for this. (See Chapter 8 under "Support Departments" for more information on accounting and auditing staff roles in TQM.)

"This was a business decision. If I'm paying people $31,000 a year, they can't just approve overtime. I changed their job from one that did not add value to DISC's services to one that did.

"Besides, the guys in the comptroller shop were not happy approving forms and pushing paper. Out in the divisions, they work on meaningful things and see results measured in millions of dollars."

Continuous Improvement

Now for an example of how TQM helped one government organization beat the socks off private industry.

The Jacksonville, Fla., Naval Aviation Depot faced a critical problem in 1988. Using TQM methods to prepare its proposal, it had won an open competition with private industry to refit P-3 antisubmarine patrol aircraft. But when work began, the depot found it was using too much labor to stay within budget.

A TQM team of managers, foremen, and artisans worked out a better way of organizing the work, which brought the labor hours per plane to the target level. Most government organizations would have stopped right there, but not the depot. It used work process tracking, a new management structure, and a proactive program to get suggestions from workers and customers (the Navy's flying units).

This generated a constant stream of new ideas for improvement. Now, the depot completes planes with 40 percent less labor than originally planned, and is still improving. At record quality levels. Without new automation. The result: millions of dollars saved for the Navy and taxpayers. The P-3 has been in service more than 20 years and has seen plenty of private contractors, but none ever came close to this level of performance. (See Chapter 8 under "Employees" for a more detailed description of the depot's improvement effort.)

Said a depot manager to Coopers & Lybrand, "This may be difficult for some people to understand, but the truth is we simply can't stop getting better. When you structure an operation with the goal of improving it, there are no brakes on the quality train."

Would your employees complain about this relentless effort to do things better? Said a depot worker, "Look, the pressure to improve doesn't come from our bosses. We put it on ourselves."

"Those are nice examples," you may think, "But why should I use TQM? No one is pressuring *me* to do this." The following information may motivate you.

WHY GOVERNMENTS NEED TQM

Private industry uses TQM to compete and survive in the marketplace. For government, the reasons are better service to citizens, tight budgets, getting and keeping the best employees...and survival, too.

Citizen Perceptions Of Government Quality

Citizens are your ultimate customers, the final beneficiaries of your products and services. How satisfied are they with what government is doing?

Only 1 in 11 Americans thinks government does a very satisfactory job in producing quality services, according to the results of a 1988 survey of consumers by the American

	Percent of Survey Respondents:			
	Level of Satisfaction			
Those who are satisfied with the quality of government services	*Very*	*Fairly*	*Not very*	*Not at all*
	8%	56%	27%	8%
	Type of Government			
Those who feel that government is operating competently	*Federal*	*State*	*Local*	
	31%	40%	44%	

Source: *Consumers' Perceptions Concerning The Quality Of American Products And Services,* 1988 survey conducted for the American Society for Quality Control by the Gallup Organization, Inc.

Figure 1-2
Consumer
Opinion of
Government
Quality

Society for Quality Control, shown in Figure 1-2. Only 31 percent think the federal government is operated competently, and just a few more hold this opinion about state and local government.

About half the survey respondents said they think governments should make more efforts to improve, but a third have given up hope and say, "Turn government services over to the private sector." If you believe that customers define quality, this is a clear challenge to improve.

Tight Budgets And Deficits

"They have lost some of their best employees, and those who remain are overburdened and disgruntled... Administered in repeated doses, (major staff reductions) can hurt product quality, alienate customers, and actually cut productivity growth. It can foster an organization so preoccupied with bean counting, so anxious about where the ax will fall next, that employees become narrow-minded, self-absorbed, and risk-averse."

– *Fortune*, April 9, 1990

Sound like government budget cutting? It is about private industry, which has made the mistake of cutting jobs, not waste. Most governments follow the same misguided course. They use the sledgehammer approach: across-the-board budget cuts, hiring freezes, reductions in force, and elimination of programs. Does this increase quality, productivity, or efficiency? Of course not.

TQM will help you save 10 to 20 percent of your operations budget by reducing your "cost of quality," at no sacrifice to performance. Cost of quality is TQM's term for money spent to prevent problems, inspect for and correct them, waste, and product or service failure. As shown in Figure 1-3, much of the cost of quality is hidden.

The cost of quality in most private companies is 20 to 40 percent of sales price (think about that the next time you buy something). The Wisconsin state government estimates cost of quality in public service to be somewhat higher than 30 percent, while a 1990 cost of quality study by Coopers &

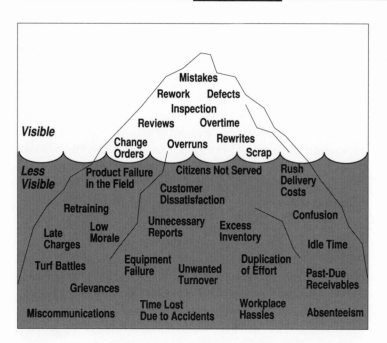

Figure 1-3
The Cost Of
Quality Iceberg

Lybrand of one government installation set it at 33 percent of budget. Coopers & Lybrand has helped private companies use TQM to reduce this to less than 10 percent, most of which goes toward prevention.

Our government clients are starting to get there, too, by eliminating or reducing the *root causes* of high cost of quality. When you remove the cause, the symptom disappears. When you treat the symptom with sledgehammers, it just gets worse.

Competition For Getting And Keeping Employees

Attracting and retaining a top-quality workforce is today's chief challenge, according to industry and government leaders. How can TQM help you do this?

"As younger people enter the workforce, they want to have immediate input into decisions, and more control over how they work," says the quality coordinator of Volusia County, Fla. "The quality movement has democratized the way we work, which helps us attract and retain bright and able young employees. It's tough for county government to compete on wages alone, so this is important."

Of equal importance is the trend in industry and government to reduce the number of middle management positions. In the modern streamlined organization, the ambitions of many workers must be satisfied in ways other than promotion to management. TQM allows every employee to make a difference, and to be part of teams that help make decisions that once were the exclusive realm of management. TQM also gives more authority to workers, which enriches jobs to make them more satisfying.

Survival

The 1988 consumer survey cited earlier showed that one-third of Americans feel government services should be contracted out to private industry. Many elected and appointed officials share this feeling and have passed rules to promote competition between the private and public sectors. Losing means firing your employees. It also means that you will not have the ability to respond to future demands for your services.

Says the TQM coordinator at NASA's Lewis Research Center in Cleveland, Ohio, "We came to realize (and this is now part of our culture) that we are not that much different from a private company, whose business can go elsewhere. Therefore, we are always vulnerable to closure. We have to do our job so well that we will be the best choice for our customers."

An agency's competitors are not always in the private sector. Says an executive at the Philadelphia Veterans Affairs Regional Office and Insurance Center, "It's a mistake for people in government to think of TQM as simply a way of dealing with dwindling resources. We have successfully resisted attempts to transfer some of our work to other government units, because we can prove we can do a better job. We also get special projects and new work because the Department of Veterans Affairs has confidence in us.

"There *is* a market of government business for which you compete, and don't forget that it includes your own work. A government office with a track record of quality can compete for parts of that market, and get more of it."

STARTING THE JOURNEY TO QUALITY

Introducing TQM is not easy, and you will not be able to do the job overnight. You may have a hard time getting started, but you will not be alone.

The **federal government** has undertaken a major campaign to introduce TQM to all parts of the executive branch. In early 1990, there were 235 federal quality initiatives under way, and the number increases daily.

State governments have done likewise. In Wisconsin, the governor leads the way in the quest for quality in all state agencies. Individual agencies in Florida, Michigan, Arkansas, and California are also posting remarkable gains through TQM.

Dozens of **town and county governments** across the country are adopting quality management as the best way of serving their citizens. Big cities, small towns, and counties are all well on their way to creating "total quality communities."

These government organizations faced every problem and obstacle you will encounter, and then some. Their collective wisdom and experience are in this book. Your journey to quality begins with learning, so please read on.

Chapter

2

THE PRINCIPLES AND ORIGINS OF TQM

- ■ Four differences between TQM and traditional management
  - – Building in quality vs. inspecting it in afterwards
  - – Employee authority vs. management authority
  - – Focus on systems improvement vs. blaming employees
  - – Continuous improvement vs. one-time breakthroughs

- ■ The history of TQM
  - – 1900-1959: Basic principles developed by Americans
  - – 1960-1979: Japan added to and improved the principles
  - – 1980-1985: Renewed American interest in quality
  - – 1986-1990: The renaissance of American quality

Many people in government feel that TQM is nothing new. In a 1989 survey of federal executives (see Appendix B), Coopers & Lybrand found that 6 out of 10 felt that TQM is just a new way of packaging tried-and-true management techniques.

The federal executives are both right and wrong. "TQM tools and procedures are not new," according to a senior manager at the Air Force Development Test Center. "What is new is our understanding of the principles and structures that stimulate quality."

The best way to explain this is to look at four major differences between TQM and traditional management and examine the origins of these differences. This will lead you to appreciate the reason for a comprehensive approach to introducing TQM to your organization.

HOW TQM DIFFERS FROM TRADITIONAL MANAGEMENT

Ensuring Quality

Traditional management tolerates errors and waste, if these do not exceed set standards and specifications. *Quality control*, or inspecting things after they are made, is the chief means of ensuring that products and services meet the old quality standards. Cadres of quality control inspectors wait at the end of production lines to examine products for defects. In white collar organizations, managers and many employees spend most of their time checking and correcting documents prepared by others.

More conscientious traditional organizations also use *quality assurance* to help guarantee quality. Quality assurance is a system of audits and other procedures, usually done by specialists, to make sure products and services are made as planned. The key flaw to this approach? The way things are planned may not be the best way. The plans allow for errors, so you still need quality control.

Anticipating errors, traditional organizations devote substantial resources to "planned rework." The money and time needed for this are formal parts of cost estimates and budgets, or simply informal "fudge factors."

TQM focuses on improving the processes that make products and services to the point that they are defect-free and yield no scrap or waste. This approach eliminates the need to inspect for defects afterward, except in critical products and services such as nuclear fuel or aircraft maintenance. Advanced TQM organizations have either put most of their quality control or quality assurance personnel back into line departments, or retrained them to help workers and vendors use TQM methods.

Management Structure

The origins of traditional management structure include the time-and-motion studies of Frederick Taylor in the late 19th and early 20th centuries. Taylor introduced the idea of studying and measuring how work is done to make it more efficient. The regional commissioner for the Social Security Administration in Dallas illustrates the impact of this on organizational structure with a story about coal shovelers.

"In 1897 a Baltimore coal yard asked Taylor to help them become more efficient," the commissioner says. "He observed and measured the work of the 500 shovelers, learning that the ideal weight of each shovel load was 21 1/2 pounds and that the workers needed different shovels for different types of coal. He also charted the most efficient movement of coal in the yard. The yard cut back to 140 shovelers, who could each shovel 59 tons of coal versus 16 tons. This reduced the cost of moving a ton of coal from 7 cents to 3 cents.

"But to do this, the coal yard needed a special staff for shovel inventory, planning, and management information. Before, this was the job of workers and foremen."

Eventually, these special staffs grew to include planners, analysts, and efficiency experts schooled in "Taylorism." The job of middle managers became making sure that workers followed the dictates of the specialists. Someone needed to make sure the middle managers were doing their jobs, and to coordinate all the specialists with the line departments. A hierarchy of managers emerged to handle this, and also rules and reports that were required for control. Management centralized authority at higher and higher levels, and in increasingly specialized departments. This is how most organizations manage today.

What are employees supposed to do in this structure? In his *Principles of Scientific Management*, Taylor says, "A high-priced man does just what he's told and no back talk... When [your manager] tells you to walk, you walk; when he tells you to sit down, you sit down..." That is the basis of Theory X management, which states that few workers want to or can handle work that requires creativity, self-direction, or self-control. Taylor's "high-priced man" was supposed to be motivated only by money; he was not expected to need any other incentive to do his job.

TQM management structure is much different. Many special staff functions go to workers and first-line supervisors, along with the authority to plan and control their work. Authority is decentralized. Instead of relying on a hierarchy of managers and specialists to coordinate things, teams of managers, specialists, and employees work together. As a result, the

Figure 2-1
Traditional
Organization

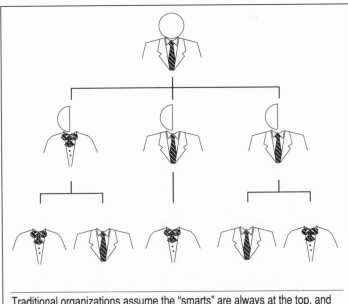

Traditional organizations assume the "smarts" are always at the top, and that employees leave their brains at home when they come to work.

TQM management structure is much flatter and more flexible than that of a traditional organization.

And TQM employees are not robots. TQM is based on Theory Y management, which assumes that all people have a natural drive for accomplishment. Part of management's job is to provide opportunities for that drive to benefit the organization.

Focus On Systems Improvement

Perhaps the key difference between traditional management and TQM is the view of individual performance. Traditional management focuses on individuals, measures their performance through periodic appraisals, and rewards or punishes individual results. Management by objectives (MBO) and employee performance standards are natural outgrowths of this approach.

TQM says that when employees do not control the systems within which they work, they cannot be held totally accountable for results. TQM says that 85 percent of the problems in an organization arise from systems, or the way management sets up the way work is done. Only 15 percent of problems arise from mistakes by employees. This is the "85/15" maxim. Some government organizations take this a step further. Israel's government-run military industries audited 900,000 worker decisions over 27 months and found that only 205 were wrong. This means workers were right *99.9998 percent of the time.*

Does this mean that the *results* of worker decisions are nearly always right? No, because these are based on instructions that may be wrong. Nor does it mean that all workers are always on time, never abuse sick leave, or are never lazy or irresponsible. It simply means that if well-planned systems do what they are supposed to, most problems will be prevented.

Another way of looking at the 85/15 maxim, according to a general in the Air Force Logistics Command, is that "85 percent of your gains are within the realm of the manager [who is responsible for systems]. The implication is that you can get 85 percent of the gain by managing harder. But the real answer

Figure 2-2
Causes of
Waste

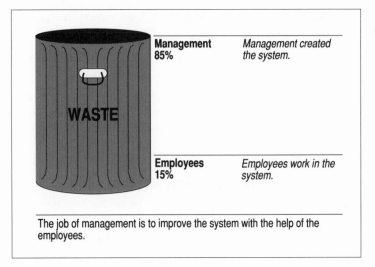

	Management 85%	Management created the system.
	Employees 15%	Employees work in the system.

The job of management is to improve the system with the help of the employees.

is managing differently. Managing harder tends to add bureaucracy and reports. This impedes progress rather than improving it."

Continuous Improvement

Traditional management depends on breakthroughs such as automation and computers to improve quality and productivity. For example, in its 1989 survey of federal executives, Coopers & Lybrand found that they think automating labor-intensive operations will contribute more to quality and cost control than anything else.

Nothing in TQM denies the worth of breakthroughs. A TQM organization is usually first in line for new technology that adds value to products and services. Although breakthroughs bring sharp and immediate rises in quality and productivity, they are followed by plateaus of no improvement. Also, true breakthroughs are hard to predict. Before one arrives, levels of performance may decline. This is because top managers focus on finding the breakthroughs, not on improving day-to-day operations.

TQM places more value on the small but regular gains made by daily attention to enhancing how work is done, or *continuous improvement*. Taken together, these small gains often exceed the level of improvement caused by breakthroughs.

An organization can buy new technology, but cannot buy continuous improvement, which comes from the dedication of employees.

John Franke, director of the Federal Quality Institute and former assistant secretary for administration at the U.S. Department of Agriculture, notes the power of this dedication: "At USDA we had an employee suggestion campaign, and were pleased that we got 2,700 suggestions in one week and put 2,300 of them into effect. Then I learned that Toyota implements 5,000 employee suggestions *per day.*"

THE HISTORY OF TQM

The mention of Toyota prompts the question, "Is TQM a Japanese business management style?" By extension, this question raises doubts about whether TQM works in the American culture or in government. The history of TQM should lay these myths to rest. It is a fascinating history, involving wartime secrets, government employees, and *considerable irony.*

Shewhart And Bell Laboratories

At Bell Laboratories in the 1920s, Walter A. Shewhart developed a system of measuring variance in production systems, known as statistical process control (SPC). TQM uses SPC to help monitor consistency and diagnose problems in a work process. He also created the Plan-Do-Check-Act (PDCA) cycle, which applies the scientific method to improve how work is done. PDCA, outlined in Figure 2-3, is TQM's basic framework for introducing improvements to processes. PDCA is a cycle; by constantly repeating the cycle on a work process, the process gains ever-higher levels of performance. This is called continuous improvement.

World War II

The War Department took Shewhart's SPC methods seriously during World War II. It hired Shewhart's student, W. Edwards Deming, a mathematical physicist and U.S. Department of Agriculture and Census Bureau researcher, to teach SPC to the defense industry. Quality control and statistical

Figure 2-3
The "Plan-Do-
Check-Act"
Cycle for
Continuous
Improvement

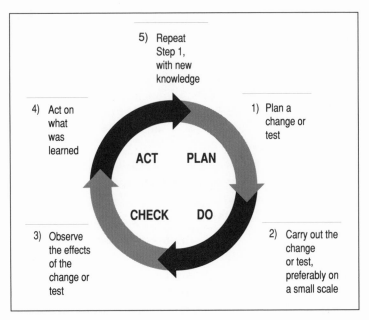

methods were such critical elements in the war effort that they were classified as military secrets, known as "Z-1" in the United States and "Standards 600" in Britain.

Irony #1: After the war most companies stopped using SPC. It had a brief resurgence in the 1950s and 1960s, but eventually was consigned to quality control departments, if it survived at all.

Reconstruction Of Japan

Irony #2: The U.S. occupation forces in Japan helped the defeated nation to apply quality control methods, including SPC, in rebuilding its telecommunications industry. The results impressed many Japanese, including a number who formed the Japanese Union of Scientists and Engineers (JUSE). The JUSE is now the most prestigious quality organization in Japan.

Irony #3: Then the occupation forces invited Deming to help Japan with their first post-war census. The JUSE asked him to lecture business leaders on SPC and quality control. He ended up teaching the Japanese much more; his lectures were the genesis of the modern quality philosophy.

Irony #4: Until this point, the Japanese, like the Americans, only applied quality control methods to production and inspection. Another American expert, Joseph M. Juran, helped them expand the methods to all functions in an organization. Armand V. Feigenbaum stressed to the Japanese the need to involve all departments in a company in the pursuit of quality. He called this Total Quality Control.

Juran also taught that quality should be defined as "fit for customer use." This changed the idea of quality from simply making products that conformed to technical specifications to looking at the entire product life cycle from the viewpoint of meeting customer expectations.

The Japanese Quality Movement

The Japanese expanded Juran's customer concept to include internal customers, those people within an organization who depend on the output of other workers. Kaoru Ishikawa enlarged Feigenbaum's idea to include all employees (both white and blue collar), not just department managers.

About this time the Japanese began to study the work of American behavioral scientists such as Abraham H. Maslow (the hierarchy of needs) and David N. McGregor (Theory Y). Basing his work partly on Theory Y, Ishikawa helped to create quality circles. These were small teams of managers, workers, and supervisors trained in SPC, PDCA, and group problem solving; they are the original model for TQM teams.

Think for a moment about what happened when Ishikawa put the teams together with TQM's tools:

• SPC and PDCA drive continuous improvement, and

• Teams at every level of an organization started using SPC and PDCA daily.

The outcome was a constant flow of new ideas for improvement, derived from objective and scientific study, coming from everyone in the organization, all aimed at satisfying customers. This is the foundation for the high rate of employee suggestions in companies that use TQM.

Now, if first-line supervisors and employees can improve how work is done, they must know enough to control it. Companies using quality practices began to give more authority to employee teams to plan and carry out their daily work.

Other Japanese enhancements to the quality movement included Genichi Taguchi's application of experimental design techniques to product design and production. These methods originated in the 1920s and 1930s at Bell Laboratories, but there they were confined to product design. The Japanese also added better and faster methods of product planning, including TQM's quality function deployment technique. Finally, they redefined their relationships with their suppliers into what TQM calls "vendor partnerships."

By the 1970s most large Japanese companies had adopted, in one form or another, what Ishikawa called "company-wide quality control." The effect this management style had on Japanese products is obvious: "Made in Japan" now stands for world-class quality.

Renewed U.S. Interest In Quality Practices

The quality and low cost of these goods sent American manufacturers scrambling to find the secrets of Japan's success. In 1980 a television program spotlighted Deming as a key reason. But U.S. companies were puzzled by his message.

John A. Betti, now under secretary of defense (acquisitions), was an executive at Ford Motor Company then. He recalls: "I distinctly remember some of Dr. Deming's first visits to Ford. We wanted to talk to him about quality, improvement tools, and what programs would work. He wanted to talk to us about management, culture change, and senior management's vision for the company. It took time for us to understand the profound cultural transformation he was proposing."

After reading this book so far, you can understand what Deming was talking about. But many people did not, and sought partial solutions.

1980 to 1985: The False Quality Revolution

Many American private and public sector organizations tried to introduce the improvement tools alone, but most of these attempts failed. For example, the American quality circles movement had its heyday between 1980 and 1985. It almost died because management confined it to employees. SPC again came into vogue, but failed nearly everywhere. One reason was that management would not let workers act on the information SPC produces. Organizations tried to apply Philip Crosby's "zero defects" concept as a motivational tool for workers rather than a management performance standard. They found that the resulting slogans demoralized people.

The Renaissance Of The American Quality Movement

Historians probably will mark the latter half of the 1980s as the true start of the American quality renaissance. About 1986, people began to understand that Deming's "profound change" meant a comprehensive approach to quality.

The reason is that quality management is a holistic management philosophy, not a set of isolated techniques. Many government organizations have yet to understand this. The 1989 Coopers & Lybrand survey of federal executives shows that only one-third who said their organizations had started full implementation of TQM had completed all the preparatory steps along the way. Experience says they will regret this. *There are no half measures in the pursuit of excellence — you have to do it all.*

Chapter
3

DEVELOPING QUALITY RELATIONSHIPS WITH CUSTOMERS

- Every government organization has customers

  - External customers: end users of government products and services
  - Internal customers: People within an organization who depend on fellow employees and managers

- All customers are also suppliers, and all suppliers are customers

- Only customers can define quality

- How to make customer satisfaction the prime focus of government

Call them clients, stakeholders, users, beneficiaries, or John Q. Public — the government has "customers" just as private enterprise does. If this idea surprises you, you are not alone. Coopers & Lybrand has found that many government organizations do not have this perspective when they first encounter TQM.

WHO ARE GOVERNMENT'S CUSTOMERS?

Your customer in government is anyone who receives or uses what you produce — or whose success or satisfaction depends on your actions. At the most fundamental level, that user will be an *internal customer*, another unit or person in your organization whose part in a work process comes after yours or who uses your output to do his or her job.

At the Crane, Ind., Naval Weapons Support Center, for example, the internal customers of the procurement office are all the line departments that work on weapons systems. These departments depend on the procurement office to order parts and materials to get their jobs done right and within deadlines. If purchasing problems put them behind schedule or over budget, they are the ones who hear from angry external customers and top management.

At the United States Environmental Protection Agency, middle managers developing policies or budgets for their units are the customers of administration officials and agency upper management who develop and communicate agency-wide policies and objectives. Department heads need clear direction and constructive feedback from the top to create effective policy directives for their staffs.

At the Equal Employment Opportunity Commission, litigators are customers of investigators. Litigators need a sound investigative memo to develop legal strategies and adjudicate cases successfully.

"On a day-to-day basis, cross-functional cooperation among internal customers is what TQM is all about," notes the chief of statistical methods at Watervliet Army Arsenal in New York State. "The more we understand the needs of our 'downstream' internal customers, the better the whole process works."

At the ultimate level, the final product or service user is an *external customer*. External customers can be direct, such as the retirees who receive benefits from the U.S. Army Accounting and Finance Center in Indianapolis and the naval commands that send ships for repair to the Philadelphia Naval Shipyard. They also can be indirect. For example, the Federal Deposit Insurance Corporation works directly with financial institutions, but the ultimate customer is the individual bank account holder.

Figure 3-1 gives additional examples of agencies' external customers.

Government Program	External Customers
IRS Service Center Ogden, Utah	Tax attorneys Tax preparers Taxpayers
Norfolk Naval Shipyard Norfolk, Virginia	Fleet commanders Type commanders Ship commanders
Johnson Space Center Houston, Texas	Congress & the administration NASA headquarters Other government agencies Scientific community Private businesses Foreign governments
U.S. Patent & Trademark Office	Engineers, scientists, and inventors Patent and trademark attorneys Private businesses Industrial information specialists Students
Defense Commercial Communications Office	Whole Department of Defense
Office of Physical Security & Law Enforcement , General Services Administration	All federal agencies that lease space from GSA (6,800 buildings) Building managers Federal employees Visitors to federal offices
Social Security Administration	Beneficiaries Congress

Figure 3-1
Government Has
Varied External
Customers

Everyone Is Both A Supplier And A Customer

It is important to note that *supplier-customer relationships for both internal and external customers are reciprocal*, as shown in Figure 3-2.

Figure 3-2
Customer-Supplier
Relationship in
TQM

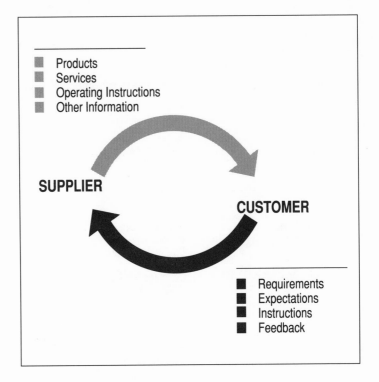

For example:

•   Although the line departments at the Crane Naval Weapons Support Center are the customers of the procurement staff, the buyers are also the customers of the line departments: for timely advance requests for materials, clear and accurate specifications, and external customer feedback on needed improvements.

•   Taxpayers are customers of the Internal Revenue Service, but the IRS is a customer for the information taxpayers give in their tax return forms.

• Managers are customers for employees' reports, but employees are customers for managers' instructions on how and when to prepare those reports.

In short, you are both a customer and a supplier for everyone you deal with. Treat your suppliers like customers, and you will have better suppliers. Make sure your customers give you the right information, and you will be a better supplier.

WHY DOES TQM EMPHASIZE CUSTOMERS?

In business, understanding the customer's idea of quality has obvious importance: if customers are not satisfied with products or services, they won't buy them — and profits will reflect their disaffection. Although government doesn't usually sell its products or services, a customer-driven process is equally critical in the public sector.

In TQM, customer needs and expectations, not agency-established standards, define quality. Remember the example of the Philadelphia Veterans Affairs Regional Office and Insurance Center (VAROIC) in Chapter 1? No matter how fast the VAROIC processes loan applications in its offices, the veterans measure turnaround from the time they mail an application to the time they receive a check in the mail. Which is the better definition of quality in turnaround time?

The commanding officer at the Cherry Point Naval Air Depot recalls, "For years, some of our operators made a component for a larger part. One of the operators asked the workers who used the component about its quality. 'Quality's fine,' said these internal customers. But could it be any better? 'Well, we have to open it up, drill an alignment hole, and then reassemble it. Takes us about an hour to do that.' Checking the component's plans, they found that the hole had been left out of the drawings. Now, the operators who make the component put the hole in it, which takes six minutes. We make hundreds of these a year; think of the time we had wasted by not finding out what the internal customers really needed."

No matter how good your products and services are, they cannot have total quality unless they meet your customers' needs and expectations. You cannot "do it right the first time" unless you know the right thing to do.

Do Customers Know The Right Thing To Do?

"Right" is relative, and is best defined through customer/supplier interaction. You have no doubt had the experience of internal or external customers asking for a product or service that is partly or totally wrong for their needs. You have to talk with these customers to help them better define what you are to deliver; often you are more of an expert on the subject than they. But ultimately the customer validates your mutual decision on what is best.

Also, customers may not realize that it is often possible to go beyond their expectations. *Customer satisfaction*, shown in the lower right-hand corner of the matrix in Figure 3-3, comes when customers expect a product attribute (physical quality, timeliness, cost, etc.), and the attribute is present in the product. *Customer dissatisfaction* comes when they expect an attribute, but it is not present.

Now, it is possible to go beyond simply satisfying customers by including attributes they do not expect in a product. This is doing that special "something extra." Examples of this include:

• The FAX machine the Philadelphia Veterans Affairs Regional Office and Insurance Center added to its loan processing permitted veterans to get quick service in emergencies (see Chapter 1).

• Opening several small license and tags offices in suburban shopping centers is something the Maryland Department of Motor Vehicles is doing to cut travel and waiting time for drivers.

When you add these types of attributes, you are *delighting* customers (the upper right-hand corner of Figure 3-3). The greatest challenge is to work on the *opportunities for delight* (the upper left-hand corner), when you find new ways of pleasing customers. This is one of the chief goals of continuous improvement.

		Figure 3-3
		Product

Opportunity For Delight	Delight	Attributes Not Expected by Customer
Dissatisfaction	Satisfaction	Attributes Expected by Customer
Attributes Not Present in Product	Attributes Present in Product	

Figure 3-3
Product
Attributes and
Customer
Satisfaction

Customer Dissatisfaction

Most organizations measure customer satisfaction by how well they avoid customer dissatisfaction. A common mistake is to think that if few customers complain, most are happy. Let us say that only 5 percent of your customers complain to you. Does this mean that 95 percent are satisfied? How would you feel if you learned that 96 percent of your unhappy customers will not complain, and that all customers with gripes will tell them to 9 or 10 other people? That was the finding of a federal consumer products study.

Multiply the number of complaints you get by 10, and you may have a more realistic picture of customer satisfaction. Multiply complaints by 100, and you have an idea of how many people out there have heard bad things about your organization. Think about that the next time you have problems getting your budget approved, or when voters fail to support your bond issue.

MAKING CUSTOMERS YOUR NUMBER ONE JOB: FOUR PRACTICAL STEPS

When government is committed to its customer, no service or process continues to exist simply because *"we've always done it that way."* Instead, the customer-focused environment is dynamic, with customer expectations spurring continuous improvement.

Taking a customer focus is a basic, common sense idea. Yet it may seem revolutionary to employees whose organizations have not yet adopted this ethic. In some pre-TQM environments, even staff who recognize that they have customers may view them with indifference, or even hostility.

"If my customers would just leave me alone, I could get some work done!"

How have governments converted attitudes and activities to make internal and external customers "job one"? Four basic steps have achieved important changes:

- Identifying customers,
- Getting (and acting on) customer feedback,
- Focusing employees on customer service, and
- Reaching out proactively.

Identifying Customers

The first step in taking a customer focus is deciding who your internal and external customers are. For many government programs, this process may be middle managers' and employees' first exposure to TQM. How does it work? When Coopers & Lybrand provided TQM awareness training to managers and employees at the Rome, N.Y., Air Development Center, some began the session by stating emphatically, "We don't have customers. The PX has customers."

Yet as they worked through the questions in Figure 3-4 and filled out the customer exercise worksheet in Figure 3-5, they soon made the connection.

Figure 3-4
Your Customer

Whom do you deal with when doing your job?

Who gets the output of what you do?
- Internal to your group
- External to your group

Whose success or satisfaction depends upon your actions?

Figure 3-5
Customer
Exercise
Worksheet

1) Identify your customers	2) Identify the products and/or services you provide to those customers	3) How would you rate the quality of the products or services you provide?
Internal:		
External:		

The managers took the exercises back to their departments to give all employees a chance to work out their unique customer orientation. Employees first defined their individual output, such as providing telephone coverage, maintaining program status data, or making engineering recommendations. Then they identified the recipients or beneficiaries of that output. They were as surprised as the managers by how many customers they really had.

Some of the insights the Rome personnel derived from the exercises changed perspectives dramatically. The security police at the air base began to see people involved in an accident or crime as their customers. Research and development staff came to see all ultimate users of their innovations as customers. Managers realized that their secretaries were among their internal customers. Knowing who their customers are, the people at Rome can learn how best to satisfy and delight them.

Getting (And Acting On) Customer Feedback

Results of customer identification often show a wide range of clients, each of whom may want something different from your program.

"When we first analyzed the needs of our external customers, it was a real eye opener," notes the chief of statistical methods at the Watervliet Army Arsenal. "We found we had many clients with different definitions of quality. The soldier, the R&D customer, clients for arsenal services, and the taxpayer will inevitably have different—and sometimes conflicting—values about our products and services."

How can you make sure your standards reflect all your internal and external customers' needs? Government organizations use a variety of customer feedback methods to get the range of input they need.

Surveys

Customer surveys help monitor perceptions and trends relating to your quality. They also describe the customer's current situation, pinpoint new or ongoing customer needs, and generate ideas for improving your products and services.

The Office of Physical Security and Law Enforcement of the General Services Administration (GSA), charged with security planning for many federal buildings, conducts biennial building surveys to assess security systems, crime-related problems, and customer satisfaction. "We put a heavy emphasis on involving our clients in this process," notes the assistant commissioner in charge of the program. "We look at their security concerns as well as recent crime trends to update our protection plan. Before we put a new plan into operation, we discuss survey results with the customers. Then they appreciate why we're taking one approach and not another to provide the right security at the lowest possible cost."

Nearly every TQM organization surveys its personnel on the quality of work life. This is important, because employees are customers, too. Some have expanded this to include in-house surveys that show where an organization can improve its ability to satisfy both internal and external customers. For example, the Air Force Development Test Center used Coopers & Lybrand's Organizational Assessment Process (discussed in Chapter 11) to learn where to focus management action, training, communication, and other internal improvement resources. This targeted action, based on employee input, helps build an environment that will support quality improvement.

Focus groups

Many agencies use this commercial advertising technique, bringing together small groups of customers to discuss a new idea, product, or service. Although results are not statistically valid, they provide specific qualitative feedback to help refine a program's approach. For example, the Philadelphia Veterans Affairs Regional Office and Insurance Center uses focus groups to assess its forms and publications. Facilitators elicit user comments on issues such as ease of use, comprehension, and tone. The VAROIC then refines the products to overcome problems identified.

The Public Building Service of the GSA used focus groups in a broader way: to help plan a comprehensive client relations program. The service established focus groups of both internal and external customers and intentionally included chronic complainers in both groups. Planners used feedback on issues these groups raised to design an in-depth survey conducted with 10,000 service employees and 4,000 client organizations.

Comment forms

Just as customer query cards help hotels and restaurants get timely feedback, they also prove useful to government programs. At the NASA Lewis Research Center, groups that serve internal customers use customer feedback forms to evaluate their services. Administration, technical services, computer services, and engineering units regularly distribute the forms, which ask customers questions about specific services, needs for improvement, and overall quality ratings.

Personal visits

One-on-one meetings and site visits are common ways to learn what customers want and need. Top management and supply section leaders from the Defense Industrial Supply Center (DISC) in Philadelphia regularly visit the military organizations they serve. The colonel who began the program says that, besides ironing out details, the visits help DISC personnel understand the customer's sense of urgency about requests. "When you see a whole aircraft carrier tied up because we haven't delivered the cable they need, you get a powerful message," he says.

The Naval Publications and Forms Center (NPFC) and the Fresno, Calif., IRS Service Center take a similar approach to working with internal customers. At NPFC, members of the Total Quality Environment Division regularly interview selected internal customers for feedback on the quality initiative itself. They use the results to make decisions on issues such as training and team formation.

At the Fresno IRS Center, the computer services division has a formal meeting every morning with representatives of each customer area. Customers discuss computer runs, printing jobs, and other problem areas, and outline their priorities and needs.

Toll-free telephone service lines

Government organizations use this mechanism to allow customers to present concerns easily. Officials at the Philadelphia VAROIC feel that important improvements in quality have come out of customers' telephone feedback. "For example, the input we received led to improving computer-generated notices that were confusing some customers," says the VAROIC assistant director. "In addition, we learned that some customers did not know about the wide range of options they had under our plans. In response, we developed a proactive information dissemination program."

Customer advisory committees

Some agencies have organized ongoing groups of customer representatives to discuss issues and offer insights for improvement. At the Ogden, Utah, IRS Service Center, the vehicle is the director's advisory committee, which includes tax attorneys, accountants, and other tax practitioners from 14 states. This forum discusses tax administration issues and keeps center officials aware of the impact IRS decisions have on taxpayers and tax practitioners. Special service programs have resulted from better understanding practitioners' needs. One such program gives them priority expert assistance in solving complex tax problems.

DISC Employees
Walk a Mile in the Customer's Shoes
Quality expert Joseph M. Juran says that the best way to understand your customer is to become your customer. Quality planners at the Defense Industrial Supply Center are helping their employees do just that under the new "Know Your Customer" program. Every weekend, supply specialists join active and reserve Navy personnel in an exercise at sea. They learn what teamwork means to ship operations and how the materials they supply can make a difference.

"When civilians see the rigors of life at sea, they're shocked," notes a Naval reserve officer who helps

---

> coordinate the program. "They develop a real appre-
> ciation of their customer's setting — and maybe the
> customer's mood when he's making a request. By par-
> ticipating in an exercise they also see the underlying
> reality of a ship's supplies and maintenance: we have
> to be battle-ready each time we sail."

Focusing Employees On Customer Service

Just as in private enterprise, the attitudes of individual government employees can affect the customer's perception of a program's quality as well as the reality. The need for active employee support of a customer focus is as important for internal customers as it is for external customers.

How do agencies make the transformation? Because each employee population is unique, different approaches work best in different environments.

One important step in most organizations is training. At the Defense Industrial Supply Center, the course "Your Partnership in DISC" teaches staff a new, customer-centered model of productivity. The course emphasizes the importance of teamwork among internal customers.

Sometimes training focuses on the "how-to" more than on the "why" of customer service. Employees at the GSA Office of Physical Security and Law Enforcement receive 24 hours of training in customer interaction techniques. The course helps them communicate the office's commitment to continuous improvement.

Another way of promoting employee buy-in is to *reward* it. This can be as informal as posting customer "compliment" letters or including customer feedback in decisions about formal recognition awards. More directly, some agencies make customer service a part of performance evaluation criteria. External customers often participate in performance reviews at the Naval Avionics Center in Indianapolis. There, promotion panels include internal and external customers of the position.

The Philadelphia VAROIC uses cross-functional process improvement teams to improve internal customer relations.

Designing teams in this way allows representatives of diverse departments to work together — often for the first time.

Getting employee suppliers closer to their internal customers was also the goal in the Crane Naval Weapons Support Center's quality improvement program. An improvement team had traced some supply problems to buyers' lack of familiarity with customer departments' varied material requirements. The solution? Let buyers specialize in meeting one department's supply needs — and put their offices in that department. "By decentralizing the purchasing function, we moved the flash point for problems back to the departments," noted Crane's procurement chief. "We could resolve problems faster or avoid them altogether as buyers became experts in their customers' purchasing needs."

Because TQM is grounded in hard facts, it is not surprising that agencies also use quality indicators to focus employee attention on customer service. At the Naval Publications and Forms Center, departments keep statistical measures of customer satisfaction such as the percentage of correct forms and publications issued and timeliness of work.

"Graphic displays of these indicators keep all of us focused on improving customer service," says one manager. "The trends give us momentum for continuous improvement in meeting — and exceeding — customer expectations."

Reaching Out Proactively

Many government programs go beyond seeking customer feedback on their efforts: they take proactive steps to make the customer part of the quality process.

One way suppliers enhance relationships is by maintaining customer awareness of their organization's activities. At the Defense Industrial Supply Center, several directorates send out regular newsletters to internal customers to achieve this end. One example is DISC's Office of Telecommunications and Information Systems' quarterly "Byte-Line," which goes to all computer users. DISC also sponsors Sharenet, an electronic bulletin board that posts minutes of the weekly meetings between the commanding officer and the directors, training opportunities, and other information to update employees on quality efforts. Employees also ask questions and make suggestions via Sharenet.

Customer education is another technique for making the customer part of the quality team. GSA's Office of Physical Security and Law Enforcement takes several approaches to this. Its previously mentioned biennial survey is used to educate customers about crime prevention. The office develops self-help security information for federal workers, such as pamphlets on crime prevention. Field staff regularly set up information tables in GSA buildings to distribute pamphlets and answer questions. The office lends its expertise to the architects who plan federal buildings; it wrote an architectural textbook chapter on security aspects of building design. The result of all this is not measured simply by better educated and happier customers. Between 1986 and 1989, reported incidents of violent crime and theft in GSA buildings fell by 16 percent, and dollar losses from crime dropped by 27 percent.

The Naval Publications and Forms Center found that many of its customers (including every organization in the Department of Defense, many foreign governments, and private companies) did not know how to ask for the materials they needed. "We do not charge our customers for the materials they order," explains the center's executive officer. "So people may take a scattershot approach to getting what they really need. To help our customers be more precise, we gave everyone who orders materials a short lesson in how to do it right, using a personal computer program and modem. This worked so well that we began giving the system to customers to promote electronic orders."

NASA's Lewis Research Center takes perhaps the most direct route to customer involvement: the center includes customers on improvement teams and other problem-solving initiatives. The chief of the materials development branch recalls one example: "We were very concerned about our backlogs in conducting tests in our metals and ceramics shop. In addition, test samples also had contamination problems. Working closely with the research customers we identified root causes of the problems and potential solutions.

"The collaboration worked so well that we eliminated the contamination. We also improved our turnaround time so much that our metals and ceramics matrix shop is now a Monday through Friday instead of a six-day-a-week operation, and we have reduced overtime by almost 50 percent."

The Defense Commercial Communications Office (DECCO) involves external customers in one of its most critical activities: long-range planning. A panel of senior executives from DECCO's varied Defense Department customers helps the office set priorities on issues such as reducing cost and enhancing technical capabilities.

THE OUTCOME: RESPONSIBLE SUPPLIERS, DELIGHTED CUSTOMERS

Government organizations that take these four steps see tangible changes — in the kinds of programs they offer and in the customer response they receive. The experience of the Philadelphia VAROIC is representative of this transformation. Since adopting TQM, the center has changed from a system that responded to written customer inquiries to one that provides personalized case management via a toll-free hotline. The new system has cut the time it takes most customers to resolve concerns from an average of 11 days to a matter of minutes. To improve continuity of service, the specialist who takes a customer's call is responsible for follow-up action to resolve the case, instead of referring it to someone else.

"This is not an abstract improvement," notes the VAROIC's assistant director. "Complaint letters are down by 89 percent, and we anticipate cost savings. We know what better service means to our customers. Most of us who work at the center are veterans ourselves."

Chapter

4

WHAT GETS IMPROVED, AND WHY

■ TQM takes a systems approach to improvement

■ The heart of the system is the individual work process

■ Process improvement can occur at any point in the system

■ The objectives of improvement are right output, consistency, timely delivery, appropriate cost, safety and well-being of personnel, positive effect on society and environment, and positive customer perception

■ Traditional performance indicators measure results; TQM measures processes, or how quality is built into output

■ Traditional government accounting is not adequate for improving quality; activity-based costing is better

Quick fix. Putting out fires. Do it over. Fix it again. Worka-rounds. Come back to it later. Garbage in, garbage out. SNAFU. Out of stock. We're out of toner. Back order. Not what we ordered. Is that the best you can do? It's the contractor's fault. Typos. Not within specs. Defective. Nobody's perfect. Lost in the system. Blame the system. Quality control. Over budget. Overtime. Off schedule. Excessive backlog. Unplanned downtime. Delayed. Late penalties.

If you have not heard any of these phrases in the last week, you are the exception. They mean a system did not produce the most desirable product or service, on time, within budget, the first time. In this chapter we will look at systems and what customers expect of them.

THE TQM VIEW OF SYSTEMS

In TQM, the basic building block of the system is the process. All other system components revolve around the process. This is why TQM improvement is called "process improvement."

What Are Processes?

Processes are the ways work gets done. Here are some examples of processes:

Simple: Writing a check, repairing a vehicle, entering data.

Functional: Accounts payable, vehicle fleet maintenance, data processing.

Cross-functional: Financial accounting, determination of how many vehicles to buy, formulation of information strategy.

Every process has *inputs,* or material from another source, such as bills to pay, cars to be repaired, and raw data to enter in a computer. Information may be included with this material, such as an authorization to pay a bill, a job order for a repair, or instructions on keying in data.

Inside the process, a *transformation* occurs. Transformations include all the steps involved in writing a check, fixing a car, and keying in data. Sometimes this is called "throughput."

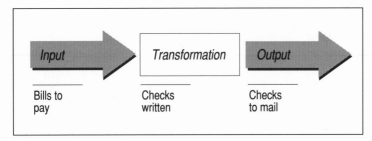

Figure 4-1
Diagram of a
Simple Process

The internal components of the transformation are people, equipment, methods, materials, and environment, which will be discussed in more detail shortly.

The transformation produces a value-added product or service, which is the process *output*. Outputs might be bills and checks to mail, a repaired car, and data entered in a database.

The term "value-added" is central to TQM process improvement. The value of each step of a process, and the process as a whole, is determined by how much it contributes to meeting customer expectations.

Linked processes

As shown in Figure 4-2, the output of one process becomes the input of the next, and so on until a final product or service is delivered to the external customer. This flow of work is the production stream. In Figure 4-2, the transformation "checks written" is the *downstream* internal customer of "bills verified and payment authorized" and the *upstream* supplier of "checks mailed."

All customers and suppliers, both internal and external, give each other *feedback*, or information such as problem reports and suggestions for improvement. Figure 4-3 shows

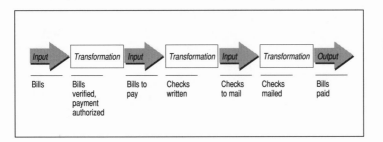

Figure 4-2
Diagram of
Linked Process

feedback between the transformations "bills verified, payment authorized" and "checks written."

Figure 4-3
Feedback in
Linked Process

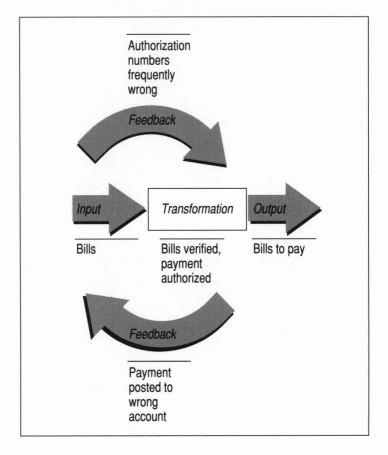

The system

Groups outside a process or series of linked processes influence the way work is done. Inside an organization, a line function (one that produces the products or services sent to external customers) may be influenced by administrative and support functions, such as the agency director, personnel department, comptroller office, or supply department. In a government organization, all functions are also influenced by outside groups, such as elected officials, oversight agencies, special interest groups, unions, and the general public. Taken together, all linked processes and these other elements are a *system*, shown in Figure 4-4.

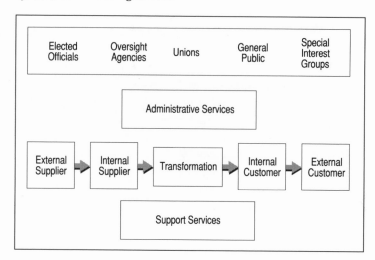

Figure 4-4
The System

THE 10 POINTS OF PROCESS IMPROVEMENT

Depending on the problem or opportunity, a process can be improved through some change in the process itself, or changes in the system. The following examples show how to improve processes at 10 different points in the system:

1. Inputs
2. People
3. Equipment
4. Methods
5. Materials
6. Environment
7. Outputs
8. Internal administrative or support functions
9. Other external groups
10. Feedback

Point 1: Inputs

Changing inputs may mean finding better raw materials or components for an industrial process, work orders in a service process, or performance reports for an administrative process. It may also include making sure that the right amount of material or information is delivered on time.

Altering the packaging of input can bring improvements. For decades, lawyers wrote court documents on legal-size paper. When federal courts mandated letter-size paper a few years ago, they put an end to the need for separate legal-size file cabinets and folders. This saves money for the courts, lawyers, and everyone else in the country.

Changing inputs is not confined to suppliers. It can also involve customers. The external customers of the Patent and Trademark Office in Washington, D.C., include people who apply for patents. Clerks were spending hundreds of hours a month matching up different parts of patent application documents. An improvement team of clerks said, "Have the applicants put their application numbers on documents they submit after their original application." There were no complaints from applicants, and now fewer than a dozen documents have to be matched each month.

Transformation

Process transformation components are people, equipment, methods, materials, and environment. Changes in each of these process components are possible.

Point 2: People

This includes everyone who is directly involved in a process, including those who make the transformation, inspect or monitor the process, support personnel, and others. The Navy Public Works Center in Norfolk, Va., reorganized its single-trade maintenance crews into cross-trained, multi-trade crews with plumbing, carpentry, electrical, and other skills. No more time is wasted waiting for one single-trade crew to finish before another can begin. This also eliminated the need for job coordinators and some third-level supervisors. Most organizations that use TQM eventually reorganize their work forces into fewer job classifications and more cross-trained personnel.

Point 3: Equipment

Equipment is the machines and hardware used in the transformation. This includes equipment used to receive materials and information from upstream suppliers, transform them, and send them to downstream customers. Examples might be local area networks, scientific instruments, lathes, or printing presses. The KEY TEAM, made up of guards in the Volusia County, Fla., correctional facility, documented that the use of radios for officer-to-officer communications meant that inmates could eavesdrop on the conversations. A security breach could result. Based on team recommendations, the facility installed telephones at key locations, including the watch towers, dormitories, and central control areas.

Point 4: Methods

This is the way that work is done. It includes operation manuals, rules and regulations, software, training, formulas, algorithms, and other procedures used in transformation. An improvement team at the Ogden, Utah, IRS Service Center found that the way the center was placing addresses on tax-payer notices caused Postal Service equipment to misread the information. The team recommended changing these procedures, and the change decreased the volume of undelivered mail.

Point 5: Materials

Materials are supplies or tools, already at the transformation site of a process, that are used to add value to input. They are not the inputs themselves. They include chemicals, forms, printer ribbons, ledgers, cleaning supplies, repair tools, and audio-visual aids. An improvement team of maintenance workers at the Volusia County public airport looked for ways to speed the cleaning of aircraft parking areas. Team research identified a degreaser that is more effective and faster in removing oil spills.

Point 6: Environment

Environment includes air temperature, noise levels, location, decor, and maintenance and other physical conditions of the area in which the process is located. Environmental factors may affect the physical properties of a product or service (e.g., dust in a paint shop) or the people working in a process (e.g., office decor). It can also mean decreasing distance to customers. For example, the Defense Industrial Supply Center transferred many of its financial analysts from a central office to internal customer divisions. The teams now work closely with customers to identify projects that lead to cost savings.

Point 7: Outputs

Altering the form or distribution of an output may also cause improvements. This can include changing a document so that it is more easily read or placing medical claims forms in high-traffic areas of a building instead of keeping them in the personnel office. Since most of its potential vendors have computers and modems, the Defense Commercial Communications Office started advertising requests for bids via an electronic bulletin board as well as through paper notices. Vendors can check the bulletin board daily and download entire requirements packages from it. This cuts lead times, mailing costs, and errors inherent in paper communications.

Point 8: Internal support or administrative functions

Improving internal administrative and support functions often has a direct impact on line function processes. Improvements may mean eliminating unnecessary reports from a line function or improving a support function process. The Cherry Point Naval Aviation Depot engineering departments had a shortage of qualified workers, though positions were available. Process improvements in the personnel office shortened the length of time needed to hire an engineer from 178 to 45 days.

Point 9: Other external groups

Government agencies must comply with rules formulated and administered by other agencies. Often these rules are seen as immutable, particularly by field operations staffs that think they lack "clout." In fact, the external agencies will usually accept reasonable arguments for change.

For example, Navy public works centers had streamlined their administrative and support functions by eliminating unnecessary work, which caused several hundred people to lose their positions. The centers wanted to place these people on temporary assignments in line functions, where more staff were needed, and gradually train and transfer them to permanent line positions, but civil service rules would not allow temporary assignments for more than 120 days. The centers persuaded the U.S. Office of Personnel Management to extend this period to one year, as an experiment with a special transition staffing pool to which they assigned the employees. Within the year, nearly all workers found permanent jobs in the centers or elsewhere. While waiting, they did needed work. The experiment led to a permanent rule change.

Point 10: Feedback

Improving feedback is key to process improvement in TQM. Every example in Chapter 3 of how organizations aggressively seek internal and external customer and supplier complaints and suggestions for improvement is aimed at doing this.

Another form of feedback is performance measurement information. The procurement chief at the Crane Naval Weapons Support Center in Indiana explains this: "We had an extensive system for measuring performance, but most of the information flowed upstairs. This was like police having radar guns, and cars not having speedometers. We decided to stop worrying so much about the bosses' numbers and focus on giving buyers the feedback they need to do their jobs right." Doing this allowed buyers to spot and solve problems early, as well as manage their work-in-progress better.

In summary, improvement in a process can occur within a single process itself, or anywhere else in the system. The point at which improvement is targeted determines who will work on it and the strategies and tactics to be used. The objectives of improvement at any point in the system come from the following short list.

THE SEVEN OBJECTIVES OF PROCESS IMPROVEMENT

Figure 4-5 lists seven expectations of customers and measurement indicators for each. These are the objectives of process improvement. Note that each relates to the *ability* of the process to meet customer expectations, not necessarily to physical output.

Figure 4-5
The Seven Objectives of Process Improvement

Expectation	Indicator
1) "Rightness" of output	Feedback from customers that product or service is the right type for their needs
2) Consistency of output	Variation in characteristics of output, such as some of those listed in items 3 through 7 below
3) Timely delivery of output	Degree of variation from normal, average, or scheduled delivery time
4) Appropriate cost, or resources required for the process	Degree of variation from normal, average, or scheduled cost, time, or materials required to produce, physical space required, etc.
5) The safety and well-being of those involved in the process	Accident rates; morale and comfort as measured by interviews, surveys, or complaints
6) Effect of the process itself on society and the environment	Risk of danger, poll of neighbors, measurement of pollutants
7) Customer perceptions of how work is done	Customers' feedback on confidence they have in processes or outputs, and their view of how service gets delivered

Objective 1: Right output

By now you have heard the phrase, "Do it right the first time." It is possible to do it right the first time, but you may be doing the wrong thing. So the first question to ask in looking at any process is whether the output is right for the customer. If it is not, then all decisions about improvement are grounded on sand.

For example, if no one needs the output of a process, why do it? Said the commanding officer of the Cherry Point Naval Aviation Depot: "We used to distribute stacks and stacks of computer reports throughout the depot. Then we found out that half the people receiving these reports threw them away, and the other half kept them 'just in case.' We don't have as many reports anymore."

Output may be generally of the right type, but not be totally right for the customer. The veterans' loan applications in Chapter 1 are an example of internal requirements not being suitable for customers.

Rightness of output is also determined by the core mission of an organization. When Volusia County public safety department deputies respond to non-police-related calls, they duplicate the services of other agencies and reduce the time available for police priorities. The department's SALT III improvement team examined the problem and recommended emphasizing non-deputy responses to nine categories of calls for service. The team then met with local service providers to ensure that they, not officers, would handle the calls.

At the macro level, strategic long-term planning determines the right things for an organization to do to satisfy customer expectations. This may mean developing a TQM approach to operations, increasing communications with customers, or developing new capabilities to meet future customer needs.

Objective 2: Consistency of output

Keeping output consistent makes sense, but it is one of the more difficult concepts for people new to TQM. Consistency has obvious benefits. You want the sugar you put in your coffee to taste just like the sugar you used last time. If you are buying a spare part, you want it to fit exactly. If you are paying bills, you want all the checks to go out exactly on time: if they are late, you will have penalties; if they are early, you lose interest payments at the bank.

Nothing is absolutely consistent; everything varies at least a little bit. But even a minor amount of variation can lead to at least some extra cost, defective parts, late deliveries, and so on, so an important objective of TQM is to produce consistent output.

Consistency does not mean that you do everything perfectly, or that you are meeting any of the other categories of customer expectations. Consistency simply means that output always has the same characteristics, and that processes operate the same way each time they produce output. Measuring and diagnosing reasons for differences in consistency are discussed in Chapter 5.

Objective 3: Timely delivery

Everyone understands the need to deliver products on time to external customers, but most people give themselves a little slack when it comes to internal customers. This is a major cause of cost overruns in many agencies, because the internal customer's meter is running during this delay. Late deliveries cause an internal customer to do expensive workarounds and issue poor output.

Late delivery also encourages customers to stockpile expensive parts and supplies, because they cannot depend on their suppliers to deliver these when needed. This practice, in turn, takes up space and ties up capital — and both are scarce resources. How serious can this be? In one government facility, Coopers & Lybrand found $150 million in unrecorded inventory of parts and supplies, in part because unneeded items were squirreled away instead of being returned to the supply system. Why? The internal customers could not depend on the supply system to deliver these items on time when they were needed. Multiplied across all government agencies, the problem runs into billions of dollars.

Early delivery can cause its own problems. For example, resources used to deliver some products and services ahead of schedule may have been needed to prevent others from being late. Early delivery also may force customers to devote extra storage space to products that arrive before they are needed.

The measurement indicator of timely delivery is its variation from the planned dates of delivery. TQM's goal for delivery is "just-in-time": all inputs to a process should arrive exactly when scheduled.

Objective 4: Appropriate cost

The objective of improvement in this area is to maximize the value of output while minimizing costs. Often costs can be reduced by automation, by using a new type of input, or even by buying a product or service instead of producing it internally. Changes such as automation also may increase the value of an output by improving precision and decreasing error. These are the easy ways, though, and concentrating on them while ignoring everything else can bring its own problems.

"Now that we've automated, we do the wrong thing faster"

The harder way to improve processes requires the removal of non-value-added steps and the introduction of new value-added steps. Typical non-value-added steps that increase costs include:

• *Unnecessary sign-offs and approvals:* Says a manager at the Johnson Space Center: "When people want something signed off on, they may not understand the time this might require. That's why you have organizations that can get things done in one or two days, and others that need two or three weeks."

• *Unnecessary paperwork and documentation:* If nobody needs them, they do not add value.

- **Inspection:** Inspecting output for errors does not add value to it.

- **Reworking:** Doing something over because it was not done right the first time does not add value to output.

- **Storage:** The only things that get better when stored are wine and whiskey. The time, money, and space needed to store any amount of input or output beyond what is needed immediately do not add value (see Objective 3).

- **Transportation:** Any engineer will tell you that no value is added to a product by moving it from one point to the next in the production line. For example, at the Pensacola, Fla., Naval Aviation Depot, a team figured out how to cut down the distance it moved aircraft landing gear during overhauls by consolidating work processes in fewer and closer buildings. This will eliminate 8 out of 42 major process steps, which reduces the time needed for overhauls by 14 percent and saves more than $1 million a year.

- **Ping-ponging:** Very often a document will "ping-pong" back and forth between two units, with slight revisions occurring each time. If the revisions can take place all at once, every "ping-pong" beyond that point is unneeded effort and delay.

- **Treating different things the same:** This often occurs in procurement functions, when large and small purchases are treated the same. The small purchases should require less effort and a lower level of sign-off authority. The same thing happens when planning departments treat simple jobs the same as more complex ones.

- **Outside coordination:** Often a coordinator is simply someone you have to go through to get to someone else. It is better to have two units do their own coordinating than to put someone in between.

- **Expediting:** If you have to make frequent special efforts to get something through the system quickly, the system probably is not working right. Signs of expediting include frequent use of expensive overnight delivery services, "walking papers through the system," and lots of overtime.

• *Fragmented responsibility*: The responsibility for seeing that a job gets done may be divided among several units. The result often is that no one is really responsible and a process is delayed.

Some people think that "streamlining" means removing all non-value-added steps in a process, system, or organization. This is a dangerous misconception that will cause you to focus on cutting, not improving. The streamlined organization is not "lean and mean." Instead, it has minimized non-value-added *and* maximized value-added steps. Additional value-added steps that may reduce costs include:

• When inspection is necessary, moving the inspection function upstream, since upstream errors are usually less expensive to fix than downstream errors.

• Using quality function deployment (see Chapter 5) to plan and design the full life-cycle of a product or service, thus preventing problems that emerge after production starts.

Objective 5: Safety and well-being

The importance of focusing on the safety and well-being of people involved in a process varies with the nature of the process. Obviously, inherently dangerous processes need extra attention to safety aspects. Creative solutions to these types of problems come from good teamwork and have beneficial side effects. For example, some workers at the Norfolk Naval Shipyard did not always wear safety shoes. Reasons they gave were the limited selection at the shipyard shoe store and complicated, slow reimbursement procedures. An improvement team recommended moving the safety shoe store to a better location and increasing its inventory and styles. Accidents from slips and falls dropped 45 percent. The team also suggested a new, streamlined reimbursement procedure, which eliminated the processing of 5,000 checks a year.

Objective 6: Effect on society and the environment

Governments are heavily aware that their policy decisions and how they work can have a tremendous effect on society. The effects of even the simplest change in a law or regulation can cause financial loss and even death for some citizens. For example, changing the laws and procedures for regulating savings and loan institutions has had one of the more major unintended effects on the economy in this century.

The side effects of a process also may affect the environment. Varying some component of the process can alleviate this. For example, defense operations are sometimes allowed to use chemicals and paints prohibited to private industry for environmental reasons. The Navy's ordnance facilities are researching substitutes for these materials and recommending the substitutes to weapons system program managers.

Recycling is a way to prevent the poor side effects that can result from a waste disposal process. Governments have started to require residents to separate newspapers, glass, and plastic from garbage, so that it can be recycled instead of dumped in bulging landfill sites. Many governments have a policy of buying recycled paper and plastic to help create a market for these products.

Objective 7: Customer perceptions

The quality of a process also must be judged on the customer's perceptions of its ability to deliver the desired output. It may matter little that a process is the best available and that the output cannot be matched anywhere. If customers have no confidence in it, they will complain or go elsewhere. For example, a research report may be technically accurate and useful, but its customers may not have confidence in it until a specific outside expert "blesses" the report.

One major downfall of government organizations is their inability to communicate quality performance to customers in a believable way. A root cause of this is often failure to measure performance the right way. For example, the opinion that building tenants had of maintenance services provided by the Navy's Norfolk Public Works Center was biased by "worst case" examples. A new performance measurement system measured all jobs done for each individual tenant. When they saw the whole picture, tenants agreed that the center's services were satisfactory, and that problems were more the exception than the rule. The tenants thus gained confidence in the center and its processes.

This ability of TQM measurement methods to increase confidence in an organization is shown by the experience of the U.S. Coast Guard. Media articles reported widespread poor treatment of boat crews by Coast Guard personnel boarding to inspect for illegal drugs. Using TQM methods, a team of Coast Guard personnel reviewed the boarding procedures and surveyed crew members of boarded boats. The survey found no instances of poor treatment by Coast Guard personnel. Giving this documentation to the media stopped adverse publicity.

Customers also must perceive that a process is fair. This is particularly true for many government functions, such as regulation, law enforcement, benefits calculation, tax assessment and collection, and health and safety inspection. Inside an organization, employees must see that performance appraisals and decisions about office space, complaints, and similar issues are handled fairly.

This sense of fairness will not come from explanatory pamphlets, published reports, and documentation. On a daily basis, it will result from polite, concerned, and informative communication with internal and external customers. The same is true with how services are delivered. An indifferent attitude by a government employee can do more to damage an organization's reputation than anything else.

PERFORMANCE INDICATORS

How can performance be measured against the objectives of process improvement? The answer can be found within the process itself.

Results Indicators Versus Process Control Indicators

Many government agencies have difficulty developing performance indicators. This is because they focus on *results indicators* related to final output to external customers, rather than on how processes are performing in making those products and services. Remember, if processes perform as intended, output should be of high quality.

You begin by moving away from the concept of results indicators to *process control indicators*. According to the Fresno IRS Service Center, "Process control indicators are used as monitoring tools to identify situations or trends before they become critical and to ensure that a process is working accurately. They are also sensors in the measurement system used to track our work and measure our accomplishments."

Developing Process Control Indicators

One way to develop process control indicators is to use flow charts to track processes and subprocesses. As discussed in Chapter 5, a work process flow chart maps out the different steps in a stream of processes or subprocesses, showing transformations, decision points, and when output of one step becomes input for another. With flow chart in hand, determine appropriate indicators for each critical task in the process. These may be time, money, or anything else that is important about that task. What determines importance? Meeting the expectations of internal and external customers.

Process indicators are not developed just for top executives. They are more important to people at the process level, who control day-to-day operations. If your measurement system is useful on the lowest level, it will be useful at the highest.

One caveat about using flow charts just to develop indicators: it can take a long time to do this for all your processes, and not all your processes will require this procedure. Do not order all your managers to employ the flow chart approach at once. Instead, apply flow charts to critical processes as they are improved (and keep the charts to the minimum detail needed).

At the Jacksonville, Fla., Naval Aviation Depot, managers base their performance reports on computer graphics flow charts of processes and subprocesses. This technique lets them easily link performance data with discrete subprocesses. The power of this link-up in diagnosing problems is significant.

Off-the-shelf computer graphics programs for flow charts are available for mainframe, mini-, and personal computers. They are an inexpensive and flexible substitute for labor-intensive hand-drawn flow charts.

One added benefit is that graphics programs permit quick distribution to employees of changes in operating procedures (the Jacksonville depot does this). Another is that some software permits you to simulate changes in a process and observe the downstream effects.

Indicators For Management

Top and middle managers do not need the amount of detail provided by process-level indicators; their indicators can be composites of more detailed data. Data may be collected for several linked processes and subprocesses on indicators such as lead times, error rates, and backlogs of each. This information can be combined into indicators for the total production stream. For example, each step in the bill payment linked process stream shown in Figure 4-3 can have its own indicator of timeliness. However, the head of the department where the bills are paid may want to see the overall timeliness of the process stream, which is the sum of the average time each process spends to make its transformation.

Activity-Based Costing

Most government agencies have difficulty in using cost as a process indicator, because their costs are accumulated by budget line items within broad categories such as personnel, travel, and contractor services. The main reason for this is the fund accounting system, which is designed to track obligations of appropriated funds and tie these to budgets. It is hard to use fund accounting to associate these costs with a single activity, product, or service. Activity-based costing (ABC) helps you discover the true costs of a process or output.

Figure 4-6 shows two different ways of looking at costs. One lists traditional line item expenses; the other lists the same expenses by activity. Which is more useful for controlling costs and making cost-saving improvements? Activity-based costing, which accumulates and reports costs by activity or process — including the costs of developing, producing, and delivering output to customers.

Figure 4-6
Annual Costs in
a Warehouse

Traditional Line Items		Activity Line Items	
Salaries	$500,000	Receiving	$65,000
Contractor Services	100,000	Receipt inspection	90,000
Travel	50,000	Storage	50,000
Facilities	30,000	Inventory controls	60,000
Supplies	20,000	Warehouse maintenance	150,000
Total	$700,000	Training	50,000
		Data entry	20,000
		Standards development	80,000
		Order processing	25,000
		Order picking	50,000
		Packing	30,000
		Shipping	30,000
		Total	$700,000

Using ABC lets you to do several things:

• Assign a realistic dollar cost to a product or service;

• Focus cost-saving measures on discrete processes or tasks;

• Provide meaningful cost data to improvement teams;

• Identify elements of a function that should be listed in cost of quality calculations;

• Compare current costs to those of other organizations, and answer the question, "why the difference?"

• Develop better cost estimates for tasks and budgets;

• Document savings of a TQM initiative; and

• Assign more responsibility and authority for cost management to middle managers, line supervisors, and self-managed teams.

This last point is the most important. The best place to control costs is at the process level. When you rely on a fund accounting system, many critical financial decisions are made on an arbitrary basis. Instead of selective and targeted cost savings, you are forced to resort to across-the-board reductions, hiring freezes, and other sledgehammer approaches. In most cases this is simply because your senior managers have no idea which parts of their processes add the most value to products and services, and which add the least. People at the process level can determine this, but they need realistic cost indicators. ABC gives them that information.

In many cases your financial personnel can work around your accounting system and provide useful data on a one-time, ad hoc basis. For example, the Department of Energy's Albuquerque Operations Office oversees DoE's multi-billion-dollar nuclear weapons manufacturing complex. The office received reports on scrap and rework costs, but knew they were only the tip of the iceberg: the direct costs contained in the accounting system. The center quality director asked one of the plants to do a special analysis of all the costs related to scrap, rework, quality inspection, engineering, management time, and various indirect support functions. Much to their surprise, the full cost came in two and a half times the direct costs.

Ad hoc studies such as this are better than no information, but you need sound, routine financial data reporting if you are to track progress over time.

CONTINUOUS IMPROVEMENT

In this chapter you read about specific things organizations do to improve their processes, but do not make the mistake of focusing on the improvements themselves. You need to put your energy in *how* to improve, because improvement is not an outcome, it is a continuous process.

For example, can you really ever completely meet your customers' expectations? Probably not. If you try hard, your products and services will come very close, but customer expectations are constantly changing, as are technology, the economy, political realities, the workforce, and every other factor that affects your organization. You will never be entirely aligned with all these factors, so you will always have a "quality gap."

The idea of *arriving* at quality is anathema to TQM. To *seek* quality is something different. That search is called "continuous improvement." The philosophy of TQM teaches that an organization must constantly strive to improve. To do otherwise would engender a sense of complacency, which leads to stagnation, which leads to ruin. In a more practical vein, perfection is impossible, so why delude ourselves by thinking we have achieved it?

Chapter

5

TOOLS AND PROCEDURES

■ TQM is an analytic approach to process improvement

■ TQM's tools include:

 – Charts, graphs, matrices, and other methods of collecting, organizing, and displaying information
 – Statistical methods for revealing underlying patterns of process performance
 – Root cause analysis methods
 – Experimental design

■ The basic TQM procedure for process improvement is a form of the scientific method

■ Government personnel at all levels have learned to use TQM's basic tools and procedures

■ Quality function deployment is the TQM procedure for simultaneous design of the entire product or service life cycle; this saves time and money, prevents problems, and ensures customer satisfaction

If it ain't broke, don't fix it: "So what if it can be done better? Nobody's complaining."

Live with it: "We don't have the power to make it better."

We've always done it that way: "We never think about doing it better."

It's state-of-the-art: "We'll wait until someone else discovers a better way."

We're no worse than anybody else: "We'll never try to be better than anybody else."

We'll correct it in the field if there's a problem: "We won't take the time to anticipate and prevent all possible problems."

It's good enough: "We can get away with it."

99.9 percent is good enough: "We're complacent."

Good enough for government work: "Nobody expects us to be any better."

Each of these phrases effectively prevents improvement in systems. The attitudes they reflect are the reasons for problems, and the eventual stagnation and ruin of an organization. TQM is about getting to the root cause of a problem and preventing it from occurring again. More than that, according to a maxim of the Air Force Development Test Center, TQM means "Even if it ain't broke, make it better!"

Motivation and hard work alone will not do this. You also need a good set of improvement tools, and procedures for using them. This chapter gives you an overview of the basic tools and a quick look at the more advanced methods. One procedure, called the "Road Map to Quality," is designed to lead you through the continuous improvement cycle. The other, quality function deployment, will save you time and money in designing products and services.

THE TOOLS

TQM benefits from any logical and proven method of

gathering, analyzing, and displaying information. The tools discussed here are among those most frequently used in TQM, but they are not the only ones. Do not be shy about including your own methods in your TQM toolbox.

The Basic Tools

Anyone in your organization can use the following tools for tracking performance, spotting improvement opportunities, learning root causes of problems, and displaying information. These tools are by no means all there is to TQM, but unless you use all or most of them, you will not be practicing TQM.

Flow charts

Flow charts are diagrams of the way in which work "flows" through a process, series of linked processes, or system. You can use a work flow chart to define a system, and to locate "fail points," redundant steps, and other problems listed in Chapter 4. In workflow analysis, you draw a flow chart of the "as is" state of an existing process, study the chart, and refine the flows to maximize value-added steps and minimize costs.

Once you have created a flow chart for a critical process, it is a good idea to keep the chart current with any changes in work procedures. If you do, you will always have a ready reference for how work is being done. As discussed in the last chapter, you also can assign process performance indicators at important points in a work process flow chart to give you and process personnel a constant stream of information for monitoring purposes.

 Flow Chart

Cause and effect diagrams

People working on improvements in process need an orderly way to arrange their thoughts about cause and effect. Cause and effect diagrams (also known as fishbone or Ishikawa diagrams) show the effect at the head of the arrow, with possible causes branching off the arrow. Use them to organize possible causes of problems or opportunities for improvement generated during a team brainstorming session. Categorize the causes by the components of the process: people, equipment, methods, materials, and environment.

Cause and
Effect Diagram

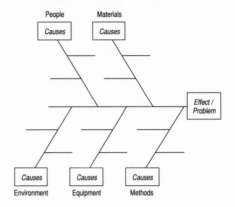

Check sheets

Check sheets are forms used to collect data on the frequency of an event or problem. Data from check sheets can be used to build many other tools: pareto charts, histograms, scatter charts, run charts, and control charts.

Check Sheet

Problem	Month			
	1	2	3	Total
A	III	II	IIII	9
B	II	I	III	6
C	⊥⊦⊦⊤	II	⊥⊦⊦⊤	12
Total	10	5	12	27

Pareto charts

Pareto charts use a rank-order approach for listing causes according to their contributions to an effect. The greatest cause is shown on the left side of the chart; the lesser causes are displayed in descending order to the right. Usually, you start improvement by working on the greatest cause, then go to the

next, and so on. For example, faced with four causes of customer complaints, you may want to start with the one that
causes the most complaints.

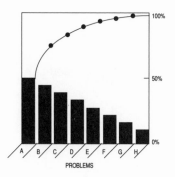

Pareto Chart

Scatter charts

Scatter charts or scattergrams help show the correlation between one variable and another. This might be, for example,
whether deliveries (variable 1) are made later as the volume of
transactions (variable 2) increases, or whether work performance increases with more training. Correlation does not mean
that one variable necessarily causes another to change; intervening variables may remove the apparent relationship. Statistics and experimental design adjust for this.

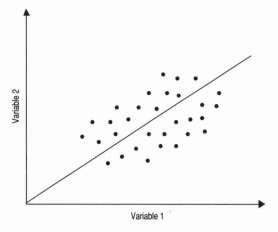

Scatter Chart

Histograms

All repeated events will produce results that vary over
time. If you record results, you will have the data to build a

histogram, a bar chart that shows the distribution of this variance. Each bar on the chart shows the frequency of results in a range of values. Histograms give you a snapshot of the way results are distributed. For example, two companies make toner for your copy machine, but sometimes their toners are a little darker or lighter (opacity) than standard. Here are histograms on the opacity of toner made by each company. From which will you buy your toner? Company B, which has the least variation in opacity.

Histograms

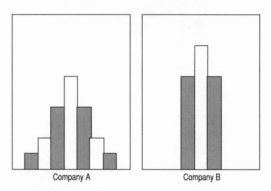

Company A   Company B

You also use histograms to determine the type of control charts or experimental designs you will use to study a process.

Run charts

A run chart plots the value of results over time: yearly, monthly, weekly, daily, or hourly. This lets you see trends, cycles, and other patterns in a process. While run charts are good preliminary tools, control charts give you much more information.

Run Chart

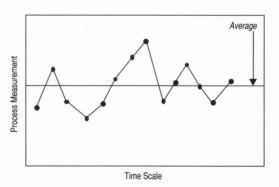

Control charts

Control charts will be discussed after you read about the principles behind them in the next section on process variation.

All statistics needed for the tools just discussed and for control charts can be calculated by hand, but personal computers make this unnecessary. You can use spreadsheet programs for all calculations and generate some charts and graphs with these programs. Many buy off-the-shelf software designed for TQM tools, a good investment if you use the tools often (and you should!).

And anybody can use TQM's basic tools. The county manager of Volusia County reports: "Some people in our mosquito control programs can't read very well, but when they are working on a problem like hitting power lines, they sound like management analysts."

Measuring Process Variation

Everything in life varies: your phone bill is different from month to month, crime rates go up and down, and reports come in early, late, or on time. In traditional organizations, people label variation either "bad" or "good." Bad variation is when this month's results are "worse" than last month. Good variation is when the results are "better."

There is a lot more to variation than just "good" or "bad." When a process varies, it is talking to you. It is telling you reasons for variation. But without control charts most of the time you cannot understand what the process is saying.

Types of variation and their causes

If you calculate the average performance of a process over a year's time, you will find that each month there is some variation in performance. Sometimes performance will be higher than average, and sometimes lower.

Abnormal variation occurs when performance suddenly shoots much higher or lower than average. You cannot predict abnormal variation, because it is due to *special causes*. For example, errors may have increased because a manager assigned a new and untrained employee to a critical process.

Other special causes may be a flu epidemic that keeps employees away from work, a sudden surge in demand, or the one-time breakdown of equipment. If a problem appears only once or very rarely, then it probably has a special cause.

Normal variation is the routine fluctuation of performance. Over time, process indicator data may go up or down, but you can predict with a reasonable degree of certainty what the range of variation is going to be (i.e., plus or minus a few percent points). Normal variation occurs because of *common causes*. These may be the level of training of all employees in a process, the reliability of equipment and methods normally used, or simply minor random events. When everyone has the same problem or makes the same error in working in a process, then look for common causes.

Special causes account for only about 15 percent of the variation in a process, and common causes for 85 percent. This is another way of stating the TQM 85/15 maxim discussed in Chapter 2. Most traditional managers devote themselves to solving special cause problems; this is "fire fighting." TQM managers work on common causes. Which type of manager will gain the most improvement?

Fixing, improving, and tampering

When you remove a special cause of abnormal variation, you are *fixing* the process. This does not mean the process is any better. When you fix a flat tire on your car, you do not have a better car. It simply means that the car will function normally again.

If you remove or reduce a common cause of normal variation, you *improve* the process. The normal operations of the process will be better.

Now, intuitively, you may know the difference between special and common causes — sometimes. But even the best managers can fail to distinguish between the two. When this happens, they start *tampering* with the process. They may or may not gain their objectives, because the approaches to reducing abnormal and normal variation are different.

Stability, capability, and reducing normal variation

Whenever you work on a process, you need to know what you are shooting for: stability, capability, or reducing normal variation.

If a process frequently shows abnormal variation (outcomes cannot be predicted), it is out of control, or *unstable*. You cannot improve an unstable process. If you try, you will not see the improvement, because it will be masked by abnormal variation. Your first objective is to make a process *stable* (outcomes can be predicted). Employees, first line supervisors, and technical experts usually can solve these types of problems quickly and easily.

However, a stable process may not be *capable* of meeting customer expectations. Say, for example, you can predict that, on average, your output is going to be delivered two days late — but your customer wants it on time. Satisfying your customer may require fundamental changes in the process. If you try any "quick fixes," though, you will be tampering with the process.

Let us say you have a stable, capable process. On average, you deliver output on time, though normal variation still makes some deliveries late and others early. You now want to *reduce normal variation*, which may also require fundamental changes.

Improving process capability and reducing normal variation requires managers to take action. Only managers can decide to form improvement teams to research the fundamental changes needed, and to act on team recommendations.

Statistical Process Control: The Basis For Control Charts

TQM uses statistics to show you the types of variation in your processes. These statistics are best understood not by their formulas, but by the information they give you when put into charts. Taken together, these methods are called "statistical process control" (SPC). SPC is simply a means of communication. It is the "voice of the process," telling you what is going on.

Figure 5-1
Control Chart

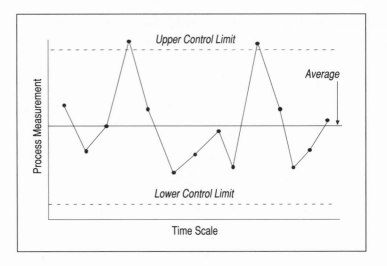

One frequently used SPC tool is the control chart. The solid middle line of the chart in Figure 5-1 marks the average variation of the process over the period measured. The line connecting the dot points on the control chart shows when the process it measures experienced abnormal variation (where the line spikes up and out of the upper control limits of the process). When the line stays inside the dashed lines of the upper and lower control limits, the process is experiencing normal variation. Control charts also show how close the process comes, on average, to meeting a desired objective (i.e., process capability).

Maintaining the process

Control charts serve an additional purpose: they help *keep* a process in control. People grow adept at spotting negative trends in the charts, so that they can take steps early to solve problems.

Statistical Process Control In White Collar Organizations

Most government organizations are white collar operations. Can they use SPC? According to the commanding officer of the Defense Industrial Supply Center, which is a white collar group, "Administrative and other white collar processes have output, the same as manufacturing or commercial functions.

Products such as documents can be sampled, and their variation charted and evaluated. A manager, employee, or work unit can take action on the basis of this analysis." He compares the objectives of improvement in white and blue collar functions to show they can be measured, and are therefore amenable to SPC:

Objectives

Blue collar functions	*White collar functions*
Reduce reject rates	Reduce document errors
Limit rework	Limit reprocessing
Minimize scrap	Minimize wasted time
Shorten manufacturing cycles	Shorten turnaround time

Even when work is non-standard, SPC can help monitor processes. For example, a comparison of the labor hours and budgets forecast for a series of jobs to the actual hours used will show variations in the job planning forecasting process, and lead the way for improving that process.

The Other Tools

Although the basic tools described earlier are sufficient for most situations, it is always good to have others. You can never have too many tools, if you know where and when to use them.

Tools to organize information

Force field analysis is a simple and easy-to-use tool that helps people list the situations and events that contribute to the problem (the restraining forces) and the actions necessary to counter these (the driving forces). This is useful in determining how best to overcome resistance to change when introducing an innovation (see Figure 9-3 for an example of this). Various types of *matrices* help organize information to evaluate the relative contributions of root causes to an effect, the benefits of working on one issue versus another, or the best solution for a root cause. Other organizing tools include simple tabular lists, tree diagrams, time-to-time analysis, why-why diagrams, defect concentration diagrams, and glossaries. *Juran's Quality Control Handbook* (see Appendix A) provides a complete listing and summary explanation of the other tools.

More statistical tools

There are about a dozen different types of control charts, each of which has its special application. Probability papers and analysis of variation (ANOVA) are other examples of statistical tools. If your processes are very high volume and repetitive, these techniques can be helpful (see Ishikawa's *Guide to Quality Control* and *Juran's Quality Control Handbook* in Appendix A for more information on these methods).

Experiments

Improvements to processes should go through an experimental stage during which they are tested and the results are compared to previous performance or some desired outcome (see "Improve the Process" later in this chapter). Generally, these are very simple experiments involving one independent variable.

With more than one independent variable, or potential intervening variables, you need more rigor in your method. When you suspect that only one or two variables are the cause of an effect, experiments that involve a few variables are a good approach. But what if you have only a general idea of what the causes are, or you have a complex process with many inputs and transformation steps?

TQM uses *experimental design* methods in such situations. Taguchi methods of experimental design are useful in solving complex production problems, and in designing new products and services. Their advantage is that employees and supervisors can run most types of Taguchi experiments with some expert guidance, since the methods are straightforward and the results clear. More traditional experimental design is equally valuable, but requires more intense help from experts (see *Quality by Design*, Appendix A).

Process simulation

Using computers, it is possible to simulate different approaches to a process to identify normal causes or optimal operation. Simulation is based on assumptions about performance, so the better you track performance of your processes, the easier it will be to use simulation. Simulation can be done on personal computer spreadsheet programs, or with more powerful personal computer, mini, or mainframe simulation programs.

Fear Of The Tools

Many people are afraid of and confused by TQM's tools. Based on interviews for this book, these reactions can be divided into two categories: simple nervousness about how to use the tools, and fear about what the tools will reveal.

The only way to overcome fear about knowing how to use TQM's tools is to use them. "The tools of TQM often seem intimidating, but once people have some basic training they see how easy they are," notes a manager at the Philadelphia Veterans Affairs Regional Office and Insurance Center. "Some of our teams stick to the basics, but some enjoy getting into more advanced concepts."

The second cause of fear is more insidious. "The problem with control charts," said the chief of statistical methods at the Watervliet Army Arsenal, "is that they show problems. Lots of them. Managers and workers may believe that these problems are going to be blamed on them, and that they will be 'beat up' as a result. SPC and any other TQM measurement tools are not about individual performance. They are about system performance. If you use the results of TQM analysis to punish people, TQM will fail in your organization."

THE ROAD MAP TO QUALITY

The foundation for all TQM improvement procedures is Shewhart's Plan-Do-Check-Act cycle (PDCA) mentioned in Chapter 2 and shown in Figure 2-2. PDCA is simply the scientific method applied to improving processes; it substitutes objective analysis for gut feelings.

The four steps of the PDCA cycle are:

1. *Plan* what you are going to do;
2. *Do* an experiment based on the plan;
3. *Check* the results of the experiment; and
4. *Act* on the results of the experiment.

To achieve continuous improvement in a process, you repeat the cycle working on different problems or opportunities, usually in order of their importance.

If this sounds like ordinary common sense, it is not. Common sense is assumptions — we *think* we know what is going on and the effects of our actions. Most people assume their way past PDCA's steps for improving a process. They assume they know the expectations of customers, how a process is behaving, the causes and solutions of problems, and that they have in fact improved the process.

Coopers & Lybrand's application of PDCA is called the Road Map to Quality, and is shown in Figure 5-2 .

Figure 5-2
The Road Map
to Quality

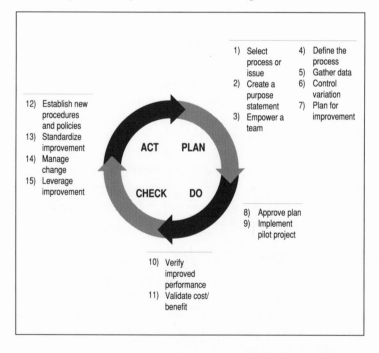

Using The Road Map

Plan

The objective of the "Plan" step is to arrive at a workable plan for improvement. Often organizations do not give this step the attention it deserves, and their attempts at improvement bog down or fail. The step's heavy emphasis on a clear purpose statement, conducting objective research, and involving the right people is characteristic of all TQM methods. This saves time and money later, and helps ensure workable solutions.

1. Select process or issue

Usually a team of managers selects the process or issue to receive attention, based on priorities: Which of many processes or issues requires attention now? Which will yield the greatest return on improvement resources? The team can use pareto charts to rank potential improvement projects by importance.

2. Create a purpose statement

The potential improvement requires a clear purpose statement. The management team writes the statement so that the results of the project can be measured in numbers: percent improvement, dollars, time, error rates, etc. Saying "improve customer service" is too broad and not readily measurable. The statement "reduce the number of customer complaints about late delivery of reports X, Y, and Z" is much better.

3. Empower a team

Next, the management team may charter an improvement team to work on the project. Let us assume that the focus of the project will be a single process. Most improvement team members should come from within the boundaries of that process, or the points at which the process gains control over input and loses control over output.

For example, in the linked processes shown in Figure 4-3, the input boundary of the "checks written" process is the point where it receives the bills and authorization to pay them. The output boundary is where the checks are passed on to be mailed. If the root causes of the problem or opportunity to be addressed lie outside the "checks written" process boundaries, a team made up only of personnel from this process will not be effective.

Depending on the issue addressed, the team may be augmented by specialists who bring technical skills, or representatives from other organizations involved in the process, such as vendors or other government agencies. These outside personnel may be formal members of the team, or advisors.

The management team gives the improvement team the resources needed for the project. This includes allowing the improvement team members the time to hold meetings and conduct research, access to customers and process managers, and money.

4. Define the process

The improvement team's first job is to define those parts of the process that affect the issue being addressed. This definition includes listing and processing process inputs, transformations components, outputs, suppliers, process managers, and customers. The team may do a preliminary work flow chart on the process at this point.

Next, the team lists the desirable performance characteristics for the process, basing them on the seven objectives shown in Figure 4-5 as these relate to the issue. The expectations of management and customers are considered during this exercise:

What do **managers** *expect from the process?*	*What do* **customers** *expect from the process?*
• Minimum rework	• On-time deliveries
• Average unit cost of $15	• No errors
• No overtime	

The team then writes process objectives, which are simply restatements of these expectations (e.g., the unit cost of the output should be no more than $15).

5. Gather data

The improvement team must now define process perform-ance indicators. As discussed in Chapter 4, these indicators are measures of performance within the process. For the improve-ment project, they also may include results indicators. The team then develops a performance indicator measurement plan.

Based on the measurement plan, the team collects data on performance indicators. Data analysis shows what customers and managers are really getting, which is the process's actual performance:

*What do **managers** expect from the process?*	*What do they get?*
• Minimum rework	• 25% of units are re-worked
• Average unit cost of $15	• Average unit cost of $20
• No overtime	• Average of 2 hours of overtime per day

*What do **customers** expect from the process?*	*What do they get?*
• On-time deliveries	• Half of deliveries are late
• No errors	• 10% of units have errors

6. Control variation

The team uses histograms, run charts, or control charts at this point to look at the amount and type of variation in the process. They immediately fix abnormal variation, because a process that has abnormal variation cannot be improved.

7. Plan for improvement

Using techniques such as brainstorming, the team may list all potential causes of unsatisfactory normal variation or of other failures of the process. Brainstorming is a structured exercise in which all members of the team suggest causes in a round-robin fashion, then discuss the merits of each. Cause and effect diagrams help classify these causes according to process components, and pareto charts rank them by the magnitude of their effect on the issue addressed.

Now the team can develop potential solutions. If there is a difference of opinion on solutions, the team must reach consensus. Consensus does not necessarily mean arriving at the most technically "right" solution. Instead, it means solutions that everyone will support, which is important since team members often are expected to implement these changes.

The team writes an implementation plan detailing its findings and suggested actions. The plan includes the estimated costs and benefits of the solutions and schedules, budgets, and other supporting information.

This completes the "Plan" step. The outcomes include a sound plan, and commitment to the plan by the improvement team members who developed it. Both outcomes are equally valuable.

Do

The objective of the "Do" step is to test the proposed solutions. The step also reduces the risk of making fundamental changes before they are proven effective, and allows for adjustments. This type of experimentation is another characteristic of TQM.

8. Approve plan

The management team reviews the plan and decides the next actions. The managers agree on a schedule for one or more pilot projects and allocate the resources for them. The original improvement team may be asked to carry out or monitor the pilot projects, or these tasks may be given to other teams or managers responsible for the process.

9. Implement pilot projects

The changes necessary to process components are made on a trial basis. Performance data are collected throughout the pilot projects, according to the measurement plan developed earlier.

One important outcome of the "Do" step is that personnel who will be affected by a change have the chance to test or observe others testing it. This increases their acceptance of change.

Check

"Checking" the validity and worth of the solutions is the objective of this step.

10. Verify improved performance

Data collected according to the measurement plan are analyzed to determine if improvement has occurred. If the improvement objectives have been met, managers will usually give the go-ahead for introducing the change throughout the process. If no or little improvement has occurred, managers may decide to modify and repeat the pilot projects, or to start again at an earlier part of the improvement cycle, such as sub-step 7, "Plan for improvement."

11. Validate costs and benefits

Based on the pilot projects, the management team recalculates the potential costs and benefits of introducing the change throughout the process. If the "Plan" and "Do" steps have been conducted well, the team will probably be in for a pleasant surprise. More often than not, the outcomes of the experiment exceed expectations and point the way to further improvements.

Act

Installing a permanent change is more than simply "rolling out" pilot projects to a process. The "Act" step considers the other changes that are often required, and the potential for maximizing return on resources invested in improvement.

12. Establish new procedures and policies

The procedures used in the pilot projects are not always the final form of the permanent change to be introduced. The procedures may need adjustment based on the suggestions of people who used them during the pilots.

The permanent procedures also may require policy changes. Most of the time the policies in question can be altered within the organization, but outside permission may be needed for some.

13. Standardize improvement

The permanent changes must be made standard operating procedure. This means recording them in operations manuals and training people to use the new procedures. The data collection method used during the pilots must be adapted to the normal performance measurement system (or vice versa). Finally, the higher level of performance achieved should be established as the new "baseline" for further improvement.

14. Manage change

Sub-steps 12 and 13 address the technical aspects of introducing change, but not the social aspects. Simply ordering people to follow new procedures does not mean all of them will do so. They often have what are to them valid reasons for resisting change, or they may simply be afraid of it.

As noted earlier, some of this resistance and fear will be overcome by involving people who will be affected by a change in the Road Map improvement cycle, and by using pilot projects to demonstrate the change. However, this is not enough when the change is complex or has negative consequences for some people. Then, managers must use the change management strategies outlined in Chapter 9 to successfully introduce an improvement. These strategies are aimed at weaning people away from old practices, drawing them into new ones, and monitoring to ensure sustained use of improved ways of working.

15. Leverage improvement

There may be other operations or processes that can benefit from the improvements just made. Management should look for opportunities to "leverage" the resources thus far invested by transferring these improvements to other parts of the organization.

Organizations with weak inter-unit communication or strong "turf" barriers often fail to realize the leveraging potential of single improvements. Improvements in one area must to be advertised to others, and top leaders must ensure that managers in all relevant units consider adopting these changes.

Is completing the "Act" step the end of the Road Map cycle? Can you relax and go back to routine? Read on to discover the secret of continuous improvement.

Repeating The Road Map Cycle

After successfully going through the Road Map cycle once, you are not "done." There are *always* other improvement opportunities within the same process or issue. You can go back to the pareto chart created during sub-step 1, "Select process or issue," and work on the next most important item. Also, during your first time through the cycle you may discover other opportunities.

Available resources and potential return on investment put limits on repeating the cycle. However, management should have a bias toward repetition, since this is continuous improvement in its most fundamental (and powerful) form.

Taking shortcuts

Everyone who uses some form of PDCA eventually is tempted to take shortcuts. You and your employees may grow impatient and want to get on to results. Be aware that skipping steps along the way increases the chance that you will assume your way past a critical point. If you take shortcuts, keep a record of them to find out if they work.

Taking the Road Map approach to process improvement gives the search for quality a rigor absent from traditional management. By following the steps in the cycle, any employee can contribute to excellence.

QUALITY FUNCTION DEPLOYMENT

The problem with the cartoon below is that it is a cliché everyone has seen. Depending on your line of work, the labels underneath the trees may vary, but the message does not: different functions in a traditional organization do not plan together.

One way of making sure they do is *quality function deployment* (QFD). QFD helps to align the goals of a stream of related processes with the expectations of both internal and external customers. The stream may include policy making and rule making; planning; product or service design; testing; production; distribution; and customer service. In industrial operations and information systems, QFD is related to and used with simultaneous (or concurrent) engineering, but does not get down to the nuts and bolts level of detail of that method. In white collar operations, QFD may be used to plan a campaign, develop a new service or revamp an old one, or consolidate and improve administrative services.

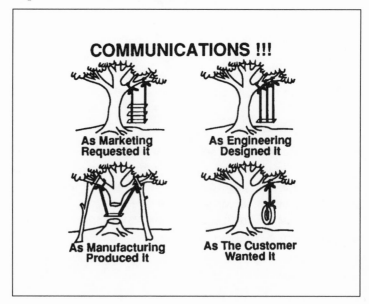

COMMUNICATIONS !!!

As Marketing Requested It

As Engineering Designed It

As Manufacturing Produced It

As The Customer Wanted It

The reason to use QFD is the complex nature of some organizations and their products and services. The probability that you can meet customer expectations and hold down costs decreases in proportion to the number of processes that lead to an output. The reason: there is often a gap between the goals for a product and service and the views, values, and goals of individual process managers. This tendency is found in all organizations, even those that follow TQM.

Like many TQM methods, QFD is a team tool. QFD team members come from each function involved in a product or service. As with the Road Map to Quality procedure, the team learns the expectations of external customers and translates these into defined and measurable goals, which are the desired characteristics of the output.

The team uses a matrix, sometimes called "the house of quality" because of its shape, to match customer expectations and the goals of different functions involved in meeting them. The team then works with all relevant functions to translate the requirements derived from these goals into objectives for each process. The process objectives are based on what downstream internal customers expect of their upstream suppliers, if the organization is to meet external customer expectations.

Later, people from each process develop these into more specific objectives. Attaining these objectives may require that some processes speed up their operations and others add equipment and steps that will save money and time downstream. This is the job of each process or function, not the QFD team.

QFD team members come from all the functions involved because this method requires good cross-functional communication, compromise, and consensus. Good *communication* helps to spot potential problems early. For example, the design of a service should be based in part on how it is to be delivered, and service delivery people have better insight to this area than planners. *Compromise* is needed because one function or process may not be able to meet the needs of its downstream customer fully, so these needs must be revised or the problem handled in another way. Finally, *consensus* about goals among representatives of all the functions involved means that all will support the goals.

QFD greatly reduces the time and money needed to put a new product or service into production. Traditional approaches tend to do this as a relay race, involving functions in the order of their position in the product stream. This can require months and even years. For example, traditional manufacturers usually use up 70 percent of a product's life cycle in the design phase. With QFD, all relevant functions are involved at the very start and work simultaneously on all parts of the product stream.

QFD also saves money, because it anticipates and prevents many problems that emerge only after production starts. As Figure 5-3 shows, it is cheaper to prevent a problem in the early stages of the product or service life cycle than fix it after production starts.

Figure 5-3
Typical Distribution
of Effort in Product
Development

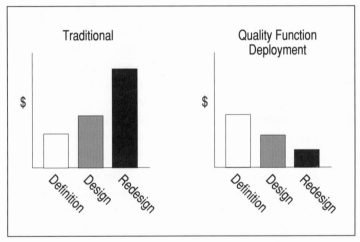

TQM Tools And Procedures Require Teamwork

Although individual specialists can use TQM tools and procedures, the effect is not the same as when teams use them. Many of the tools are designed to bring out the thoughts of people involved in a process. Procedures such as the Road Map to Quality and QFD are team exercises for the same reason; they are also designed to gain consensus on solutions. Consensus implies groups, and teams are structured groups. The next chapter shows how to form these teams.

Chapter

6

PROMOTING TEAMWORK

- TQM uses teams to make improvements at all levels of an organization

- TQM teamwork is structured around its tools and procedures

- The *executive steering committee* plans and manages organization-wide improvements

- *Management teams* plan, manage, and make improvements in their units

- *Improvement teams* focus on special issues

- *Self-managed teams* consist of a supervisor and employees who control and improve one or a few processes

- TQM teams need special training and support

This story is told of Werner von Braun, pioneer of America's space program. Someone once found him lying on the beach at Cape Canaveral, staring out at the waves. "What are you thinking about, Dr. von Braun? Are you dreaming about an innovation in space flight, or how to solve some problem?"

"No," he replied. "I am thinking about something much more important: my team."

TQM cannot happen without teams. They are the key to unlocking the potential of all personnel, from the top executive to the lowest paid worker. Teamwork is the glory part of TQM, its most stimulating (and fun) activity. Guiding and supporting teams are the most serious business of management, and the most rewarding for managers.

WHAT IS A TQM TEAM?

A TQM team is a group of people, each affected by the same process or processes, working toward a common goal and using common methods. They may include executives, managers, supervisors, employees, external customers, vendors, and partner agencies.

Figure 6-1
Types of TQM
Teams

Types	Membership	Focus
Management teams	Executives and managers	Manage quality activities
■ Executive steering committee	Top executives	Guide the organization
■ Issue management teams	Top and middle managers	Work on key issues of the strategic plan or other special issues
■ Unit management teams	Top and middle managers	Guide and support quality progress in their units and work on systems issues
Improvement teams	Anyone, including customers, vendors, distributors, and partner organizations	Conduct improvement projects
Self-managed teams	Employees and first line managers	Manage and improve their specific processes

TQM organizations use many different names for the teams shown in Figure 6-1. The executive steering committee may be called the quality council or quality board. Issue or management teams may be called subcouncils or boards. Improvement teams have the most names: process action teams, quality improvement teams, quality circles, cross-functional teams, interunit teams, or quality function deployment teams are among the most frequent. Self-managed teams are sometimes called super teams or natural work groups.

When an organization starts to introduce TQM, the teams listed in Figure 6-1 are an overlay of existing management structure. The interaction of the teams is driven by the improvements on which they are working. Gradually, this way of working becomes the normal style of managing most operations. The exception is the self-managed team; the reasons for this exception will be discussed later in this chapter.

WHY TEAMS?

The reasons for TQM teamwork are many and, above all else, practical.

Maximizing Skills And Insight

The aim of TQM teamwork is to maximize insight into improving quality. Traditional organizations usually put individuals in charge of quality: specialists and managers. TQM does not deny the skills of specialists and managers, but it realizes their natural limitations. Specialists tend to have a narrow range of skills, and managers often see things only in terms of their units or are removed from day-to-day operations. Teaming them with employees and other managers overcomes these limitations.

Breaking Down Structural Barriers

The flow of work in an organization goes across departmental boundaries. Teams made up of people from different departments are a way to break down the structural barriers of an organization.

Increasing Acceptance Of Change

People do not resist change, they resist *being* changed. No matter how logical, rational, and beneficial a change in operations is, they will resist it if it is imposed from without (Chapter 9 discusses why). When people affected by a change participate in planning and introducing it, it will be more acceptable to them. Teams are a way of ensuring this participation.

Creating Structure

TQM uses a disciplined approach to teamwork. Methods such as the Road Map to Quality, training in group dynamics, the use of facilitators, and documenting all give form and structure to TQM teams.

Bringing Out Hidden Talents

Often employees want to contribute to improvement, but do not know how. The discipline and group dynamics methods of TQM teamwork help bring out their hidden talents.

Training For Leadership

Improvement teams are training grounds for future managers. As one Coopers & Lybrand TQM consultant notes: "Every team has a team leader, someone responsible for scheduling meetings, conducting them, and keeping the team on target. This is valuable experience in group management and leadership. That this happens in a controlled setting using top-notch decision tools is a plus. The team leader learns the right way to lead, which is more than can be said for how many managers learn this."

Does an organization have the time for TQM teamwork? As several government managers interviewed for this book said, there is a tremendous power in having people do their work for 39 hours a week and spend one well-guided hour figuring out how to do it better.

TQM TEAMWORK AS A SYSTEM

As a system, TQM teamwork has several components. These include the teams themselves, their internal structure, team management, and team support.

Internal Structure Of Teams

All TQM teams have a leader and members. Often they have a facilitator and may be helped by other specialists.

The *team leader* is responsible for calling meetings, making task assignments, and keeping to the schedule. A team leader might be an employee or a manager; sometimes managers are team members and their employees team leaders.

Team members are people who are directly or indirectly involved in a set of processes or in a problem area. They may include the people who operate or manage the processes, and sometimes their internal or external customers, suppliers, and partner organizations.

Team facilitators are from outside the process or problem area, and so have no vested interest in it. They are trained in TQM problem-solving methods and group dynamics. They help in selecting and using problem-solving tools, often train members in their use, and help guide discussions.

Teams may call on the skills of a *statistician* or *consultant* for the more advanced TQM analysis and process design techniques.

Types Of Teams

Figure 6-1 showed the types of TQM teams. Each will now be discussed in detail, except quality function deployment teams, which are covered in Chapter 5. Please note that the lines between different types of teams are often blurred; some may share responsibilities or do the same types of tasks.

The executive steering committee

The key tasks of the executive steering committee are to develop an organization's TQM philosophy, policy, and strategic plan, and to identify major quality projects. It also monitors the progress of introducing TQM, and the key quality indicators of the organization. Finally, it works on major systems issues that require top management consideration, and often takes the lead when working on quality issues with partner organizations or high-level appointed or elected officials.

Sometimes this team will form a quality council made up of its own members and others inside and outside the organization. This council may include other managers, union representatives, and top support contractors. This larger body will assume some specific tasks involved in introducing TQM, or serve as a "board of directors" for the organization's quality effort.

The executive steering committee charters other management and improvement teams. These are usually issue management teams and some cross-functional improvement teams.

The job of the executive steering committee is serious business. Its importance should be first among equals to the other pressing needs of its members. According to the commanding officer at the Cherry Point Naval Aviation Depot, "I am on the executive steering committee here, and we meet every Monday morning, although this may not be absolutely necessary. We have found this to be productive, and a signal to others of our willingness to tackle problems." If the executive steering committee does not meet, neither will lower-level management teams. When this happens, the organization's entire quality effort will fizzle out.

Management teams

Management teams are charged with management and oversight of quality of work and quality activities for a specific issue or for the units they represent. They act on higher management directives, solicit suggestions for improvement from managers and employees, and may be in charge of the formal suggestion programs in their units. They also maintain contacts with customers, vendors, and other organizations to obtain information useful for planning quality actions. As needed, they pass this information up the line to the executive steering committee, or down to employees.

Another important job of these teams is management of change. Using such techniques as force field analysis (see Chapter 9), they form strategies for overcoming obstacles to introducing innovations to their units and the organization. These may include unneeded rules, "turf" issues, and departmental barriers. If management teams do this well, TQM and the process improvements that come from it will easily fit into the organization.

The management team reviews feedback from any source in the organization. There will always be many opportunities for improvement (if there are not, something is wrong), so the team must select those it will work on through systematic examination aimed at separating the significant from the trivial. Methods such as pareto analysis help to do this.

In selecting projects to work on themselves, or to assign to other teams, managers may benefit from the criteria given to us by the Fresno IRS Service Center, presented in edited form in the box below.

A Guide For Selecting Team Projects

Team projects should be:

Important: The vital few projects that will result in significant benefit in achieving an organization's mission, improving services for customers, or reducing the cost of quality.

Chronic: If several attempts to solve a problem have failed, the problem will probably benefit from using a team approach to get to root causes.

Systemic: The prime goal of TQM is to improve systems. Issues selected usually should not be limited to a few people, cases, or situations. For example, if all employees face the same problem or make the same error, the root cause is probably systemic. A few isolated problems *may* have systemic causes; if their negative consequences are severe, this may justify a team approach.

Customer oriented: Management goals are important, but team issues should focus most often on meeting customer expectations. This means learning first-hand what customers want.

Measurable: The problem or issue, and the changes made to it, must be measurable — "good feelings" about results are not enough

Source: Adapted From the Fresno, Calif., IRS Service Center.

Unit management teams work on systems issues within their units. When doing this, they may follow a procedure such as the Road Map to Quality from start to finish. If they find issues specific to one or a few processes within their units, they may charter an improvement team to work on it. They also may ask other management teams to help form a cross-functional team when an issue requires this approach. Finally, they charter the self-managed teams in their unit processes.

Managing lower-level teams

The management team ensures that lower-level teams have the resources they need for their projects. This includes training, meeting time and space, and access to information. Sometimes the management team or its leader must counsel supervisors and middle managers to allow employees to participate in teams.

The management team monitors lower-level teams, asking for periodic progress reports. If some technical or procedural problem arises that is beyond the ability of the lower-level teams to solve, management must come to their assistance.

A management team also hears presentations by lower-level teams. If it is within the power of a management team, it may decide to put these recommendations into immediate action. If not, the management team will arrange for a presentation of findings to the appropriate group within the organization.

Managers must follow the rules, too

Do not think that somehow management teams can gloss over the normal process improvement procedures and still do their work right. Whenever they do, both their solutions and their purpose statements to lower-level teams are usually suboptimal. Also, if they skip steps, so will their lower-level teams. TQM is a *management* approach, and managers should follow it.

Another mistaken notion is that a team of managers will be immune to group dynamics problems. As one quality coordinator pointed out, "Managers are used to having 51 percent of the vote, or following the directions of a senior manager. Put them in a team situation where everyone is equal, and you can imagine the struggle."

Improvement teams

Improvement teams can include anyone in the organization and representatives of outside groups such as unions, vendors, distributors, customers, or other government agencies. Each team member is closely associated with a particular process or small group of processes, either working in it or serving as an internal customer or supplier. Together, the team members represent all processes or subprocesses that are the targets of their improvement project.

Improvement teams are temporary groups, operating only until they have completed a project. However, some organizations interviewed for this book have permanent improvement teams similar to quality circles. These permanent teams often will generate issues they wish to address, and suggest these to management.

When improvement teams meet

Improvement teams meet over several months until they complete their project. Usually, these meetings take place once a week for one or a few hours. The exception is where management needs faster action on a critical process, in which case the team will meet more often.

Teamwork is part of the members' jobs, and they should not be expected to put in after-hours time. In good TQM organizations they do because they want to, but they should receive normal compensation for this.

Reporting to management

Management teams should have a bias toward accepting the recommendations of lower-level teams. If management has done its job right in training and supporting lower team members, the results of improvement team efforts should be acceptable. If they are not, you can usually trace the reason to management.

An improvement team's (and all other teams') presentation of findings to management should have hard data and convincing arguments. It should show that the team has followed the appropriate procedures. Management should feel free to question any assumptions and recommendations, but should do this positively.

Team presentations should be as easy as possible. In some organizations interviewed for this book, the presentation procedure is formal and structured. Teams present their recommendations in a set format, such as a report or series of charts. In other organizations the presentations are less formal. The choice of presentation style should strike a balance between the need for management to review a team's methodology as well as its results and the need to minimize burdensome paperwork.

Presenting their plans is easy for some teams and hard for others. For example, a team composed of managers or professional white collar workers should have no problem with this. As the quality coordinator at NASA's Lewis Research Center said, "Here, we live by the overhead projector. There is no need to train most of our managers and specialists how to use it. Young specialists, clerical employees, and blue collar workers may need some coaching, though." Several quality coordinators interviewed said that they devote a small amount of time to training workers how to present results. For example, the Quality Room at the Cincinnati IRS Service Center has a video camera to help team members practice their presentations.

Management should never view a presentation as a waste of time. It is an important event for employees, one that they may have practiced for at length and look forward to with joy and pride. For example, a team of librarians and volunteers at Volusia County's New Smyrna Beach Public Library worked on improving the "traffic flow" of library users and on finding a better library cart. They presented their findings to management using video tapes, charts, overheads, and a felt board. They also served a cold buffet lunch at the meeting. This and similar presentations are celebrations of the struggle to arrive at a good solution. Talking about the struggle is the core of the celebration, so management should listen.

Cross-functional improvement teams

Cross-functional improvement teams consist of managers and key employees from several different functions working on an issue that involves all of them. The chief of statistical methods at the Watervliet Army Arsenal explains: "We have executive/middle manager teams working on several fundamental cross-functional systems. We call one of these 'acquiring,' or how we obtain the external inputs we need. The team includes managers from such departments as engineering, product assurance, manufacturing, procurement, and accounting. Each of these departments affects and is affected by the 'acquiring' system, so the members of the team are at once customers and suppliers to each other. If we limited this team, say, to the procurement department, we could not deal with the whole system of 'acquiring.'"

Other examples of cross-functional teams found among the organizations interviewed for this book include:

• Representatives from sheriff and fire departments, radio dispatchers, and medical response personnel working on 911 emergency calls;

• Managers from data processing departments and their internal customer departments working on improving information systems;

• Line managers, union representatives, personnel managers, and employees working on employee performance appraisal systems; and

- Transportation agency personnel working with utility companies to develop a better way to coordinate repair and maintenance of power, water, and gas lines.

Issues that are not for improvement teams

Improvement teams should not be used to deal with *individual* workers' personnel problems, performance appraisal, union grievances, or adverse actions. However, an improvement team can work on the policies related to these issues. Improvement teams cannot be used for quick and decisive action in times of emergency — managers must do this.

How many improvement teams?

Some organizations, including a few interviewed, try to maximize the number of teams in the belief that this fosters improvement and a spirit of teamwork. This can be a mistake. The number of teams should be limited by the number of important issues for them to work on, and by management's ability to support and monitor team activities. Keeping teams "busy" with low-priority projects wastes resources, lowers morale, and will doom a TQM initiative.

Self-managed teams

Self-managed teams are the natural long-term outcome of effective TQM. Self-managed teams consist of a line supervisor or lead employee who is the team leader, and all other employees who work on a specific process or major subprocess. The team is responsible for operating and monitoring the process, coordinating with adjacent processes, and making improvements.

These are some of the characteristics of self-managed teams:

- They are found in complex processes. They are not usually found in processes where everyone uses simple repetitive motions (i.e., a simple assembly line). Some examples:

  - Federal Express formed 1,000 of its Memphis, Tenn., clerical workers into teams of 5 to 10 people trained in TQM and given authority to manage their work.

- Some employees and managers at NASA's Lewis Research Center are organized into natural work groups that use TQM to manage operations.

• The processes the teams manage are well defined. The teams and higher managers have developed performance indicators for these processes and track them routinely.

• The teams are supported by management teams.

• The team leader is more of a coach than a boss. He or she trains the team in TQM methods, helps them make decisions, and carries their concerns and suggestions to management.

Though these teams are the natural outcome of TQM, this is true only when you have done a lot of work in preparation for them. They operate best when their development is preceded by the activities discussed in Chapter 11. If you try to set up such teams throughout your organization immediately, you will probably fail.

Forming self-managed teams

During the first year or so of an organization's TQM initiative, it will form many improvement teams made of employees and first line supervisors of individual processes or subprocesses. If these teams do their work well, they are natural candidates for self-management. Making this shift requires:

• Defining a team's process, including its boundaries, and developing process performance indicators;

• Providing special training in TQM tools and procedures for the process supervisor or lead employee;

• Briefing and gaining support for the self-managed team concept from middle and upper managers in the unit where the process is located;

• Establishing rules, procedures, and other guidelines for team operations; and

• Developing incentive plans that reward both group and individual effort in the team (see the Chapter 10 section on

"Redesigning performance appraisal and monetary reward systems to reflect TQM principles").

Further transition to self-management teams should occur on a unit-by-unit basis, after each unit has management teams, experience with several improvement teams, and at least a few pilot self-managed teams.

QUALITY CIRCLES: A LESSON IN HOW NOT TO RUN A TEAM

The American model of quality circles came into vogue during the 1970s and 1980s. These were small groups of employees engaged in similar work who met once a week, often after hours on their own time, to discuss improvements. Sometimes they were led by facilitators.

Although hundreds of thousands of quality circles started in this country, almost all have died out. This is in distinct contrast to the experience in Japan, where quality circles began, and where 6 million of these teams thrive today. The reasons for their demise in this country provide a valuable lesson in how not to run a team:

• *For employees only:* U.S. quality circles were limited to employees, and managers were often told to keep hands off. As a result, quality circles did not have management support, nor were they seen as part of management systems. The Japanese quality circles have always had supervisor and management participants. (In Japan, there are also quality circles for supervisors, managers, and top executives. These are analogous to the management teams described earlier.)

• *Management resentment and fear:* Said the chief of statistical methods at Watervliet Army Arsenal, "Quality circles did what managers were supposed to be doing, which ticked off the managers." His counterpart in the city government of Wilmington, N.C., said this management feeling went even deeper: "Quality circle members made long lists of problems. Most of these were problems of the system, and managers saw themselves as being blamed for them."

• *Lack of training:* Most quality circle members did not receive adequate training in problem-solving tools and procedures. They took shortcuts, which led to poor and insupportable recommendations.

• *Nature of problems addressed*: Many quality circles focused on quality of worklife issues. They did not address problems that directly affected the performance of their organizations. Also, because they were limited to employees, the circles could not address problems that needed management input, so their efforts were never taken very seriously.

• *Voluntary participation:* Said a manager at the Defense Industrial Supply Center, "I think one reason the quality circle program did not work optimally is that it was seen as voluntary. If volunteers handle a task, then it is not always seen as that important." Japanese quality circles were never "voluntary" in the sense we think of the term. Instead, management asked a supervisor to form a circle with his workers, and you can bet he persisted until they "volunteered."

The quality circle concept is not wrong, and there are many well-run quality circles in this country today. But the way the concept usually was executed in America weakened it. Japanese experts point out that quality circles are the last component to be installed in their quality systems, while here they were the first. Thus, the U.S. circles had no foundation.

If you have a quality circle program in your organization, its teams may be apprehensive about TQM. Your top executive should take care not to belittle their accomplishments. They should be integrated with the TQM effort, supervisors and managers added to the circles, management team tasks added to their work, and the groups encouraged to continue.

TRAINING AND FACILITATING TEAMS

Figure 6-2 outlines the characteristics of successful and unsuccessful TQM improvement teams. Success requires management support, which includes training and guidance in using tools, following procedures, and group dynamics.

Figure 6-2
Successful and
Unsuccessful
Teams

Successful Teams...	Unsuccessful Teams...
Are focused. The more the issue has been defined for the team members before the start of a project, the less chance they will get off the track.	**Are unfocused.** Teams spend much effort trying to narrow the scope of the issue, and often head out in the wrong direction.
Have the right members. People on the teams represent the processes involved and the skills needed to address the issue.	**Do not have all the right members.** The team does not have representatives from key processes, or the right skills. Any solutions they develop will be less acceptable to the organization.
Have time to work on the issue. The issue does not require an immediate solution	**Must look for "quick fixes."** The team is pressured by management to look for quick solutions or to "fire fight" a problem.
Make teamwork a priority. Teamwork is at the top of the team members' "to do" lists and is seen that way by management.	**Feel pressure to do other things first.** Team members feel that other things are more important, and may be pressured by their superiors to put other tasks first.
Are backed by committed management. Management sets high expectations for the team; instills confidence; provides oversight, guidance, and recognition; and demands excellence.	**Have little management commitment.** Management does not make demands on the team or provide it with support and guidance.
Have excellent communication. Team members communicate well in meetings, and with management and other parts of the organization.	**Work in isolation.** Team members do not get along, and work in isolation from management and the rest of the organization.
Have good information. The team has enough information to deal with an issue, or the skills and resources to gather this information.	**Have little information.** The team does not have hard facts on an issue, nor can it obtain this information. Any solutions are based on guesswork.
Follow the improvement cycle. The team uses the appropriate TQM tools in the right sequence to address an issue.	**Skip steps in the cycle.** The team does not follow the cycle; results do not get to root causes.

Training

The crucial part that training plays in TQM teamwork cannot be overemphasized. People have to learn new ways of approaching problems and issues, unfamiliar terms and techniques, and how to conduct themselves in a meeting. The what, how, when, and who of TQM training are somewhat different from formal classroom instruction.

Curriculum

The key subjects of training for TQM are the improvement cycle and how to use the basic tools of TQM (discussed in Chapter 5). Every member of a team, and eventually all employees from the top executive down, should be familiar with these tools. More specialized training includes in-depth study of statistical process control, quality function deployment, and advanced tools. Training also should cover group dynamics, in order for teams to understand how best to run their meetings.

Beware of canned courses. A host of companies will sell you standard, off-the-shelf courses on TQM. Their trainers (who are simply trainers) will deliver these by rote to your personnel. The effect will be neither satisfactory nor long-lasting. Everything taught should reflect the mission and situation of an organization. Instruction need not be tailored from scratch, but it does require some customizing.

Materials

Like their courses, most of the organizations interviewed for this book customize TQM materials they obtain from outside groups. These materials are roughly divided between team leader and team facilitator workbooks, and those used by team members. The materials contain examples relevant to the organization, often drawn from previous teamwork.

Timing

The consensus among the people interviewed was that training for improvement teams needs to be "just in time." That is, teams should receive training as they need it, and must apply it immediately. Some estimated that team members start to forget what they learned in classrooms in no more than three weeks. The world of TQM is full of horror stories of organizations spending vast amounts of money on training, then seeing it go to waste when people did not use it quickly.

Most training should be on the job, using actual data from the process under examination. The only way people understand TQM is to use it, and they understand it best when they use it on a process with which they are familiar.

Instructors

Managers and supervisors should be the principal instructors of their employees. They should know the information employees need thoroughly and completely — because they should be using it, too, every day. Not only does this ensure that everyone has a common language and understanding, it also sends a clear message to employees: this is important.

Until managers and supervisors have the knowledge and skills to do this, special internal instructors can be used. All the organizations interviewed for this book started with outside consultant trainers, but only as an interim step while they trained their own. The exceptions are advanced courses in highly specialized methods. Many organizations certify managers and instructors as qualified to teach TQM methods.

All people tend to give their own interpretation of TQM when they are instructors. There is nothing wrong with this when it simply reflects the style of the instructor. But people can stray from the basic messages, so certification and periodic refresher courses help keep them on track.

The ideal TQM instructor also can perform the job of facilitator, which is discussed below. However, at the start of TQM implementation, you may have to use different people to serve as instructors and facilitators.

Facilitators

If the idea of an outside facilitator for a team meeting seems alien to you, consider how meetings are run in your organization right now. Does everyone contribute freely to them? Do they stay focused? And do they always deliver? If so, send us an application form — we want to work there, too! If not, you will need facilitators. People are not used to the structured team style of TQM — few people interact in this way until they join the quality movement.

The best TQM team facilitators know how to use the right tools, follow the improvement cycle, and handle the dynamics of group meetings. They attend team meetings, observe the group dynamics, recommend ways to help teams work more effectively, and advise the team leader on how to get individual members to work together. Facilitators stay in the background if things are running smoothly, and come forward to help when they are not. (Keep these qualities in mind: they are how you want all your managers to manage.)

Choosing facilitators

A person from outside a process area who has no vested interest in an issue makes the best facilitator. He or she will bring an objective view to team meetings. All the organizations interviewed for this book had several facilitators that they assigned as needed to different teams. Most of these facilitators were managers, or had management experience.

Some of these organizations use full-time facilitators selected from among their staff, while others use part-timers who hold other internal jobs, or a combination of both. It is also common to use outside consultant facilitators during TQM implementation. A few organizations, such as NASA's Johnson Space Center, use permanent outside facilitators.

Training facilitators

Many people interviewed report that the early training they gave to their internal facilitators lacked balance: they concentrated too much on the tools and procedures, or too much on group dynamics. Facilitators need both sets of skills. Several organizations require that their internal facilitators be certified in both by outside consultants.

The instructor and facilitator roles as management norm

As discussed in Chapter 11, eventually you want to do away with special instructors and facilitators. All of your managers should learn to handle both roles, both in assisting a team outside their unit and in their day-to-day management of their subordinates. This is true participative management.

Other Support

Other support an organization needs to provide its teams includes time and space for meetings, travel to remote sites if this is necessary, materials, and technical assistance. As indicated in Chapter 5, team members should always be given access to internal and external customers and suppliers, if this is necessary for working on an improvement issue.

ISSUES AND PROBLEMS IN WORKING WITH TEAMS

People interviewed for this book identified several other issues and problems in working with teams. Their observations and Coopers & Lybrand's are presented below.

Scope Of The Purpose Statement

The major reason for delays and failed efforts in TQM team work is that the scope of a purpose statement is too broad. Nearly every organization we interviewed reported horror stories like this one told by a facilitator from the Fresno IRS Service Center: "One team I worked with was charged with reducing undeliverable mail. Sounds simple, doesn't it? It turned out that there were many types of undeliverable mail, and many causes that required action and authority beyond the ability of team members. The team spent a year and a half just narrowing down the possible actions they could take." *It is management's job to develop clear, concise, and measurable purpose statements for all teams.*

Politics

Part of a team's job is to be sure the solutions it proposes are acceptable to management, other employees, and the organization as a whole. This is the "politics" of quality. Teams made up of managers and white collar professionals may readily understand this, but other employees may need to be coached. A solution that is unacceptable is a bad solution, no matter what its technical merits.

Management Interest And Involvement

The strongest support managers can show for teamwork is to be on teams themselves and promote teamwork throughout their units. Also, says the quality coordinator of the Florida Department of Transportation, District 5, "Managers must be interested in teams, know and talk with team members, and look for areas to appoint teams. One way you can tell if there is management support for teamwork is when a manager walks in and sits down at a team meeting. In some meetings, the workers keep talking as if he isn't there. In others, they clam up."

"Quick Fixes" Derived From Team Work

While addressing an issue, a team will turn up dozens of small problems and opportunities. Many will be within the jurisdiction of managers close to a process, non-controversial, easy to implement, and of no or low cost. There is nothing wrong with taking action on these immediately without experimenting with them — if you are confident of the results. If you are sure a small idea like this is a diamond, fine. If not, take it to the jeweler (i.e., the Roadmap to Quality).

Teamwork Versus Regular Work

Teamwork *is* part of the regular work of all employees. One objective of any quality improvement effort is to convince both management and workforce of this. Making teamwork seem too special is a mistake. An organization must send out this message loud and clear: "This is the way we do business."

Voluntary Versus Appointed Participation

Should the members of improvement teams be volunteers, or should they be appointed by management? Coopers & Lybrand's position tends toward appointing members — teamwork is regular work. However, no employee who is truly opposed to the idea should be forced to join a team.

The Cincinnati IRS Service Center keeps files of applications of employees who want to serve on teams. Management teams choose improvement team members from among these volunteers, and also appoint employees with special expertise. Other agencies simply put out a call for volunteers whenever

Other agencies simply put out a call for volunteers whenever a team is being formed and screen the applicants for the appropriate skills and positions.

Managers are a different story; teamwork is part of their job. Resistant managers should be educated and counseled on the importance of their participation. This is doubly true for competent and skilled managers who could add much to a team and are admired by their employees. The chief of statistical methods at Watervliet Army Arsenal puts it this way: "A strong horse is worth taming. I think you have to make extra efforts to bring your best on board."

A group of employees who are candidates for a self-managed team can decide not to participate. However, if they do elect to join, every member of their work group is, by definition, a member of the team.

Re-energizing Teams

Even in a mature TQM organization, teams require periodic revitalization. Holding refresher courses and sending members to conferences help. Volusia County has an annual QualityFest, a day of seminars and presentations, to which it invites all team members, managers, and outside organizations. This costs Volusia County less than $1,000 a year, yet the impact on employees (and the private sector of the Volusia economy) is tremendous. Other groups, as mentioned in Chapter 3, send their employees to visit customers, which increases the desire for excellence. There is nothing like seeing your product in use to make you want to make it better.

But the most important energizer costs much less. When top managers serve on teams, ask employees how their teams are going, and, most of all, enact team recommendations —that is energy.

Chapter

7

EXTENDING QUALITY OUTSIDE THE ORGANIZATION

■ A public organization is part of an enterprise that includes these partners:

- Other government groups with similar missions or interests
- Groups that distribute its funds or services to the public
- Vendors and contractors
- External customers

■ An organization's ability to improve is limited by the quality practices of its enterprise partners

■ Government organizations have improved quality in enterprise partners by teamwork, incentives, mandates, and other formal and informal cooperative arrangements

You can practice the most advanced TQM in the world, but if you ignore your partner organizations, you will eventually run into a dead end. Do not be myopic. You are not part of an organization; you are part of an enterprise. That enterprise includes you, your customers, and your partners: other government agencies, groups that distribute your funds to the public, and your vendors and contractors.

Who Are Your Partners?

Here are some examples of enterprise partners, besides external customers, in government:

- Other government agencies or branches of your own agency that affect your work processes;

- Local or regional offices that provide central agency products and services to a program's ultimate customers; and

- Vendors, contractors, and other external suppliers.

These are not always "natural" partners. Other government offices may not understand or care about your needs, and interagency turf battles may be long-standing. Your agency may have an us/them view of your distributors. Procurement regulations and ethics concerns may make it difficult to define and pursue proper cooperation with your contractors.

Despite these obstacles, governments are forging new and better relationships with their partners. TQM is helping to lead the way.

GOVERNMENT PARTNERS

Many of the organizations interviewed for this book have used TQM methods to form partnerships with other government agencies. For example, coordinating with the Federal Reserve Bank allows the Ogden IRS Service Center to make daily tax receipts available to the Treasury one day earlier, for a savings of $1.4 million annually. Several IRS Service Centers include representatives of the U.S. Postal Service on teams working on undeliverable mail.

Without this type of partnership with other government agencies, you will rapidly hit a stone wall. Your ability to improve your own operations is limited by how much you depend on these other agencies. This dependence extends horizontally to organizations working on the same issues that you are; it is also vertical, going up all the way to legislators and other elected officials. To succeed in quality improvement, you must begin to analyze what you need from these partners, and what they need from you.

The only way to do this is to begin talking with them about shared issues of quality. TQM methods and procedures will help you prepare for those meetings, so that you can define clearly the issues that affect you most. You can use educational strategies to bring these parties on board, or you can even force them to comply with your quality needs — but only if you have the facts.

CHANGING RELATIONSHIPS WITH DISTRIBUTORS

In government, distributors are organizations that receive resources from funding agencies and give them to the final recipients. For example, local Food Stamp and Women, Infants, and Children (WIC) programs are distributors for the U.S. Department of Agriculture. Local community health clinics are distributors for federal- and state-funded health care resources.

Distributors are, in a sense, like the service stations in an oil company's network. The oil company may not own the service stations, but needs them to do a top-quality job if the company expects to sell its gasoline. If government distributors do their jobs right, the funding agency will meet its objectives. If not, both the funding agency and the final recipients are in jeopardy.

One model for distributor relations is the detailed and inflexible procedures manual combined with massive documentation. The other is the grant that has few controls attached to it. Neither model is satisfactory, since neither does anything to promote true quality practices among the distributors. A new model is emerging.

Empowering Distributors To Create Their Own Quality Systems

Each year, the Department of Education gives or guarantees $18 billion in grants, loans, and work-study assistance to college students. It depends on thousands of schools to help administer the various financial aid programs. The predominant department strategy for working with the schools includes prescriptive regulations, massive documentation, after-the-fact inspection, multiple process checkpoints, and minimum standards and quotas.

The new strategy, still being tested on Title IV student aid programs, is to deregulate the process and give the schools the authority to determine on their own how best to accomplish financial aid program objectives. And instead of quotas and minimum national standards, the effort pushes for continuous improvement. The department exempts the 60 schools in the pilot project from some federal regulations that prescribe in inflexible detail how to verify student application data before awarding financial assistance. Instead, the schools can design their own verification programs. In return, the schools develop a formal quality system that includes management self-assessment, error measurement, corrective action management, and monitoring. The department trains and consults with the schools in setting up these systems.

According to a recent evaluation of the pilot program, most schools found that the new system helps them manage their financial aid offices better. In addition, the system consistently identifies chronic problems, which lets the schools target corrective action at process improvement, not individual mistakes. According to a department report, the pilot project has the potential to be a government-wide model for reducing procedure-oriented regulations while maintaining accountability.

TEAMWORK WITH VENDORS AND CONTRACTORS

The true price of purchased products and services is the total cost of owning them. This includes the actual bid price, plus the cost of inspecting for defects, poor performance, and correcting errors made by contractors and vendors. Also to be considered is the relationship between the customer and the vendor. If it is negative, costs invariably are higher because neither party will help the other improve quality (which reduces cost). If it is positive, open, and sharing, the total price of goods actually becomes lower, because quality will improve. Only recently, however, have both public and private sector organizations started to take this more holistic view of the cost of purchased goods and services.

This change is difficult to make. Buying from the lowest bidder and keeping an arms-length relationship with vendors are ingrained tenets of American business and government — and principles that audit agencies and inspectors general take seriously. For the rest of this chapter let us examine two new approaches: partnership and mandating quality.

Team-Building With Vendors

The whole notion of team-building between customers and vendors revolves around recognizing that a team relationship can and should exist. Such a relationship is characterized by open communications, trust, common understanding of roles and responsibilities, and common quality goals.

But to arrive at this point, the customer must practice TQM. This means that customers see themselves as suppliers, too.

Treating suppliers as customers

When the Air Force Systems Command (AFSC) asked the chief executive officers of its largest contractors what the AFSC could do better, contractor response was loud and clear: clean up your requests for proposal (RFPs).

"We recognized that when it came to RFPs the contractors are our customers," said an assistant deputy for contracting at Wright-Patterson Air Force Base. "To get quality proposals we had to give quality RFPs."

To do this, the Air Force developed an ongoing cross-functional government/contractor team that works for continuous improvement in RFP form and function. "Before we took a TQM approach," a contracts manager said, "I would not have considered the RFP process a high priority. I would have said, 'Go away, I'm busy doing my job.' Today it's clear that working with suppliers to make the process effective is a critical part of my job."

Planning together

NASA's Johnson Space Center includes contractors on the working groups that carry out fundamental planning tasks, such as the strategic planning support team, the technology support team, and the contractor incentive working group. The center director also holds periodic meetings with contractor executives to share information on NASA and center strategic plans. "We have about 50 contractor organizations at Johnson Space Center, and we have to have a structured system to use their expertise," says a management chief. "Like employees, contractors perform better when they understand how they contribute to the big picture. How can they do that if you don't give them the big picture?"

Training together

When Coopers & Lybrand conducted TQM training for the Air Force Electronic Systems Division, three partners took part: the division, the 3245th Air Base Group, and the Mitre Corporation, a major contractor. Contractor and client personnel interacted as each learned about the new approach the division would follow.

Coopers & Lybrand also facilitated two-day team-building exercises for the Air Force Development Test Center and its major contractors, Magnavox, General Dynamics, and Harris Manufacturing. After these meetings, everyone was able to answer clearly and succinctly these two questions: "What do you need from me?" and "What do I need from you?"

The answers were not found in test center contract documents, and usually people were too busy to ask the questions. Worse, they assumed they knew the answers. The participants of the center exercise say the major benefits are vastly improved communication and a crystallization of their roles and responsibilities. As a result, the center and its contractors have formed more and better improvement teams. For more information on team building, see Chapter 11.

Working cooperatively

In the past 20 years government has increased the number of specifications and required management procedures that contractors must follow. Some organizations are finding that the end result improves when contractors help agencies develop the rules they have to live with. For instance, the National Security Industry Association and the Aerospace Industries Association worked with the Department of Defense (DoD) to develop a national certification program for products and industry quality systems. DoD and the defense industry have also developed a 10-point quality excellence program that focuses on eliminating unnecessary contract requirements.

Prime contractors and subcontractors of the Air Force's Advanced Cruise Missile program have met as a group with program officers and contract personnel on several occasions to work out approaches to problems and opportunities. The focus of these meetings is quality, and the methods of conducting it are those of TQM.

Providing Incentives To Quality

Both government and industry customers are giving their suppliers and distributors special incentives to improve quality. These include flat-out requirements, negative sanctions, and positive rewards.

Basing buy decisions on past quality performance

The Department of Defense is reconsidering its whole approach to contracting; it wants to reward quality, not just low price. Plans are under way to base source selection for new weapons contracts as much on the quality of work contractors have demonstrated in the past as on the cost bids they offer.

Defense Department planners believe that quality pays. "If we can get contractors following TQM principles," says one DoD quality advocate, "ultimately the highest quality company is also going to be the lowest bidder."

Every month, the Defense Logistics Agency circulates a list of suppliers that do not provide high-quality material. The

Navy is going one step further by testing a contractor evaluation system that rates bidders according to their past performance in delivering quality goods and services. The rating system is based on the risk to the Navy of dealing with a contractor: red means high risk, yellow means medium risk, and green means low risk.

In the test, the Navy adds the cost of additional quality control measures it must take to the quoted prices of the red and yellow contractors. In addition, awarding a contract to a red contractor requires approval by the head of the contracting office.

Giving warranties

One method the DoD is working on is the exemplary facility concept. Under this approach contractors give the agency a warranty that everything they turn out is fit for its intended use.

"If you have a contractor that's doing an outstanding job, you can put him in charge of his own processes. You do not spend extra money sending quality assurance inspectors to his facility," a DoD planner explains. "Then you hold his feet to the fire based on the warranties. This program could also allow many of our 7,200 quality control inspectors to stop rejecting defective finished products and start helping contractors develop processes to 'do it right the first time.'"

Mandating quality

In June 1987, the Pentagon took a major step in raising supplier quality: it changed its specifications to require defect-free products. For 40 years before that, the military used "Acceptable Quality Level" standards. "By specifying no more than say, 2 percent defects [under the old system], we often ensured that two defective items out of 100 was precisely what we got," the DoD director of industrial production and quality explained. "What you expect in quality is what you get."

Earning more money for better quality

NASA's Lewis Research Center has had good response to its quality and productivity award fees program. This incentive lets a contractor earn additional money, over and above the regular award fee criteria, based on a solid quality and productivity program and verifiable improvements.

The center gets more than one-time gains from this approach. It has motivated its contractors to make fundamental TQM changes in their own organizations. The center's major contractor for logistics and support services received the special award after it adopted TQM principles such as employee participation and team action for process improvement, which resulted in benefits to the government.

One indication of the company's cultural change was distributing all of the quality and productivity award fee money to employees. "Management wanted results and the employees got us there," the contractor's quality and productivity manager explains. "They got the money because they earned it."

The most important point of the NASA example is that part of the award is for introducing quality practices. This is a real motivator for adopting TQM.

About all these initiatives, a member of DoD's Quality Assurance Council says, "Survival is a great motivator. What we're telling our contractors is that you might as well get on the quality bandwagon, because if you produce shoddy, low-quality products, expect to get no business from us."

Vendor Partnership: A TQM Approach

"Vendor partnership" is the TQM term for a formal system of dealing with companies that sell you goods and services. The advantages of this approach have been proven repeatedly in industry and include:

- Improved product quality;
- Reliable delivery performance;
- Reduced lead times;
- Increased vendor service;
- Extended technical capabilities; and
- Lower product cost.

The price of products and services from a vendor partner tends to be lower than open-market prices, because the vendor is guaranteed a large portion of an organization's business for a long period. True cost is also lower because these products and services can be designed to fit a customer's processes precisely, and the customer receives better service. Figure 7-1 compares traditional relationships with vendors to the TQM approach.

Figure 7-1
Traditional Versus TQM Vendor Relations

Traditional	Total Quality Management
Multiple vendors for the same types of products: The reasons for this are leverage in price negotiations and an assumed protection of the flow of supplies.	**Number of vendors minimized:** This creates a vested interest in the mutual success of both customer and vendor. It also allows the vendor to increase the level of specialized services to a customer.
Ignorance of the vendor's quality system: As a result, an organization must use incoming inspection to determine quality. The relationship between customer and supplier becomes one of blame versus assistance for achieving quality.	**Specific quality systems requirements:** The customer requires proof that vendor processes are in control. No incoming inspection is needed. Both parties combine problem-solving resources.
Poor communications of standards and specifications: The arms-length posture between traditional organizations and their vendors means that the vendors cannot become involved in the setting of standards and specifications. The results are confusion and frequent change orders in contracts to correct these mistakes.	**Mutual agreement on standards and specifications:** Customers and vendors work together to set standards and specifications. There are no misunderstandings.
Short-term contracts: Contracts are for a few months or years.	**Long-term contracts:** Contracts are for several years; commitments even longer.
Emphasis on price: Particularly in government, price becomes the overriding factor in selecting vendors. The quality of vendor products and vendor reputation often take a back seat to price.	**Emphasis on value:** The customer considers the overall value of vendor products, customer service, and vendor participation in the production process.

Vendor partnership may at first seem an alien concept, given government acquisition regulations. The fact is that many of its methods have just been described earlier in this chapter as part of what government agencies are doing today.

Perhaps the major barrier remaining to vendor partnerships in government is the legal requirement to open competition to all qualified vendors and contractors. Private companies are under no such obligation, and those that practice vendor partnership tend to give their business to vendors with which they have long-term relationships. They do this as long as the vendors maintain commitment to quality and offer a fair market price. It is only natural for such vendors to help customers set standards and specifications and plan projects. This information is a closely held secret in most government agencies, until requests for bids are made public.

Despite these differences in the private and public sectors' procurement environments, vendor partnership has many features that work well in both. Among these are the up-front work customers do to improve buying practices, teamwork with vendors, and certifying vendors.

Starting vendor partnerships

An organization begins a vendor partnership program by forming an internal cross-functional team of high-level managers. This team provides program direction and resources, and evaluates and resolves issues that arise. The organization then sets up several commodity teams, which focus on particular categories of purchased products and services. The commodity teams establish goals and objectives for vendors, coordinate vendor TQM activity, and report progress to the cross-functional team. Internal users of products serve on the commodity teams, provide pertinent data, and assist in evaluating vendors.

The commodity teams identify improvement opportunities in current purchasing practices and products for their area. They work with vendors to identify causes of and potential solutions for problems, and measure and evaluate results of vendor improvement. The purchasing department is responsible for introducing the vendor partnership program to vendors, and works with them to implement TQM practices.

Vendor representatives form vendor partnership teams with an organization's personnel. They work on common issues and problems, and are available to participate on improvement teams when the need arises.

Vendor partnership is appropriate only when you buy a large volume of a particular product or service, or when a product is critical to operations. Exceptions to this are commonly available raw materials, paper, etc. The higher the percentage of the vendor's sales to you, the better, since the vendor becomes dependent on your business and will be more motivated to meet your expectations.

Selecting vendor partners

Vendor partners are selected on the basis of their historic performance in quality, delivery, and price; ability to produce the needed volume; quality attitude; expertise; use of statistical process control; proximity; stability; and financial solvency.

Under vendor partnership, vendors are classified into three categories, based on audits and vendor documentation:

• **Certified Vendor:** The vendor's quality system is accepted; proven quality, delivery, and value; the customer does not inspect supplies when they aredelivered.

• **Approved Vendor:** Quality system acceptable; quality, delivery, and value under review; use statistical sampling for incoming inspection.

• **Additional Vendors:** Quality system unknown or under review; quality, delivery, and value under review; inspection is increased until reduction is justified.

This classification scheme is much like the Navy's red-yellow-green system. Adding requirements for quality practices to the Navy system (parts of which are already on the DoD's books and have recently been introduced at NASA) would come very close to making this a true vendor partnership arrangement.

Contracts and trust

Contracts are definitely part of vendor partnerships. The difference is that, for U.S. private industry, these tend to be for longer periods than in the past. However, industry's definition of short-term contracts is usually six months to a year, and long-term is often only two years. Government contracts tend to be longer. This is especially true for large and complex buys such as weapons systems, data processing systems, and facilities support.

The very long-term relationships between customer and vendor under this approach are based on trust, not contracts. Each party in a vendor partnership has a degree of commitment to the other (and to the end user) that goes far beyond the typical arms-length buyer/seller arrangement. This is why great thought must be given to selecting a vendor partner, and why vendor attitudes toward quality are so important.

TOTAL QUALITY MEANS EVERYBODY

Your organization is not an isolated agency or program; it is the hub of an enterprise. If you take this enterprise view, you will want your partners to adopt TQM, too. If everyone in your enterprise practices quality, you cannot help but achieve continuous improvement.

Where to start? First, you have to introduce TQM at the hub — your own organization. The next four chapters discuss how to do this.

Chapter

8

THE QUALITY TEAM — KEY PLAYERS, KEY ROLES

■ All groups within an organization must adopt new roles in order to support effective quality management. These groups include:

- Top executives
- Middle managers and supervisors
- Employees
- Support departments
- The quality resource group
- Unions
- Expert consultants

The first questions government staff ask about TQM are, "How will it affect my job?" and "What will I do differently under this approach?" This chapter answers those questions by outlining the new roles and responsibilities of key players in a TQM environment. These important actors include:

- Top executives;

- Managers and employees at all levels;

- Support departments;

- The quality resource group;

- Unions;

- Internal and external quality consultants; and

- Other members of the organization's enterprise.

TOP EXECUTIVES: CREATING THE VISION, DRIVING THE CHANGE

"Top management is the first through the third steps in quality. You can't begin to estimate the value of a leader who is involved...If executives are committed, it doesn't matter how many mistakes you make along the way; eventually you will succeed."

– Quality coordinator, Florida Department of Transportation District 5

"The key area is executive management, because the middle managers respond to what the leaders do."

– Quality coordinator, Cincinnati IRS Service Center

Top Government Executives: Who Are They?

Cabinet officers, assistant and deputy secretaries, agency directors, assistant directors, division chiefs, regional office directors, military installation commanders, hospital chiefs of staff, research center directors, governors, county executives, mayors, and city administrators.

Government agencies and quality experts agree that the critical prerequisite for successful TQM is top management commitment. Someone has to be willing to make a career stand on the effort — to lead with a sense of mission, to take the variety of actions required. When a top executive fulfills this commitment, he or she shapes and sustains the quality process.

Key Roles: Initiating TQM And Following Through

At many agencies, one of top management's most basic responsibilities is starting a TQM program, according to a recent survey conducted for the Naval Postgraduate School. In the 30 responding organizations, top executives had initiated more than 80 percent of TQM programs.

Committing to TQM

In committing to TQM in the 1985 filing season, the Internal Revenue Service faced a crisis. The IRS had installed new computer equipment and written 2,000 new software programs to run it, but a mountain of systems problems led to chaos. As a result, angry taxpayers waited for refunds, and angry Treasury officials waited for revenue. The IRS Commissioner announced an agency-wide TQM initiative soon after that.

Not all TQM initiatives begin this dramatically, but visible agency problems are often an important spur to action. The first task of an organization's leaders is to discover and publicize the reasons for change. Then, they must show that TQM is effective.

Getting quality expertise

Once upper management becomes interested in TQM, the next step is to provide TQM awareness training for top aides (e.g., assistant directors, regional office directors, division chiefs). Leaders also assemble a pool of experts, including internal or external quality consultants, to help guide planning and implementation. With this cadre of top management and consultants on board, the initiative begins to take shape.

Developing a vision

Before you can find the right path, you have to know where you are going. Creating the agency's vision for change — and then empowering your staff to achieve it — is arguably management's most important contribution. Quality visions are broad, but they point where to go. Developing a vision includes writing specific statements about desired results, which lead to identifying internal and external barriers to success; and framing general strategies for overcoming the barriers. All TQM actions should contribute to making the vision a reality.

Visions of Government Quality

Veterans Affairs Regional Office and Insurance Center, Philadelphia, Pa.

"Our mission is to accurately and efficiently provide benefits and services to veterans and their families in a manner recognized as fair and responsive. Our vision is to be the finest provider of services in VA and to be recognized as such; to have a culture which respects both our customers and our staff and which earns the trust of veterans and their families."

North Island Naval Aviation Depot, San Diego, Calif.

"We are vital to our nation's defense. Our highly skilled, multi-cultural workforce is dedicated to producing quality products and services on schedule and at lowest cost to our customers. Through creativity and teamwork we will be the leader in aviation maintenance, logistics management, and engineering. We are committed to continuous process improvement to ensure Fleet readiness."

City of Wilmington, N.C.

"We want Wilmington to be recognized as a great place to live, where our customers receive high-quality services, our employees work in an environment of respect and support, our leadership stimulates coop-

> eration and innovation in our community, and our gift
> to future generations is an even better city than was
> given to us."

Energizing the effort

"Top managers cannot mandate TQM and expect it to
succeed, because the only changes people really support are
the ones they help create," the quality coordinator at the
Philadelphia Veterans Affairs Regional Office and Insurance
Center believes. "In trying to institutionalize the approach, you
have to use its techniques — you encourage, enable, and
exemplify the principles you promote."

Every executive has his or her own style in persuading
others to support TQM. Some rely on their charismatic leadership abilities and conduct visible "campaigns."

"When our new commanding officer came to the Defense
Industrial Supply Center the quality movement solidified,"
DISC's quality coordinator explains. "He took such a visible
role in articulating his vision, training others, and modeling the
behaviors that all the department directors wanted to be visible
too.

"Up to this point there was little push from the outside and
our efforts were disjointed. Once our new commanding officer
became personally involved, an internal 'pull' for quality was
apparent."

Visible, dynamic support for TQM does not mean being a
"cheerleader," however. As VAROIC's late director Robert
Carey said, "One thing we learned from our research is that
quality slogans are everywhere. We almost took a sloganeer-
ing approach. We had an advertising committee come up with
banners, logos, and motherhood and apple pie speeches.

"But the consultants we brought in convinced us that
cheerleading for quality is hollow. So is slapping a 'quality'
label on something you've already done. We truly energized
our effort when we began planning concrete steps to help us
reach our vision."

Working on systems issues

"I can tell how committed top managers are to TQM by looking at their calendars," says the chief of statistical methods at Watervliet Army Arsenal. "If they are spending most of their time working on system-wide quality issues, then they are committed. This means they are removing obstacles to improvement, helping managers and customers with quality issues, and doing other quality work that only people in their positions can handle. If they are spending most of their time fire fighting, attending endless meetings on other issues, or just making speeches about quality, then you have to question both their understanding and commitment to their role as quality leaders."

MIDDLE MANAGERS AND SUPERVISORS: TQM'S FRONT LINES

"Middle managers may feel most threatened by changes like these, since they may fear that TQM will take away some of their power. They are used to telling people what to do and how to do it. What we are hoping for in the future are leaders and guiders who listen to and act on the ideas of employees."

– Assistant commissioner for administration,
U.S. Patent and Trademark Office

"Often, middle managers are willing to go into process improvement, but higher management keeps hitting them with short-term projects and reports. Too often they have to stop working on TQM to work on yesterday's problem."

– Quality administrator,
Sacramento Army Depot

Government Middle Managers and Supervisors: Who Are They?

Office or department heads
Branch chiefs
Foremen
Work unit leaders and supervisors

Whom would you expect to be the greatest source of resistance to TQM? If you said employees, you are wrong, according the Naval Postgraduate School Survey referenced earlier, and Coopers & Lybrand's 1989 survey of federal executives. Employees in fact appear to offer the least resistance, while middle management has been the major obstacle.

Why? Too often top managers and quality resource groups have not paid enough attention to middle managers and supervisors in their enthusiasm to set TQM in motion. Quality leaders have learned the hard way that middle managers need to be involved in planning change and given the training to understand and function under the new approach.

"When we began our effort, funding limitations forced us to put some middle managers and supervisors on process improvement teams before they were adequately trained," says a top executive at the Philadelphia Veterans Affairs Regional Office and Insurance Center. "They were already giving up some control to allow more employee participation, and they were very frustrated. Later we realized that we needed to train them fully before expecting them to take action — and before their employees are trained or encouraged to participate. Nothing stifles employees' enthusiasm more quickly than a first line manager's rejecting their improvement ideas — or their right to offer them."

Key Roles: Manage For Improvement, Guide Process Change

Managers and supervisors have the greatest day-to-day influence on employees. They can help the workforce make quality and improvement top-of-mind issues, or they can undercut this effort and hope it goes away. But the style, attitudes, and actions of middle managers may have to be very different from the way they were before.

Developing a participative management style

"The role of supervisors and middle managers changed dramatically at the Forest Service when top management empowered our employees," the director of a forest experiment station recalls. "They had to change to a more collegial, collaborative style. They had to loosen up, accept change, and trust employees to do their jobs when given the proper means."

Managers also review the performance of employees according to different standards. Their own performance is assessed differently — and employees may contribute to their evaluation.

"Under TQM," says the chief of statistical methods at Watervliet Army Arsenal, "the standards for evaluating managers should include how well they perform in cross-functional cooperation and systems improvement. And instead of treating quality improvement as an 'extra-credit' assignment, they should see it as part of the job."

Middle managers and supervisors must learn, follow, and teach the team approach to process improvement. This can be a big leap for people accustomed to making their own decisions, but it is as critical for them to "walk the talk" as it is for top leadership.

The goal of developing these qualities is to move employees from willingness to cooperate to active involvement to dedication and self-motivation. First line managers thus can tap into a valuable quality resource for the organization: employees' discretionary effort to give their best instead of doing the minimum to get by.

Buying In: One Manager's Journey

"My first experience with participative management was as a field office employee. I submitted a suggestion through the channels and it ultimately went to Washington. They bounced it back with a reply that made me wonder if they could understand English. So I wrote it up again. This time someone in Washington called me — and chewed me out for 45 minutes for wasting their time. That was 11 years ago, and I haven't submitted a formal suggestion since then.

"My early team involvement as a VAROIC manager didn't sell me on the participative approach either. At first I wanted to solve the problem myself rather than

---

take time on the group process. But at one meeting the idea finally hit home. What I had thought was the solution to the problem turned out to be very wrong. That's where I began to see the power of teamwork.

"I realized that no one is in a better position to see the need for improvements than the employee. Upper management actively wants employee suggestions at VAROIC. I now encourage them by allowing employees and teams to implement their good ideas.

"And one side benefit of TQM is that it's a lot more fun to come to work than it used to be. That's important when you're going to be at a place for 30 years."

– Manager at the Philadelphia Veterans Affairs Regional Office and Insurance Center

EMPLOYEES: THE HEARTBEAT OF QUALITY IMPROVEMENT

"I think there is a tendency for managers not to see their employees as capable of making suggestions to improve things. We tend to forget that employees manage their families and are community leaders. If they use their brains to solve community and family problems, then they can certainly do this at work."

– Assistant commissioner for administration, U.S. Patent and Trademark Office

"The average worker in our survey readily accepted the ideas of quality management. Several [quality] coordinators said that workers were positively ecstatic. It was the first time anyone at work had ever asked their ideas on anything."

– Larry Johnston, "The TQM coordinator as change agent in implementing Total Quality Management," master's thesis, Naval Postgraduate School

Key Roles: Tracking Change, Making Suggestions

Ultimately, the success of TQM depends on individual employees. When they put the customer first, customers are more satisfied with government's services and products. When they make continuous improvement a personal priority, quality will follow, *but only if management carries out its TQM roles.* No, employee contributions are not automatic. So do not be surprised that this section mostly addresses what *management* must do if employees are going to be able to contribute.

Collecting and analyzing data

Employees who are responsible for a process are the main trackers of process performance, not managers. Line staff at the Yorktown Naval Weapons Station contribute to designing process performance indicators, tracking information, and analyzing the trends. Yorktown began with 196 indicators but is now down to 64, based on employee review of their usefulness in practice. Employees also save managers time by acting on the immediate problems that performance indicators show. The deputy ordnance officer at Yorktown says, "Top managers see only the big picture now. We leave the details to the people who do the work — they know what to do."

Setting up monitoring systems so that employees can quickly see process performance is fundamental to their being able to control their work. Whether you decide to use SPC or another approach, make sure employees get the data immediately.

Participating in quality teams

Chapter 6 covers employee involvement in teams. Should all be involved at once? Not necessarily. Employees need training before they can participate, and management must ensure that there are meaningful assignments for the teams. But, as Chapter 6 says, teams are the glory part of TQM, and every employee should be encouraged to participate.

Making suggestions for improvement

In TQM we talk a lot about teams, but individual suggestions outside the team framework also can be a driving force for improvement. Employees have the ideas and should be encouraged to suggest them. The job of mining those gems belongs to management.

In its "Idea Express" suggestion program manual, the U.S. Coast Guard gives this message to managers: "The Japanese consider suggestion programs to be the cornerstone of their success...The average Japanese employee submitted 24 ideas in 1987. Many private sector companies in the United States have experienced the same success. These groups believe, and invest in, the development of ideas. With your help, the Coast Guard can enjoy the same success."

The best suggestion programs are not simply a slot box in the hallway. The key is management's commitment to make it easy for employees to suggest improvements, and to review these promptly and put innovations into practice. Continuous improvement at the Jacksonville Naval Aviation Depot, discussed in Chapter 1, was largely due to these management actions:

• Every week all employees were asked, individually, for their suggestions for improvement.

• Teams of employees engaged in friendly and informal competitions to see who could work smarter. The rewards: teaching the other team and, as one worker said, "...that pat on the back you get."

• All workers had a computer graphic printout of their work process. They could point precisely to where improvements could be made.

• Process performance data were quickly collected, analyzed, distributed, and discussed among supervisors and employees.

• Managers acted within days, and sometimes hours, to put employee suggestions into action.

This was not a one-time campaign. It had no banners and slogans. Instead, the suggestion program at Jacksonville was *a daily, automatic, and relentless pursuit of employee improvement ideas.* Is there any wonder that the depot reduced labor hours on aircraft refits by 40 percent?

The TQM Prescription for Employee Suggestion Programs

1. Make them proactive. Have managers and supervisors ask each employee regularly for suggestions. Make sure to ask them how management can help make their work easier.

2. Break down the fear that employees have in making suggestions (and it is a real fear). Don't shoot the messengers when they tell you problems. Instead, help them work out the solutions.

3. Eliminate the paperwork, and have managers take notes instead.

4. Act quickly on suggestions. If you can't act quickly, tell the suggestor why, quickly.

5. Do not reward suggestions only with the small amount of cash that management usually gives to its most sincere and dedicated workers. Give employees a chance to tell other people about how they figured out the problem. This will reward the suggestor and inspire everyone else.

If individual workers sincerely believe that management will listen to them, they will deliver the goods. When this happens, you have arrived at continuous improvement.

The value of employee involvement in TQM is arguably greatest to employees themselves. Commitment to quality gives them a sense of mission, belonging, and accomplishment. It is as an employee at the Ogden IRS Service Center says: "It feels great to know that management really wants our ideas. I'm doing more that just putting in my time: I'm making a valuable contribution to the team."

SUPPORT DEPARTMENTS: SPECIAL SKILLS FOR QUALITY IMPROVEMENT

> *"We are trying to reorient the quality control depart-
> ment to start auditing further upstream, and to make them
> educators about quality instead of quality police."*

> – Chief of statistical methods,
> Watervliet Army Arsenal

Support Departments: What Are They?

Accounting and comptroller, quality control, quality
assurance, human resources, procurement and contracting, planning, and management analysis.

Besides adopting TQM themselves, support departments
can make a direct and significant contribution to your quality
initiative:

• A new role of your procurement and contracts department is to establish and maintain vendor partnership programs, as described in Chapter 7.

• According to a 1990 survey of 800 human resources
and quality control professionals by Zenger-Miller, Inc.,
human resources groups must begin to champion training that
supports the strategic issues of service and quality. To do this,
they must learn the strategic needs of their organizations and
form long-term training plans to meet these needs. They also
must shift their emphasis from classroom training to preparing
managers and supervisors to be effective TQM "just-in-time"
instructors for employees.

Two support functions are particularly important — accounting and quality control/quality assurance — but their
roles may not be as obvious as the others.

Accounting

TQM is about satisfying customer expectations. Does your
accounting system give you any clues about this? Can you

isolate non-value-added activities and assess whether they are worth their cost? Probably not. So you are flying with some of your most important controls out of operation.

For example, *no one* interviewed for this book said the organization's accounting system can support cost of quality calculations. According to *Juran's Quality Control Handbook* (4th edition), Reason #1 that attempts to use cost of quality fail is that the accounting department will not cooperate. By now you understand what a serious shortcoming this is for a TQM initiative.

Poor management accounting weakens the impact of TQM. Comptrollers, controllers, and accountants must change their current roles as "bean counters" and "money police." They must become the source of information you need to control and improve individual processes and your whole organization, such as:

• The cost of quality in the organization, and in its subunits;

• The most economic combination of labor, material, equipment, and purchased goods and services for a process, product, or service;

• Sound financial background for make or buy decisions; and

• Financial indicators that track process performance.

Where can financial professionals begin? By helping to introduce activity-based costing (see Chapter 4), and by getting out of their offices and helping other groups, as did accountants and analysts at the Defense Industrial Supply Center (see Chapter 1).

What is the payback for financial personnel? There is both a carrot and a stick. The carrot is more meaningful work and major contributions to improvement. The stick? *Job security.* Modern computer-based accounting systems count beans thoroughly and efficiently. Coopers & Lybrand is a Big Six public accounting firm, and computers have reduced the number of people *we* need to serve our government and private audit clients! On the other hand, Coopers & Lybrand spends an increasing amount of time teaching modern financial analysis methods to these same clients. The message to financial personnel is clear: your profession is changing; change with it.

Quality Control/Assurance Personnel: A Resource For TQM

Traditional organizations often delegate the job of ensuring quality to a quality control or quality assurance department. Says the statistical methods chief at Watervliet Army Arsenal: "There is no question that TQM can scare a quality control department, since statistical process control and process improvements reduce the need for inspections."

This is a reasonable fear. Although it will take years of hard work, eventually a TQM organization will need very few quality inspectors. When people strive to "do it right the first time," errors and defects are few. Quality assurance also will be in less demand. When employees and supervisors (and vendors and distributors) become adept at monitoring processes, they do not need an outsider to check these against formal quality assurance manuals.

Meanwhile, like accountants, many quality control/quality assurance (QA/QC) professionals must change the way they work, or start training for other careers. But they can be a genuine asset to TQM. Quality control personnel already use some tools of TQM and can help teach and consult about them. Quality assurance specialists can help managers and workers examine their processes, and give them information they need to set improvement priorities. They also can be the "front line troops" for extending TQM to vendors and distributors. To do this, QA/QC personnel must:

• Learn new TQM tools and procedures, and how to teach them;

• Learn group dynamics and communication skills needed to work with teams and individuals; and

• Learn to apply their special knowledge to administrative and support functions as well as production departments.

Even if TQM succeeds throughout an enterprise, some types of inspection will still be needed. According to the director of quality at the Norfolk Naval Ship Yard: "Some processes and products that involve nuclear fuels, flight safety, or other critical elements will always require 100 percent inspection. But with TQM, the time between defects will go from hours, days, and weeks to years." The way to make this happen is teamwork between production and inspection personnel.

QA/QC professionals are well aware that TQM is changing their world, and the content of their journals and conferences reflects this. They can be a tremendous resource: use them.

THE QUALITY RESOURCE GROUP: TQM'S CHANGE AGENTS

"I consult with people, keep them informed, and watch the schedules. Many quality coordinators might characterize themselves as facilitators. I think of myself as a catalyst."

– Chief of statistical methods,
Watervliet Army Arsenal

The Quality Resource Group: Who Are They?

Quality coordinator or administrator, quality advocate, instructor, internal consultant, facilitator.

These are TQM's change agents. This means that they must:

• Understand and support top management's vision;

• Know their organization's structure well enough to lead change productively;

• Understand the players involved in the change, including their attitudes and fears; and

• Grasp the politics of change.

Most of the medium-sized and large organizations interviewed for this book have full-time "quality coordinators," often with a small staff of full- and part-time facilitators, instructors, and internal consultants. This quality resource group coordinates, trains, and facilitates meetings of teams. Its members also consult with managers, and otherwise provide support services to an organization's quality initiatives.

The reason for appointing a special person or group to do these things is summed up by the quality coordinator at the Cincinnati IRS Service Center: "When you first start out and say, 'Quality is everybody's job,' then it's nobody's job. You need to have a full-time person dedicated to the quality improvement effort as a focal point. Maybe someday the position won't be needed, but we aren't there yet." Others disagree with this practice, saying that this work should go to each department head, and that coordinating functions should be integrated with existing structures.

Deciding which route to take is up to each organization, but the fact remains that these important jobs must be done. The key thing to avoid is explained by the chief of statistical methods at Watervliet Army Arsenal: "I am the full-time quality coordinator here. Though 'chief of statistical methods' conjures up green eyeshades, I didn't want to be designated as the person responsible for our quality effort. I have a staff of one secretary. My shop was designed to have five to seven people, but I requested that this not be done. Not only would I have to pull people off other staff, it would mean I had a 'department.' Then all the other departments would say, 'The quality department is going to do the quality program.' I don't want this to be a program.

"And I was right in doing this: now all the department directors have had to develop their internal capabilities, not just depend on me."

Whatever your choice, most quality experts believe that quality coordinators' ultimate success will be putting themselves out of business. Broad-based ownership is important to long-term success; this means transferring quality resource group duties to managers when they can handle the responsibility.

Quality Change Agents: Do You Have the Right Stuff?

What does it take to be a successful quality change agent? Government responders to a survey conducted for the Naval Postgraduate School ranked the following items most important:

- Integrity and perseverance, to stand up for TQM principles that shake up entrenched cultural values;

- Knowledge and credibility to gain the confidence of staff;

- Effective interpersonal skills, and a belief that people are the organization's greatest source of strength;

- Communication skills, especially in talking and listening to people; and

- Motivation and the willingness and creativity to take the initiative, because many issues encountered will have no precedents.

Key Roles: Leading The Way, Supporting The Journey

Quality staff make many key contributions to TQM success, yet their position is a delicate one. Although they direct change daily, they cannot appear to command it. "I emphasize that the people I'm working with are the leaders. I am their advisor," says the quality coordinator at the Aeronautical Systems Division of Wright-Patterson Air Force Base.

Providing quality expertise

Quality coordinators need to become experts in quality management. According to the Naval Postgraduate School survey, most gain their expertise from formal courses, lots of self-study, or training by another quality specialist. In their "expert" capacity they advise management where the quality program should go next and how it should get there. They also help teams in selecting the right tools and procedures to tackle an improvement project.

Being able to do this requires constant study. "When I attend conferences and courses outside of government," says the quality coordinator of the Defense Industrial Supply Center, "I'm ever mindful of the necessity to keep us up-to-date with the evolving quality discipline."

Removing the obstacles

"The problem we hear most often," say members of the Total Quality Environment staff at the Naval Publications and Forms Center, "Is that people can't participate in quality activities because they already have too much to do.

"Sometimes this is an excuse, and sometimes it's the sign of an unsupportive supervisor. We view our job as facilitating participation. We intervene with supervisors, division leaders — even the commanding officer if necessary — to allow staff to make process improvement a priority. And our commanding officer has made it clear to all managers that TQM team meetings should always come first if there's a conflict of responsibilities."

Providing access to top management

"As part of my role I attend team meetings to represent county leadership," the quality coordinator in Volusia County, Florida, says. "Employees often come up to me and say, 'I know this stuff is important, if they've sent management to work with us.'"

Most quality coordinators have regular, direct access to their organization's top management. As such they become two-way information conduits and can link elements of the organization that may have little day-to-day interaction. Direct access shows the organization how seriously top management takes the effort, and it also has practical value.

"I meet with our commanding officer every two weeks for an hour, besides being a member of his top management quality council," DISC's quality coordinator notes. "This ready access is critical for my credibility, but it's also critical for the commanding officer in keeping his finger on the pulse. Because we have regular, open communication, he understands what the quality initiative needs, and we understand his priorities."

Using facilitators and other quality helpers

Process facilitators are also part of the quality resource group. Whether full-or part-time, they need training in both the tools and group dynamics of TQM teams. An organization also may need statisticians and experts in specific TQM methods. Chapter 6 has more details on their roles.

Coordinating the resources

Quality coordinators spend much of their time arranging for and scheduling training and facilitators. They also may help to develop training materials and curricula, track the progress of teams, help team leaders select members, and keep files of people who want to join teams.

Coming From The Right Place

"Every day you have to take the temperature of people you are working with, approach them from where they are, and relate to them at their level of commitment," the quality coordinator at the Cincinnati IRS Service Center notes. "When you are at this full time, you have to realize that no one will be as enthusiastic about it as you are."

UNIONS: ESSENTIAL PARTNERS FOR QUALITY

"In the abstract, there is nothing wrong with the idea behind [quality improvement programs], but our response must be conditioned by an awareness of management motives. At best, the motive is improved productivity. At worst, the motive is to establish lines of communication that circumvent the established union-management structure."

– United Steelworkers Policy Paper, 1987

"Before TQM and our quality of worklife program, the dialogue between management and labor was usually initiated by the unions, and it was adversarial. TQM has allowed progress based on mutual interest: union and management cooperate."

– Director of quality, Norfolk Naval Shipyard

About 60 percent of federal workers belong to unions, as do many state and local employees. White and blue collar unions' acceptance of TQM is sometimes a prerequisite to success. Quality enthusiasts may see improvement as a "motherhood and apple pie" issue; unions do not always take that point of view. Some unions have actively opposed quality improvement initiatives such as joint labor/management teams, statistical process control, and gain-sharing.

Why? Unions, which are often accustomed to regarding management as an adversary, have two major fears about quality programs: threats to job security from heightened productivity, and concern that TQM will weaken collective bargaining and grievance procedures:

• TQM reduces non-value-added work and, through process improvement, increases productivity. This may mean fewer jobs.

• Much of union wage negotiation revolves around the old guild system of specialized job positions. TQM emphasizes multi-skilled workers. Negotiating wages for such workers may or may not be more difficult for a union, but it is different.

Left unspoken is the fear that, with TQM, employees will no longer want unions, since they will be satisfied with management.

Managers interviewed for this book offer different views of union involvement in TQM. In some settings in which unions are strong, their participation and support in TQM are imperative. For example, at a Navy facility that was piloting TQM in one unit, managers discovered that the union had printed up and was ready to distribute flyers calling TQM anti-labor. "We invited the shop steward to join the team," said a manager. "After the union understood what was going on, they threw away the flyers."

In other organizations, unions are less of a factor. At another Navy installation, the union has never made an active show of support for TQM, and it does not contribute in any formal way. Yet when union members rated unsatisfactory did not share in a quality bonus, union leadership offered only superficial resistance. In some environments this backhanded support may be the most a union can offer. "The union here isn't a major power" a Navy manager explains. "As long as they give us tacit support, we have no problems."

Many agencies have several employee unions. It is not uncommon for some unions to support TQM while others in the same workplace oppose or are indifferent to it. Organizations that are successful in bringing their unions on board have addressed the unions' fears and made them partners in change.

Creating Union-Management Partnerships for TQM

Quality expert John Persico, Jr., suggests the following actions for management and unions to create a positive environment for TQM.

Management Should:

- Find out about union's concerns over changes related to TQM

- Understand how labor relations laws may affect union leaders' options

- Give the union time to work out its position on TQM

- Treat the union as a partner, educating its leadership about the effort

- Create a quality management structure that allows regular union participation

- Negotiate to determine how to handle overlaps between TQM and collective bargaining

- Allay union fears such as loss of job security

Unions Should:

• Learn about TQM and how it may affect labor

• Develop policies to help them take an active role in TQM (including modeling participative management within the union management structure itself)

• Define a role for all levels of union leadership in TQM

• Keep their members informed about TQM issues

• Work with management on job security issues and overlaps between collective bargaining and TQM

Key Roles: Letting It Happen, Helping It Happen

Management should understand what unions can do to help promote quality, then seek labor leaders' assistance to introduce quality management.

Mobilizing the membership

Unions often have better lines of communication with some employee groups than management does. A good example of their reach is the union's contribution to the cultural awareness survey at the Watervliet Army Arsenal.

"We briefed the union before we did the employee survey," the chief of statistical methods explains. "As a result we got 790 questionnaires returned out of 850 distributed. That showed us the value of getting the union on board." Coopers & Lybrand found the same to be true when helping managers at the Air Force Development Test Center conduct a similar survey. The lesson: unions can help you assess the "quality baseline" at your organization.

Participating on teams

In many government agencies, unions make important contributions to shaping TQM by being part of teamwork efforts. At NASA's Lewis Research Center, the American Federation of Government Employees has joined with management on the union/management committee. Instead of negotiating disputes every three years in contract talks, the committee resolves problems as they arise; labor/management participation teams often research the issues and recommend solutions.

The Ogden IRS Service Center involved the National Treasury Employees Union (NTEU) from the very beginning of its quality program. The union president was a member of the original steering committee for the center quality council, and union representatives are members and leaders of teams.

The relationship changed slightly when the IRS as a whole negotiated a cooperative agreement with the national NTEU in 1987. Every quality council and subcouncil now routinely includes two union representatives.

The director of the center notes, "We are witnessing more interaction between union and management than ever before. Because we are talking more, fewer formal grievances have had to be filed."

The center's chief of quality assurance adds, "Our quality councils work by consensus, which means that before they make a recommendation all members must agree they can live with it. Our union representatives are very supportive on the teams, and some of our best individual employee suggestions have come from union members."

EXPERT CONSULTANTS: GUIDES TO QUALITY

"Getting information at first was like pulling teeth. We really had to scramble."

– Assistant commissioner for administration,
U.S. Patent and Trademark Office

"I was skeptical at first. I didn't believe that outside consultants could teach us anything about our own organization. But when they helped us lay out our processes in a work flow chart, we saw things we hadn't realized about the way we did business."

– Deputy ordnance officer,
Yorktown Naval Weapons Station

"We knew we needed expert help, but we didn't have any idea where to look. I got plenty of information about TQM consultants, but we didn't know how to evaluate their services."

– Executive officer,
Naval Publications and Forms Center

How do government organizations get the expertise they need to organize and operate TQM? Most use a combination of internal and external quality consultants.

Internal consultants are the quality resource group, who are, or become, knowledgeable in TQM principles and techniques. Internal consultants have the best understanding of the organization, its structure, and its culture. They know the people and the politics, and they have access to the people TQM needs. However, internal consultants may start out with little training or experience in organization development, teamwork, or group dynamics. They also may have a hard time remaining — or being seen as — objective.

External consultants may be government employees from other agencies who are veterans of quality improvement initiatives, or private consultants experienced in TQM. They offer some advantages that internal consultants may not have. Their specialized knowledge and outsider's objectivity can inspire confidence. Because they are outside the organization's norms, they often can push for change more easily than an insider could. They bring a fresh perspective, varied experience and skills, and a commitment to change based on results they have helped create.

External experts are most effective when teamed with internal consultants, who can help them understand the organization from an "insider's" perspective.

Key Roles: Planning, Training, Applying Effective Methodologies

One or more expert consultants can provide services at different points in TQM program development, depending on an organization's needs. They may offer comprehensive start-up through implementation assistance, work only on certain aspects of the process, or build in-house capacity.

Consulting for start-up

Expert consultants can help senior managers understand what to expect from TQM: the implementation process, the needs, the costs. They may have proven methodologies for assessing an organization's quality baseline and identifying targets of opportunity.

Facilitating the planning process

Depending on organization needs and preferences, consultants can do structured planning tasks themselves, provide the tools to internal staff, or work cooperatively to develop goals and strategies to promote top management's vision. They also may facilitate strategic planning sessions, team-building exercises, and other initial meetings.

Conducting training

Training is usually the consultant's most visible role. At the Equal Employment Opportunity Commission, a cadre of Washington-based staff trainers brought quality skills to the commission's regional and local offices. At the Philadelphia Veterans Affairs Office and Insurance Center, private consultants trained top and middle managers. They then trained selected managers as an in-house resource for teaching TQM techniques to the rest of the organization.

Helping during implementation

Various consultant services are available throughout TQM implementation. They include helping to set up procedures to promote continuous improvement, quality function deployment and vendor partnership, and helping to select pilot projects. Other services include helping to develop quality support systems for management information, employee performance appraisal, and other functions discussed in Chapter 11.

Coopers & Lybrand helps many of its government TQM

clients by facilitating initial improvement team projects. This ensures that these organizations can get under way quickly and provides on-the-job training for internal facilitators.

Expert Consultants: What To Look For, Where To Look

Government staff who have used internal and external consultants offer the following suggestions:

- *Look for flexibility.* Make sure consultants will adapt their program to your organization, instead of the other way around.

- *Look for experience.* Some consultants have only recently jumped on the quality bandwagon. A proven record is the best credential.

- *Do not expect too exact a "fit."* Although it is important to find a consultant with experience in government TQM programs, you probably will not find one with experience in exactly the kind of work you do. The uniqueness of your program is an advantage: with a good consultant, you will get a program designed specifically for you, not a carbon copy of "what worked for Agency X."

- *Compare value.* Consider the *value* that different TQM consultants will add to your organization, not just the cost. Choosing the low bidder for the most important change your organization will undertake may be a mistake.

- *Watch out for gimmicks.* Anyone promising a quick path or a magic bullet will not help you create lasting, continuous improvement.

- *Do not assume you will get more from firms that have best-selling quality book authors or gurus on staff.* The people you work with daily will be more important to you than "celebrity" drawing cards.

- *Tap into the growing "quality network" of government organizations.* Ask those with experience for recommendations.

- *Talk to the Federal Quality Institute* (see Appendix A). People there can tell you if a contractor has qualified for the Federal Supply Schedule for TQM consulting services. Many state and local governments can also use the schedule as an alternative to the request for proposal process.

What Is the True Value of Consultant Services?

Someone once said that quality is free—until it is time to pay the consultants. In truth, private consulting fees will be a minor part of the total cost of introducing TQM to your organization. You will spend much more on the time executives, managers, and workers take to learn how to use TQM, which will easily average from $500 to $1,000 per person. Although this is a "different color of money" from contractor costs, it is just as real. The true value of both internal and external consulting must be measured in how it will help you control this greater cost, and whether it will help you gain success.

ENTERPRISE PARTNERS: COMPLETING THE EQUATION, SPREADING THE IMPACT

When you take the enterprise view discussed in Chapter 7, you can see that your success depends on your partners playing new roles in quality improvement. For your partner agencies, distributors, and vendors, these include:

• Taking action to reduce the cost of quality of their products and services, and to improve these outputs to meet your and your external customers' expectations;

• Joining your improvement teams (and you, theirs);

• Sharing information on problems and opportunities for improvement; and

• Helping to form and pursue enterprise-wide goals for better quality.

They can do this best by adopting the quality philosophy, just as you have.

Your external customers have new roles, too. If they are other organizations, they also should join your improvement teams and respond to your questions about their expectations. Individual and organizational customers alike must learn (and you probably must teach them) that customers are suppliers, too.

Chapter

9

MANAGING CHANGE

■ TQM is a major change for an organization

■ *Change management* is a set of strategies and methods for introducing change

■ Executives and middle managers must know how to use change management

■ Experience shows common reasons why people resist, reject, or accept TQM; knowing how to diagnose the reasons is a critical skill needed by executives and managers

■ An organization that can constantly change to meet new challenges or take advantage of new opportunities will achieve the TQM goal of continuous improvement

■ Frequent changes in government or organization administration can imperil TQM; there are methods to overcome this problem

"There is nothing more difficult to take in hand, more perilous to conduct, or more uncertain in its success, than to take the lead in the introduction of a new order of things."

– Niccolò Machiavelli, *The Prince*

Machiavelli was a government executive in Renaissance Italy. You would do well to heed his words as you introduce TQM to your organization. Fortunately, there are many tools and procedures you can use to ensure your success.

ADOPTING INNOVATIONS

When you follow a comprehensive plan to introduce a change, you are practicing *change management*. Change management is based on a set of theories about how people adopt innovations. You may already know about change management under the names "technology transfer," "knowledge transfer," or the "diffusion of innovations."

Innovations

Innovations, or changes, are new ideas, tools, or procedures. They consist of processes and methods, whether these are "hard" (machines) or "soft" (management approaches). Introducing an innovation to an organization consists of technical and social activities.

The technical activities may be installing a machine, preparing manuals, or adjusting existing procedures to the innovation. The social activities include getting people to adopt the innovation, training them how to use it, and making sure they use it over time. *Coopers & Lybrand's experience is that 95 percent of the problem in introducing innovations is due to poor management of the social activities.*

The Adoption Process

When individuals and organizations start using an innovation, they have *adopted* it. Usually they go through an adoption process, as shown in Figure 9-1.

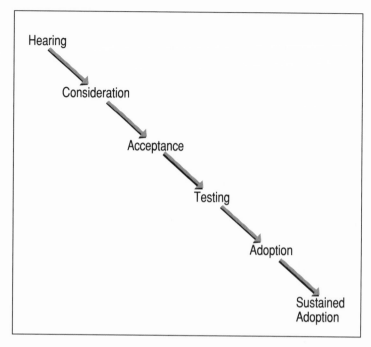

Figure 9-1
The Innovation
Adoption
Process

- *Hearing:* People learn about the innovation. They learn about TQM from you, and (do not forget this) from the media, other people in the organization, and outsiders.

- *Consideration:* They consider whether the innovation will benefit (or threaten) them. They may do this as individuals or in groups.

- *Acceptance:* They accept that the innovation will or may benefit them.

- *Testing:* They may test the innovation in a way that does not mean great risk.

- *Adoption:* They start regular use of the innovation.

- *Sustained adoption:* They continue (or do not continue) to use the innovation over time.

At any point in the process, people and organizations may *reject* an innovation. At any point, they also may stall and need your stimulation to get started again.

The objectives of change management are to guide people and organizations through the adoption process so that the outcome will be sustained adoption of an innovation, and to ensure that people use the innovation as you intended.

THE STRATEGIES AND TACTICS OF CHANGE MANAGEMENT

You cannot simply order people to adopt TQM. Although orders hold persuasive force, they are best combined with the planned use of other forces for change.

Creating The Planned Change Framework

All sound approaches to introducing a complex innovation have the following criteria:

• The sponsors of the innovation (your top executives) know and plan the direction your organization needs to take. This has nothing to do with a specific innovation. Instead, it means general direction as expressed in a strategic plan (see Chapter 11).

• The innovation supports going in that direction.

• The sponsors understand both the nature of the innovation and its effect on the people to whom it is directed (the targets).

• The sponsors know the level of both sponsor and target commitment to the innovation.

• The sponsors prepare a written plan for managing change.

• The sponsors allow the targets to experiment with the innovation in non-threatening environments, such as classroom exercises, pilot projects, and demonstrations.

• Targets participate in making a change.

Describing the "As-Is" State

The Coopers & Lybrand approach to change management begins with gaining understanding of the "as-is" state of your organization. The "as-is" state is your baseline, the point of departure for the change. Chapter 11 discusses ways of determining your "as-is" state when introducing TQM.

Describing The "To-Be" State

Next, you need to know where you want to go. This is the desired or "to-be" state after you introduce an innovation. The "to-be" state can be expressed in a simple statement, such as, "We produce documents on time with no errors." You may find, though, that it is difficult for everyone to agree on the "to-be" state. People may have different ideas of this as a result of their position, their background, or other reasons. If you cannot get the sponsors to agree on the "to-be" state, you are in trouble.

Selecting The Innovation

There is usually more than one innovation you can use to go from the "as-is" to the "to-be" state. You have to review several candidate innovations to find the most appropriate; avoid arbitrary choices.

This is no light matter. People tend to assume that a specific innovation will get them from the "as-is" to the "to-be" state. This is the "READY-FIRE-AIM" approach to change. If you do a quick history of previous changes in your organization (which will be discussed in a moment), you will probably find ample instances of this approach.

Describing The Innovation

To describe the innovation and its effect on the target population, it is necessary to spell out the "hard" and "soft" components of the innovation and the desired behaviors of the people who will use it.

Listing desired behaviors means writing down what you expect people to do. Include specific steps and tasks that may later appear in a procedures manual. Also include such items as people attending briefings and training, reporting problems, asking for support, and other actions needed to introduce the innovation.

Looking At Previous Changes

"TQM is not the first 'quality' program our agency tried," the quality coordinator of the Ogden IRS Service Center says.

"When we introduced TQM, we had lots of people who thought it was the flavor of the month, and that it, too, would pass. Some of them gave lip service to it, others figured they could 'wait it out.' It's taken hard work and results to change these attitudes."

You never start a change with a clean slate. You will always operate with a background of history that can aid or hinder your efforts. If your organization has a good history of introducing change, you will find it easier to introduce more change. If not, you will encounter resistance.

The key is to research the background. Before introducing TQM, for example, you can profit by reviewing previous attempts to change management style, such as participative management, quality circles, or management by objectives. This may require no more than jotting down a few notes from memory or talking with people who have been around awhile.

Very quickly you will develop a sense of what was attempted in the past, and whether and why this succeeded or failed. You can expand this procedure in a meeting of top executives. Remember, though, that their perceptions of success or failure may not be the same as those of people in other parts of your organization. Well-designed cultural surveys (see Chapter 11) will help you flesh out your knowledge of this history.

Analyzing Results

Follow your research with a review of the degree of support and resistance to the change by both sponsors and targets, based on information you collected during an assessment. Figure 9-2 gives you a framework for this analysis: the change prognosis grid.

Please note that the grid leaves open the possibility that sponsors may not fully support the change. For example, top management may give lip service to the need for TQM, but actually be neutral or covertly resist it. *It is essential to change this attitude to strong support before you start introducing TQM.* Moving the organization to the upper right-hand block of the prognosis grid, sponsor support/target support, is the ultimate aim of preparing for change.

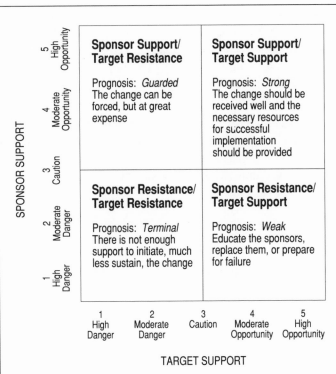

Figure 9-2
Change
Prognosis Grid

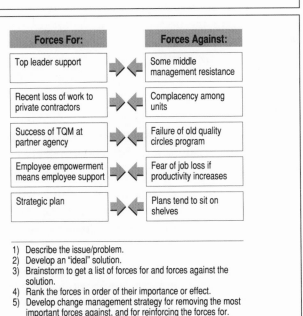

Figure 9-3
Force Field
Analysis
of Introducing
TQM

Force field analysis can be used to collect and organize the information needed for the prognosis grid. To do this, chart the forces for and against the change on a form such as that in Figure 9-3. List negative forces on the left, and postitve forces on the right. You also may want to use cause and effect diagrams to get to the root of both negative and positive forces.

With the information from your prognosis grid and force field analysis, you will have identified the obstacles you will face in introducing a change and the positive forces you can use to overcome them. This knowledge will help you develop strategies for the change.

Developing Strategies

Three basic strategies, used more or less in sequence, influence the target population to adopt an innovation: wedge, transition, and magnet. When you plan your change, write down what you will do for each of the actions below marked with a double asterisk (**).

Wedge strategy

The *wedge strategy* focuses on convincing targets that the "as-is" state of the organization is no longer viable. This promotes movement away from current cultural and expectation patterns. But rather than try to shatter belief in the desirability of the "as-is" state, you would use a wedge-like approach to nudge people away from what is known or comfortable. This includes:

** *Explaining* to the targets the problems and opportunities facing the organization. Sometimes people just need to know "why."

** *Validating* the targets' history. People will tell you in detail all the reasons the "old" way is better. Acknowledge this, and validate that it is a good way. Never say that people are doing something wrong.

** *Presenting* an optimistic vision of the change, expressed partly by the "to-be" state and the positive consequences for individuals and groups. It always helps people to see how things might be even better than they are now.

** *Specifying* the necessary changes. Share as much detail as is appropriate to help avoid confusion or misunderstanding. Your list of desired behaviors will be useful here.

** *Using* consequence management. Decrease the awards for following the old way, increase the punishments for not following the new way, and increase the effort people need to stay in the "as-is" state.

Consequence Management

An example from Ford Motor Company illustrates consequence management. Top executives wanted to see long-term contracts with vendors, but managers persisted in writing short-term contracts. The executives found that they had forgotten to remove a policy that required detailed justifications for long-term contracts. The executives switched this requirement around — middle managers had to detail justifications for short-term contracts. The result: more long-term contracts.

Similar types of consequence management may be to waive requirements for detailed reports when managers adopt quality practices, giving awards for using TQM improvement procedures, or assigning new programs (and the resources for them) to units that adopt TQM.

Transition strategy

Using a combination of wedge tactics can help to dislodge people from the "as-is" state. Once this is done, sponsors can move on to the *transition* state. In this state, sponsors initiate actions that provide structure, guidance, confidence, and trust in the change, while encouraging forward momentum. Tactics of transition include:

** *Continuing* to reinforce why change is necessary, and reminding people of the benefits of the "to-be" state.

** *Looking* for opportunities to make symbolic decisions that send clear signals reinforcing the change. A symbolic decision for TQM might be when your chief executive holds weekly meetings of key staff to talk about quality and allows nothing to interfere with these meetings.

** *Providing* as much accurate and timely information as possible.

** *Involving* targets in planning action steps.

** *Allowing* targets to ventilate their fears, concerns, and insecurities in an environment that treats these feelings as legitimate. You must respond to these feelings with action.

** *Focusing* targets' attention on the future, not the past.

** *Rewarding* those who support the change and applying pressure to those who resist.

** *Assigning* roles, tasks, and responsibilities so targets feel that they are involved and have influence.

** *Providing* targets with the logistic, economic, and political resources needed to do what sponsors ask of them. Also, providing them with training in how to understand their own reactions to the change, as well as those of others.

Magnet strategy

The transition state leads to the "to-be" state. As targets begin moving toward this state, you can use *magnet strategy* and tactics. The magnet approach draws targets away from transition and into the new state. This calls for actions that confirm the validity and promote acceptance of the "to-be" state. The tactics of this phase are:

** *Showing* sponsor commitment to the new state.

** *Using* consequence management by increasing rewards, decreasing punishments, and decreasing the effort to enter and stay in the desired state.

Finally, you must monitor a change over time to ensure that it does not slip into misuse.

Involving People

If you involve people in shaping and introducing a change, they are more likely to adopt it. This is called "ownership." First, you must make sure you are sincere about wanting their involvement; if you are not sincere, everyone will know it.

Second, you must make sure that involvement is possible. For example, if you have not made people aware of what TQM is, how can they comment on it? If you hold a meeting where people are afraid to voice their opinions, you will receive no input. Sometimes using a facilitator and a structured format will help solve this problem.

Choosing The Right Messenger

The chief of management analysis at NASA's Johnson Space Center talks about the need to choose a credible messenger to convince people they need to adopt TQM:

"The motivation for change can be like appendicitis or cancer. If you are trying to create change, appendicitis is better — it's sharp, apparent, and everyone who has it knows it's there. You don't have to be an expert to figure this out, and you don't need an expert to tell people they need to do something.

"Now, a cancer is different. It's not visible; people may not know they have it. You better have someone credible — a doctor — to convince people they have cancer.

"It's the same with changing an organization that is becoming overly bureaucratic — a slow management disease that will eventually kill it. If the problem isn't visible, you'll need expert peers and colleagues to help people understand they have it."

DIAGNOSING AND ACTING ON REACTIONS TO TQM

People will resist change, but they can be persuaded to accept it. Acceptance, however, does not mean they will adopt an innovation. Even when they do, they may not use the innovation in the way you intend, and they may stop using it.

When you start to introduce TQM, you will find a small cadre of people who are strongly for it, and another that is dead set against it. Most of the people who seem neutral really are not; they lean one way or the other, but they have not yet expressed their feelings. You need to be able to read people's true feelings and reactions, and diagnose the reasons for them. Then, you can reinforce positive feelings and overcome negative ones.

Resistance

Resistance is any conduct by people that serves to maintain the status quo when you try to change it. Resistance is not rejection. It is a natural phase in the process of adopting a change.

There are several reasons for resisting change in an organization, which include fear, resentment, and technical considerations. Each of these can come from individual's perceptions of how the change affects them, or from the influence of a group.

Fear

People do not accept or resist an innovation. Instead, they accept or resist the way it changes their lives. For example:

- TQM may reduce the need for some types of jobs.

- Shifts in communication patterns, organizational structure, influence, authority, and control also accompany TQM.

- People need to learn new skills in TQM, and their jobs may be redesigned.

These are *social consequences of change*. For some people, they will be positive changes, and for others, negative. Negative social consequences are at the heart of any fear of change you encounter. Whether the fear is real or imagined, you must always treat it as real.

When there will be only positive social consequences of a major change (and this is rare), your best approach is education and demonstration. When a change will mean negative consequences, you reduce fear by removing any uncertainties about this. Uncertainty paralyzes people. Certainty frees them, and you, to take action. Your challenge is to make this action constructive.

For example, if quality control specialists know that TQM will reduce the need for their jobs, they can do many positive things. These include retraining for other jobs or finding a niche in the TQM initiative (see Chapter 8). Even leaving the organization may be a positive step for some. If they are uncertain, they will take no action, or worse, try to sabotage the initiative.

Resentment

People resist change imposed from without. Nobody likes to be ordered to change, especially if this means radically altering how the work is done. There are very sound reasons for managers and employees to feel this way:

• In the past, top management has ordered them to do things that just did not work. Those related to TQM may have been quality circles, some forms of participative management, statistical process control, and strategic planning.

• Nearly everyone in an organization has had the experience of soaring hopes that maybe top management is serious this time...only to see an improvement program canceled.

• Middle managers who must set up TQM in their units and document activities are already busy.

Technical considerations

Finally, there are valid technical reasons for resisting change. Most people can evaluate an innovation on its technical merits (though this may require some help from you) and judge whether it will make their work better. You should have this information before you start changing things.

How people voice their resistance

People often will express their overt resistance with technical objections to the change. For example, whenever Coopers & Lybrand works with clients to develop a new information system, many client employees say the new hardware and software are not appropriate for their work. We help the client to separate these complaints into two categories:

- Valid observations of the capability of the technology, and
- Observations based on social consequences.

The first category requires improving the technology, while the second requires a strategy to win acceptance for the technology. You have to know the difference.

People also may resist change while seeming to agree with it in principle. You *will* encounter this statement: "TQM is a wonderful idea and I know it works over there, but we're different." The differences Coopers & Lybrand hears most often are that an organization has a unique way of doing business, that employees are too individualistic, or that TQM does not work in a government environment.

Finally, there is covert resistance. People may not voice objections to TQM, but will not cooperate in introducing or using it. In the extreme, some people will try to sabotage your efforts to introduce change. You should be less worried about the sabotage than the lack of cooperation. The sabotage quickly becomes visible; detecting more benign resistance is your greatest challenge.

Resistance as feedback

When people resist your attempts to introduce TQM, do not think that they are being unreasonable. Accept their resistance as a natural thing, and learn to interpret it. By resisting change, people give you vital information. They are telling you who they are — their resources and limitations, and their attitudes toward new ideas and the sources of those ideas (i.e., you and top management). More specifically, they are telling you what you need to do to introduce change successfully. For example, read the box entitled "Allowing People To

Ventilate." Can you think of management actions that can overcome the resistance expressed by the employees?

Allowing People To Ventilate

The Florida Department of Transportation asked its employees to comment about its quality improvement initiative. The department published both positive and negative feedback in its monthly quality newspaper. Some negative comments were:

"...each district has their own problems to deal with and should not let each others' problems filter through our offices or our thoughts."

"State employees will be paid the same if they do it the old way or the new way."

"I have seen employees work on improvement projects eight hours a day for several days instead of doing the job they were paid to do. Often someone else has to do the team members' work."

Once these feelings were out in the open, the department could deal with them. Also, this action showed that the department permits criticism. (By the way, there were many positive comments. In later issues of the newsletter, the department printed employees' replies and rebuttals to all of the comments.)

You will never overcome all resistance

You will never bring everyone on board. Some members of your organization complain about how you manage now, so expect people to complain about TQM, no matter how well it performs. What you want is a *critical mass of acceptance*. In TQM, a critical mass is the point when most people believe that enough of the *right* types of managers and employees have adopted this change to make it seem viable and permanent.

If you can get key and influential people to adopt TQM, you do not need great numbers to gain critical mass. Some key people are in formal positions of power. Others have informal power and influence, or are simply considered wise. Win them first, and the rest will follow.

Acceptance

You will find many people who accept TQM but do not adopt it, and people who adopt TQM but do not accept it, because there are two types of acceptance: attitudinal and behavioral.

Attitudinal acceptance means that people believe TQM will work for them. *Behavioral acceptance* means that they will use TQM, whether or not they believe in it; people who do this are "compliers."

Behavioral acceptance without attitudinal acceptance means that an innovation has been forced on people (see the upper left-hand box in the change prognosis grid, Figure 9-2). You have to expect some compliers in TQM. Over time, many will come to accept and appreciate it. But too many compliers means that TQM implementation will slow down, or even stop. Compliers often "bad mouth" TQM, and this negative communication will affect others. Too many compliers also means that a new administration that does not support TQM can easily kill it. Finally, having only behavioral acceptance means that TQM may become a ritual. When that happens, TQM is a waste of time and money.

Attitudinal acceptance without behavioral acceptance is in fact rejection. Some people in a unit may want to adopt TQM but feel pressure from their peers or managers not to do so. Other people may want to but lack the means (i.e., training, time, and other resources).

Rejection

Resistance means conduct aimed at preserving the status quo; rejection *is* preserving the status quo. Do not confuse the two. Rejection means that the outcome of the adoption process is totally negative, at least as far as you are concerned. Just remember that this rejection probably seems positive to the rejectors.

You can diagnose reasons for rejection and take steps to correct them. Five common reasons follow.

"Don't know about it"

People may reject TQM, or any other innovation, simply because they have not heard anything about it. Ask people in an isolated department or field office why they have not introduced TQM, and they probably will tell you they know nothing about it.

As obvious as this may seem, it may be the chief reason people reject TQM. Awareness activities (see Chapter 11) give people information they need to consider whether they will accept TQM.

"Wait and see"

You will find this reason for rejection among managers who want to make sure that TQM works, that it will be around awhile, and that top management is serious about it. To convince them that it works, you need to give evidence (examples from inside or outside the organization), testimonials from other managers or their external peer group, or persuade them to accept a pilot or demonstration project. If you did your homework and have strong sponsor support, you can convince them that it will be around awhile.

Finally, you can get their boss, or their boss's boss, to counsel them to take action. If you cannot do this, break contact because you will get nowhere, and come back later.

"We're not convinced"

Here, managers may say that the status quo is as good as what you are proposing. They also may point to rules, regulations, or part of their situation they believe precludes adopting TQM. Finally, they may say that TQM costs too much.

You can use the tactics discussed under "Wait and See" for this category of rejection. Unless you know the specifics of their situation, do not try to refute their reasoning by yourself. Get help from their boss, or someone in a similar situation (see the box entitled "Choosing The Right Messenger"). You may be able to help them to see the payback of TQM with examples, and help them secure truly needed resources.

In a few cases, a manager may be absolutely right that the situation will not permit TQM. For example, if an office has severe personnel problems, TQM may have to wait until the problems are solved.

"I'd like to, but..."

Managers and employees may be afraid of TQM because they doubt their ability to use it. They may feel they simply do not have the personal time to learn and use TQM. Finally, they may be afraid that TQM will cost them their jobs, influence, or power.

Education and practice will solve the first problem; real examples of how TQM will benefit them will take care of the second. A nudge from their boss will help them find the time, but if the boss is the reason, you must work on the boss. Deal with fear of job or status loss realistically. If the fear is well grounded, education and examples will not help. You must take this to top management for resolution.

"Tried it before, didn't work"

You can be fairly confident that people who claim to have tried TQM have tried only one or two of its tools (e.g., quality circles, statistical process control). Ask them to explain how they tried TQM, and show them the benefits of a comprehensive approach. If they have been part of a failure in a comprehensive approach — and there are some — show them how your approach takes care of the causes of that failure.

Organizations have a tendency to ignore or even deny these negative outcomes. Doing so sets up failure. After all, if one unit can get away with *not* using TQM, why should not the others?

Finally, you cannot overcome rejection unless you know the reasons for it. Like resistance, rejection contains the information you need to do this.

Adoption

There are seven types of adoption, and some are not desirable. You can learn to diagnose each and act appropriately.

Partial adoption

People use only some parts of TQM, leaving out others that would help them do a better job. At the organization level, partial adoption may mean that only some units use TQM. Since the work of an organization flows across departmental lines, this may mean poor cross-functional teamwork, or that you cannot address some opportunities for improvement. In a team, examples might be skipping steps in the Road Map to Quality or not collecting quantitative data to monitor a process.

Partial adoption is a major problem. When you start to implement TQM, you may be tempted to accept partial adoption as an interim phase in development. Half a loaf, you may reason, is better than none. But partial adoption at best yields suboptimal results; at its worst, the teams will not be effective and will stop using TQM.

You would do better to work on complete adoption, even if this means taking more time and money. If you must accept partial adoption, closely monitor what is going on and be prepared to step in with emergency help.

For the organization, skipping a step in the process for implementing TQM (outlined in Chapter 11) is a partial adoption of the change management process. Most of the organizations we interviewed are finding that they have to go back and do steps they skipped, because they cannot make further progress without them.

Interrupted adoption

People start to use an innovation, but stop. This may result from a unit manager's disenchantment with TQM, a new manager, failure of an initial attempt, or an emergency that pulls people away from using TQM. Monitoring how units and teams are using TQM will help you detect this problem.

Incorrect adoption

People use an innovation the wrong way. This can be as simple as using the wrong TQM tool or method. Training and technical assistance readily solve this problem. More difficult is when managers use TQM to force through their ideas, paying only lip service to employee involvement. The managers must revisit the fundamental principles of TQM, and you may need top management support in these cases.

Complete adoption

People use all TQM tools, methods, and procedures appropriate for their work. You want to encourage this through positive reinforcement. However, it is not necessarily the best form of adoption; sustained and continuous adoption are better.

Modified adoption

People modify TQM to fit a specific situation. This can be substituting one tool for another that is equally good or better. For example, cause and effect diagrams and structure trees do the same job. This is different from partial adoption, because you maintain a holistic approach. Support modifications when they work; to confirm that they do, document the change and monitor results.

One caution: TQM tools and methods are a means of communicating across unit boundaries. Exercise some control over substitutions so that one unit can understand another.

Sustained adoption

People continue to use TQM over time. This is included because it is important to ensure the sustained use of TQM. If you monitor, you will know if there is a problem with sustained use.

Continuous adoption

People use the appropriate TQM tools and procedures the right way, and constantly search for better ones. *This is the most desirable state; do everything you can to promote it.* People should, of course, experiment with changes to TQM in the same way they test a change in a process. You will want to monitor such innovations over time.

CONTINUOUS CHANGE MEANS CONTINUOUS IMPROVEMENT

An organization capable of continuous adoption, in TQM or any other area, will always maintain self-control, exploit opportunities, and meet customer expectations. TQM will never degenerate into rituals.

Encourage people to experiment, take risks, and, most of all, take charge of improving the way they improve. The results can only be positive. This is true for changes that lead to improvement, and even those that fail during the experimental stage — people try, they learn, and they want to learn more.

Promoting Continuous Improvement Of TQM

Here are some concrete things you can do to promote continuous adoption:

• Hold meetings, discussions, and seminars about TQM even after everyone has adopted it. Invite outside experts to speak, show films, and encourage people to share enhancements they make to improvement procedures.

• Send people to outside conferences and seminars, and have them brief their colleagues on what they learn. Do not limit these trips to a few managers or executives; send employees and supervisors, too.

• Tour nearby organizations that have introduced TQM. Even if yours is a white collar organization, you will benefit from seeing how manufacturing firms practice quality improvement (and remember, they have paperwork functions, too).

• Subscribe to periodicals such as *Quality Progress* and *Quality* (see Appendix A), and circulate articles of interest. Even better, encourage employees and managers to write articles. This sets them thinking about how they operate; it is also good publicity.

SUSTAINING TQM IN THE FACE OF A CHANGE IN ADMINISTRATION

Many governments face the challenge of getting TQM values to "take." If they succeed, however, the challenge of maintaining this change will loom large. Monitoring how TQM is being used within your organization is one way to do this. But external factors can pose problems, too.

One award-winning agency quality initiative, for example, recently stopped dead after several years of success. The agency's quality assurance branch chief cites contributing problems that could occur in any agency.

"Although we had instituted programs, such as a large-scale training effort, we never succeeded in changing fundamental attitudes about the quality initiative. Before the program had a chance to show it was a long-term reality, the chairman who started it left the agency. The new appointee is still awaiting confirmation, and no one knows what his priorities will be.

"Two other events precipitated the program's decline. The quality assurance function, which had been an autonomous department in running the TQM effort, was folded into another office. Then Congress cut our budget. At that point, TQM lacked real advocates, so decision-makers dropped those activities from the budget."

How can you preserve TQM in the face of obstacles such as these? Well-developed TQM programs offer the following advice.

"Make sure you have broad-based support. We've made a conscious effort to get buy-in at all levels and across all functions, so that no one person 'owns' the quality program — it's a value we've adopted almost across the board," says the quality coordinator at the Philadelphia Veterans Affairs Regional Office and Insurance Center.

Reports the quality coordinator at the Naval Publications and Forms Center: "We recently had a new commanding officer *and* executive officer come on board. Could they sabotage our program? We don't think so. We've created a number of quality 'champions' here who passionately believe in the TQM approach.

"I'm one of them, and I set up an appointment with the new commanding officer before he joined us. I found out what he knew about TQM, and promoted the concept vigorously before he arrived. He recognized how committed many of us are, and he gave us a chance to show him how well the philosophy works."

Says the quality coordinator of the Ogden IRS Service Center: "We continue to make a point of publicizing our successes. With results like these, why would anyone want to go back to the old days?"

Finally, a manager at NASA's Lewis Research Centers says, "Just keep doing it, and pretty soon you won't remember any other way of working. Quality has become second nature here; I don't think we could stop it now if we wanted to."

Chapter

10

PROMOTING QUALITY AS AN ORGANIZATION VALUE

- *Corporate culture* is the set of formal and informal beliefs, norms, and values that underlie how people in an organization behave and react to change

- Most traditional organizations' cultures do not fully support TQM; some parts of the older cultures are obstacles to quality improvement

- Executives can learn to treat corporate culture as a manageable variable in the quality equation

- Cultural areas needing special attention include:

    - Management behavior
    - Organizational structure
    - Rules and regulations
    - Employee performance appraisals
    - Budget practices

"Quality is a habit, not an act" — Aristotle.

As organizations acquire the habit of quality, TQM becomes more than an abstract set of principles. It is expressed every day in employees' satisfaction with their work, their positive relations with colleagues and customers, and their contributions to their organization's mission. In other words, they work in a corporate culture that supports quality.

WHAT IS CORPORATE CULTURE?

What makes your organization's environment different from any other's? Answering that question is like looking at an iceberg. One-tenth of an agency's individuality is visible: its organization chart, rules, regulations, and other public pronouncements. The other nine-tenths is hidden from outside view. These are managers' and employees' values, habits, ways of thinking, and unofficial operating principles that, combined with (and sometimes contradicting) the official view, constitute an organization's *culture*.

Like the culture of a society, an organization's culture is so deeply ingrained that it is taken for granted. You know what your agency's culture is, because you live and operate in it every day. But to define the elements of culture, you may need to step back and isolate the beliefs, policies, and practices that shape it.

What style of management does your agency use? How does the agency approach problem solving? Who defines quality — management or customers? How and for what are staff rewarded? How do individuals and departments interact? What do managers and employees see as the agency's mission, and how do they perceive their own roles? The answers to these questions start to describe your organization's culture.

The relationship of an agency's culture to TQM is reciprocal. TQM creates cultural change by introducing new practices and new ways of thinking. Yet the lasting success of TQM depends on how firmly these cultural changes take root. When managers and employees adopt values that support a quality culture, striving for excellence becomes an organizational way of life.

WHAT DOES A TOTAL QUALITY CULTURE LOOK LIKE?

Because each government agency is unique, no one "quality culture" will ever exist. Coopers & Lybrand's experience has shown, however, that nine values and behaviors are necessary for successful TQM. None of the organizations in the examples that follow started out with these cultural features, and some do not yet have them. Instead, they are developing them in stages as their TQM initiatives progress, based on what they learn about themselves.

Figure 10-1
Cultural Change
Under TQM

"As-Is" State	"To-Be" State
From an environment that...	**To a culture that...**
Has many different and often conflicting goals among its divisions and departments	Has a common vision shared by everyone
Punishes mistakes, hides or rationalizes problems	Openly discusses problems, rationalizes problems, sees defects as opportunities for improvement
Rewards following established policies	Rewards risk taking and creative thinking
Lets short-term problems drive and dominate work activity	Focuses on long-term continuous improvement
Relies on inspection to catch mistakes before the customer receives the product	Improves work processes to prevent mistakes from occurring
Gives management full authority for top-down decisions for change	Trusts and empowers employees to contribute to decision making
Tolerates turf battles as inevitable	Facilitates and rewards cross-functional cooperation
Makes decisions arbitrarily	Bases all decisions on objective data
Has a negative or indifferent self-image	Feels like a winner, with achievements creating good morale

In keeping with the change management approach in Chapter 9, Figure 10-1 shows what organizations do before TQM (their "as-is" state), and what they do afterward (their "to-be" state).

Everyone Has The Same Vision Of Quality And Strives To Make That Vision A Reality

Different groups in a traditional organization have different ideas about quality. Similarly, they define where the organization should be going in terms of their own narrow interests.

Says one Coopers & Lybrand TQM consultant who has facilitated hundreds of top management strategic planning meetings: "Invariably, at the start of the sessions people are not on the same wavelength. I can't blame them for that. Their entire culture is based on isolation in 'departments' and 'divisions.' There may not be any payoff for trying to improve the organization as a whole. In fact, maybe they've tried it before and gotten 'beat up' for infringing on someone else's 'turf.'

"Now these are the top executives who should be working toward common goals. Can you imagine how things are at the bottom of their organizations?

"One of my first tasks is to help them form a common vision of 'success' for their organization. This is a hard, time-consuming job. You should see the way they jockey to have their personal interests included in the vision statement. But eventually everybody realizes, 'We are all in this together.' Once that happens, things move quickly."

The result is critically important. A common vision means that decisions are made for the good of the entire organization and its customers. It means that people have the same idea of success. It leads to unity of purpose.

Management And Employees Openly Discuss Problems And Mistakes, Without Fear Of Being Punished For Them

According to Japanese quality theory, a problem is a gem to treasure because it signals the opportunity to improve. But Deming says that, for an organization to succeed in quality, it must first drive out the very real fear people have of pointing out problems.

The Veterans Affairs Medical Center in Kansas City, Mo., was convinced that patient mortality would be reduced if it could prevent problems and improve processes in giving health care. "To do this, we had to call a spade a spade," said the chief of its quality management service. "We had to say, 'We — as a hospital and as individuals — may not be doing the right thing.' That is a tough statement in any field, but in medicine, giving 'less than best' care can mean your patients' lives — and your career."

In most hospitals, physicians are not willing to criticize their peers' performance directly, and no one else on staff would dare. The medical center overcame this problem by guaranteeing anonymity to doctors whose practices were substandard, and to the other doctors who pointed this out. This drove out the fear of both punishment and retribution.

Quality staff could do detailed reviews of every death in the hospital, looking for recurring situations that were the root causes of problems, because people were willing to share their thoughts openly and freely. With this knowledge, the medical center made improvements in policies and procedures, then trained people in their use and monitored the results. In two years, the center reduced patient deaths by 20 percent. Using the same methods in other areas, the center reduced the length of hospital stays, saving money needed for increased services to veterans

Few government organizations may require the special steps needed at the medical center. The point is that simply vowing never to "shoot the messenger" is not enough. You must remove both the real and imagined obstacles to free discussions, encourage people to call attention to problems, and treasure their messages as much as you would a solution.

People Are Willing To Take Risks To Achieve Quality Results

In many organizations, following established patterns is rewarded, whether or not those patterns make sense. But quality comes from risk taking, because new approaches are the basis for quality improvement.

The Navy's nine public works centers are located throughout the nation and overseas. They all used to work under NAVFAC 450, the thousands of pages of detailed regulations and task specifications developed in Washington, D.C. As long as people did things "by the book," they could not be criticized.

Problems were inevitable: the situation for the center in Guam is different from the one in Norfolk, Va., and the Atlantic Ocean is not the Great Lakes. How could each center adjust to different situations, when the inflexible "book" spelled out precisely what they all had to do?

So the Naval Facilities Engineering Command took a risk. It threw out NAVFAC 450 and gave the centers a short list of business principles instead. The list was so short that nervous senior officials persuaded the authors to publish it in a format that at least looked bigger.

The centers all reorganized to match the type of work local customers needed. They told their work planners to stop using "book" procedures to specify how to paint a door — they figured good painters would know how. Customer satisfaction went up, and costs went down. Employees began to innovate, and their morale increased.

Was this a risk? It is for any organization that is used to tight central control. At headquarters, it means you have to trust the judgment of the field operations. In the field, it means you have to make (and live with) your decisions. Life may not be as comfortable, but *progress goes to the risk takers.*

Instead Of Fighting Fires Or Relying On Breakthroughs, Managers And Workers Focus On Continuous Improvement

Juran calls it "the disease of immediacy": designing quick-fix solutions without understanding the work process. Many traditional organizations reinforce this attitude by the way they look at problems. TQM organizations cure the disease by getting to root causes.

One Coopers & Lybrand TQM consultant, formerly the quality director at a major federal facility, tells this story of his old job: "Once a month the department heads met to go over production figures. If your figures were worse than the previous month, you got heat from the boss. The meetings were often witch hunts, with people scrambling to blame others when their figures fell off.

"You better believe we tried to 'solve the problems' that caused those figures to drop. We bought new equipment, which took extra time to install and train people how to use, when they could have been doing their main work. We changed a process, sometimes causing problems in other processes. We alternately chewed out subordinates and gave them pep talks, which confused and demoralized them. The next month, maybe the figures went up, or maybe they went down.

"Then we started using statistical process control. We found that most of the fluctuations in our figures were simply normal variation (see Chapter 5). What caused figures to vary from one month to the next? Hey, most of the time *nothing* caused them to change! In all those previous years, much of the time we had been trying to solve problems *that were not there to begin with.*

"There were no more witch hunts at the monthly meetings. The department heads began to consider how we could improve our processes, rather than attempting to 'fix' them."

The Focus Is On Preventing Mistakes And Deviations, Instead Of On Correcting Them After They Occur

When managers and employees believe that they should "do it right the first time," their perspectives start to change. Tolerance for rework goes down, and people look for ways to build quality into processes, instead of inspecting them in.

The Naval Publications and Forms Center (NPFC) is the distribution point for tens of thousands of documents, and it had a problem. In a warehouse football fields long, thousands of boxes of materials lay unidentified, misidentified, or marked too cryptically be identified. When customers requested documents stored in these mystery boxes, filling the order was like an Easter egg hunt.

"We used to open all the mystery boxes, find out what was inside, and relabel them the right way," said a NPFC manager. "But this took too much time, and wasn't really solving the root cause of the problem: the government programs that sent us the boxes did not label them correctly."

At first, the NPFC took an education approach. It sent out 6,000 letters explaining its labeling needs and introducing a new bar-coded system that suppliers had to follow. It held conferences and made personal phone calls to repeat offenders. The situation improved.

But finally the NPFC took the ultimate get-tough policy: it refused to accept any improperly identified packages and sent them back. "We didn't win any popularity contests at that time," the policy's architect notes. "Some of the less charitable suppliers suggested that the idea was a great career breaker. But walk around our warehouse today, and you'll see the results."

Managers Trust And Empower Employees To Make Improvements

In a traditional organization, managers see their primary roles as controlling workers and telling people what to do. According to quality expert Myron Tribus, in a TQM organization, "Workers work in the system; managers should work on the system and improve it with [employees'] help."

When managers take the TQM view that "the worker has the answers," they harness an enormous reserve of knowledge and experience about individual work processes.

"We take the approach that deficiencies are not the mechanic's fault," says a foreman at the Norfolk Naval Shipyard. "Instead, we look for defective material, bad processes, inadequate training, or poor instructions. When we examine the process, we see that most of the time the mechanic has done a 100 percent job of doing what he's supposed to do. If what he's supposed to do is wrong, whose fault is that?"

Individuals And Departments Cooperate For A Mutual Goal Instead Of Defending Their Turf

It is a familiar situation. You need the cooperation of the department down the hall, but helping you does not appear to be in its self-interest. It values its independence, meets its own goals, and resents outside interference or oversight.

When the Defense Industrial Supply Center (DISC) rejected this "isolationism" as part of a TQM initiative, it found out how much better processes can work if departments take on interactive roles.

"Our team structure now forces cross-functional cooperation," notes DISC's quality coordinator. "Management emphasizes that we're all here to pursue the organization's goal, taking good care of customers and employees. We conduct cross-department training to let everyone learn what others do and talk face-to-face about meeting shared needs. We don't have a perfect situation yet, but mutual understanding is growing. The results of cooperation — measured in morale, savings, and improved customer service — are our best selling point."

Decisions Are Based On Data, Not On Opinion Or On Intuition

Because TQM emphasizes quantitative measurement systems, gathering data about a process becomes a way of life. Managers come to demand hard facts for planning ahead and responding to problems. Employees also learn to appreciate the power of objective documentation.

The chief of statistical methods at Watervliet Army Arsenal says that its employees want to increase the use of statistical process control methods. "Before TQM there was a lot of subjectivity in deciding how to solve a problem or improve a process. Now they have hard data to go on — and it gives them control over their work."

The Agency Has A Positive Self-Image, And Morale Is Good

When people focus on quality and get good results, they feel better about their co-workers, their jobs, and themselves.

According to a top manager at the Naval Publications and Forms Center, "The other organizations at this installation have mostly white collar employees; we're blue collar. When we had a shooting on the installation, even our own employees assumed that someone from NPFC did it. Talk about low self-esteem — we had it!

"Now everything has turned around. We act and feel like winners. Employees are more enthusiastic about their work, and it carries over into other aspects of their lives. Although our employees are the lowest paid in this installation, they contribute more to the Combined Federal Campaign than any other outfit. We give more blood in blood drives; we have a higher level of community service. The commitment to total quality seems to make us want to do our best in every arena."

CREATING A QUALITY CULTURE

Although cultures change slowly, they can change. During the transition, agencies create change gradually by taking positive steps to overcome the barriers to change. Nine key steps are listed in Figure 10-2.

Figure 10-2
Action Steps for
Cultural Change

1) Planning for cultural change
2) Assessing the cultural "baseline"
3) Training managers and the workforce
4) Management's adopting and modeling new behaviors
5) Making organizational and regulation changes that support quality action
6) Redesigning individual performance appraisal and monetary reward systems to reflect TQM principles
7) Changing budget practices
8) Rewarding positive change
9) Using communication tools to reinforce TQM principles

ACTION STEP 1: Planning For Cultural Change

Advanced organizations understand that they must plan for cultural change. Chapter 9 discusses change management at length.

ACTION STEP 2: Assessing The Cultural "Baseline"

How much cultural change does your organization require? How do managers and employees feel about quality? What is their perception of the quality of your organization — and of their workplace environment?

To direct successful cultural change, planners need the answers to questions such as these. To get them, organizations often survey their workforce to document their cultural baseline before introducing TQM. They repeat the survey over time to assess the progress of change. Chapter 11 discusses survey techniques many agencies are starting to use.

The results of cultural surveys often hold surprises for organization management. At the Defense Industrial Supply Center, for example, a baseline survey showed that values and perceptions differed substantially among staff at different levels of authority. Although top management was highly receptive to the quality initiative and gave DISC high marks as a work setting, the degree of enthusiasm dropped at each successive level on the organization ladder.

"By our second survey, we'd made some progress, but supervisors still had major concerns about the managerial style of their middle management superiors," DISC's quality coordinator recalls. "As a result, middle managers became a high-priority target in our efforts to change attitudes and behaviors."

ACTION STEP 3: Training Managers And The Workforce

TQM training is often the starting point of cultural change. Training raises awareness about TQM principles and gives the skills needed to succeed in a participative, cooperative environment. The training experience brings people with diverse roles together to work on constructive tasks exemplifying the ethic it teaches.

Job-related training also can help institutionalize an organization's emphasis on quality. Employees need the proper skills and instructions even to begin doing a quality job.

"Before TQM our 'training' was one worker telling another how the job had always been done, which often institutionalized methods that never should have existed," a Naval Publications and Forms Center manager says. "We knew training was important, but in the press of everyday business, training schedules often fell behind. Now, every Tuesday we shut down the operation for 45 minutes of training. Each department designs its own training plans, and our training coordinator finds the expertise. We also require certification of competency, which shows our commitment to doing the job right."

Deming emphasizes this point frequently: An organization that uses formal job-related training ensures that people know how to "do it right."

ACTION STEP 4: Management's Adopting And Modeling New Behaviors

No single aspect of management support is more important than leadership for cultural change. Managers provide this leadership in two ways. They make or allow functional changes that support TQM, and they offer a personal example of the TQM ethic (see Chapter 8 for a more detailed discussion of management's role). This behavior modeling is "walking the talk."

Management by example makes for success. At the Philadelphia Veterans Affairs Regional Office and Insurance Center, the director, assistant directors, and division chiefs were the first to receive TQM training. Then several division chiefs became the trainers for the next level of management. Top managers also made up the first quality improvement teams. "We believe it's important for top management to get its hands dirty to show everyone that we're serious about TQM," explains VAROIC's assistant director.

When top managers use participative management styles, so will middle managers and supervisors. The same is true when they spend most of their time working on systems issues instead of fire fighting, when they take a long-range view instead of focusing only on today, when they accept and act on ideas from lower levels, and when they take risks.

When executives do not follow the TQM principles they espouse, managers and employees know it is really "business as usual." People imitate what they see their superiors do, because they know this is the road to personal advancement.

ACTION STEP 5: Making Organizational And Regulation Changes That Support Quality Action

As form follows function, so the structure and rules of an organization should promote and reinforce its cultural values. Some changes that organizations we interviewed have begun to make point the way to a new framework for quality.

Restructuring individual work processes

The U.S. Patent and Trademark Office increased the continuity of its work processes by reformatting lines of responsibility. Now one employee or one team "owns" a discrete, start-to-finish process. This restructuring enhances both accountability for quality and job satisfaction. As management expert Tom Peters says, "Quality begins with emotional attachment."

"Flattening" the organization chart

When private companies adopt TQM, they tend to reduce the number of management layers between leadership and employees. Although this tendency has not occurred as widely in government, some agencies have changed to a more horizontal approach.

"Making participative management work had been complicated by too many levels of supervision," a quality coordinator at NASA's Lewis Research Center recalls. "The structure really got in the way of communication between upper management and employees. We solved the problem by cutting out one supervisory layer.

"Naturally, people at first viewed the move with suspicion and fear, especially those directly affected. But we addressed concerns by beefing up our dual career program, which allows some classes of employees to receive supervisory grade levels without holding supervisory positions."

Cutting down on red tape

Externally imposed regulations often are barriers to quality, not incentives. One example of this, the Navy's public works centers, appeared earlier in this chapter. Another is the U.S. Forest Service, which recognized that empowering its units to get the job done meant freeing them from traditional bureaucratic controls. As a pilot test, three national forests and a research station received full authority to change or eliminate any process.

According to a manager interviewed in Tom Peters's film, *Excellence in the Public Sector*, "Prior to the pilot we relied heavily on our manuals and handbooks, and it was easy for some managers to deal with that. If it wasn't in the manual, it was an easy answer: 'No.' Now 'no' is a forbidden word."

The Forest Service found that lifting the bureaucratic burdens freed staff to spend more time "on the ground." New projects developed, customer service improved, and the culture now reflects an ethic of faith and trust in the employee.

You may object that you have no control over your regulations and procedures. But, if you look at them closely, you will usually find that half, and sometimes more, were imposed by your own organization, not by some outside authority. You will find rules that were made to deal with a specific situation that never recurred. You will find others for which no one really knows the reason. Finally, if you look at the regulations imposed from without, you will always find that they can be interpreted in several ways — you may have taken an overly conservative approach.

ACTION STEP 6: Redesigning Individual Performance Appraisal And Monetary Reward Systems To Reflect TQM Principles

Nothing sends a clearer message to managers and employees than the rewards they receive and a superior's evaluation of their performance. The measures an organization chooses to evaluate should show its real priorities — because they are the expectations employees will try to meet.

Organizations in this country that have introduced TQM are still struggling to develop incentive systems compatible with TQM. They know their old way is not having the desired effect. In *The Deming Management Method* (see Appendix A), Deming states the reason: "The effects [of evaluation by performance, merit rating, or annual review of performance] are devastating — teamwork is destroyed, rivalry is nurtured. Performance ratings build fear, and leave people bitter, despondent, and beaten."

Here is insight for aligning your method with TQM, and several examples of how government and industry are addressing the issue.

Individual performance appraisal

The following is from *A Study of Performance Management Systems Compatible with TQM;* Coopers & Lybrand helped design and manage this study for the Naval Industrial Improvement Program. The researchers looked at the appraisal methods of eight private companies and four government organizations that use TQM and reviewed them against TQM principles. In deciding how to handle performance appraisals, you might ask some of the study's questions about your existing method.

Does it do what it is supposed to? Under TQM, this would be to gain continuous improvement in meeting customer expectations — which is different from rewarding people for sticking to rules, fire fighting, or just making managers happy.

Does it consider the 85/15 rule? As you recall from Chapter 2, a TQM maxim is that 85 percent of problems (and therefore potential improvements) are caused by systems issues beyond the control of individual employees. Individuals in such systems can only solve 15 percent of the problems (or create 15 percent of the solutions). In this case, appraisal based on individual results does not consider the system barriers to good performance.

Does it consider variation? Individual performance varies from the average performance of the group. If you accept the principles of variation discussed in Chapter 5, you have no real basis to reward or punish an individual whose performance is within the normal bounds of average group performance.

The study recommended testing a new system that divorces individual performance from pay (base salary, bonus, and monetary rewards). In this test, all performance improvement rewards should be divided evenly among all employees in the form of base salary increases and bonuses. The salary increases would be percentage of base, which adjusts for seniority.

The test also would require managers to review employees continually (not annually), based on whether their performance is within the normal variation of the group. If it is below the lower limit of normal, employees need training, counseling, and other assistance. If this approach fails, the employees should be transferred, demoted, or let go.

Two organizations that were part of the study had already made some of these changes. At the Naval Avionics Center, organization goals now drive performance measures. Criteria for evaluation include TQM priorities such as customer service, degree of participation in quality activities, and spirit of cooperation. They also recognize that "the system" affects the employees' ability to perform, and they use a "predicted variance" approach that views individual performance within broader trends.

The Cherry Point Naval Aviation Depot eliminated the link between performance appraisal and pay or promotion. Deming supports this approach, because he believes a focus on performance is usually a misguided focus on outcome — when process is the key to quality.

Individual versus team rewards

Beyond the Bottom Line: Measuring World Class Performance (see Appendix A) is a joint Coopers & Lybrand and National Association of Public Accountants study of five Coopers & Lybrand private industry clients. Part of the book looks at performance appraisals of self-managed teams. The authors suggest that rewards to such groups should be based on total performance improvement against a series of indicators that measure quality. These might be cost, production (throughput) time, on-time delivery, defects or errors, or some other customer-oriented measure.

Individuals should be rewarded for improvement in personal knowledge, say the authors. This means learning new skills and tasks that contribute to group performance. Much of this new knowledge should come from cross-training in the skills of other group members. Cross-training creates the flexibility needed in TQM; it is also a form of job enrichment.

This method creates a "competition-cooperation" tension that is healthy for the group and the individual. The competition is to gain more individual knowledge, the reward for which is advancing in pay grade or classification. However, the knowledge gained by individuals helps the group.

The need for hard data

The recommendations of both the Naval Industrial Improvement Program and the Coopers & Lybrand/National Association of Public Accountants studies assume adequate data on process, group, and individual performance. Collecting these data is discussed in Chapter 5, under process performance indicators and activity-based costing. Obviously, if you are going to use any of the methods just described, you will need to collect this information. Setting up your incentive system is one more reason to add these valuable measures.

ACTION STEP 7: Changing Budget Practices

Because money is power, the way an organization's budget operates paints a telling picture of its priorities. Changing budget practices to support a total quality environment can be a powerful tool for reorienting organizational values, as the Defense Industrial Supply Center has learned from experience.

"Your budget structure has to follow your organization's structure and promote its goals," says DISC's comptroller. "We now develop flexible budgets, based on business volume. To promote interdepartmental cooperation, we've removed many fences that had existed between various 'pots' of money. To foster participative management, we began to delegate budget authority to the departments. We removed budget limitations and centralized review. Our central staff now provides budget support rather than oversight."

The Dallas Regional Office of the Social Security Administration is piloting giving its field offices more control over operations budgets. "Keeping the budgetary decisions as close to the point where services are provided and relying heavily on judgment of employees providing the services will ensure more service value for the dollar spent," says the regional commissioner.

Activity-based costing as cultural change

Activity-based cost data (see Chapter 5) make it possible for employees and line supervisors to control costs at the process level. This, in turn, permits a more decentralized organizational structure. Both changes are cultural shifts.

In addition, activity-based costing will help you eliminate across-the-board budget cuts within your organization. These types of cuts are demoralizing and say that an organization does not care to make hard, fact-based decisions about distribution of funds.

ACTION STEP 8: Rewarding Positive Change

Most managers know that what you reward is what you get from your employees. TQM organizations find that the nature of the reward is less important than the gesture. Government agencies usually cannot give large cash awards, and employees appreciate non-monetary recognition of their value to the organization.

Symbolic recognition is a common approach. For example, the Fresno IRS Service Center sponsors a "quality employee of the month" program, which offers small awards such as engraved pen sets, reserved parking spaces, and lapel pins. In addition, every employee who suggests an improvement idea receives individual recognition: a thank-you letter for ideas not used, and tangible rewards (including cash) for suggestions that are adopted.

The chief of quality management services at the Kansas City Veterans Affairs Medical Center highlights the need to match the right reward to the right staff groups. "We've found that nurses appreciate public recognition of contributions at a meeting or event. Physicians, on the other hand, would rather receive a private compliment from a peer or the chief of staff. What one group values may be meaningless to another. Ultimately, the most important 'reward' is feeling like a valued member of the team."

Having employees make awards to their peers is a powerful way to reward positive behavior. U.S. Forest Service workers in the Ochoco National Forest in Oregon each have an annual award certificate that they can give to any employee or manager they think is special. Called the "Groo Award," after its inventor, forest technician Tyler Groo, it is the most coveted prize at Ochoco. To get it, you have to make someone else's life better. Managers wanted to get in on the action, and employees let them — but the employees would not permit their superiors to use the name "Groo" for their award. That belongs to the workers.

Other agencies recognize employee contributions within the work environment. At the Navajo Area office of the Bureau of Indian Affairs, the area director asks employee teams to make formal presentations to agency staff about their experiences. Employees have responded positively to this professional recognition of their expertise.

Employee Recognition: Getting Emotional About Quality

Quality is hard work, and we should share the joy of success. So concludes a recent AT&T study, which found that celebrating quality is a powerful way to reinforce it as an organization value.

How does your agency celebrate quality? Here are a few ideas that other government programs have used with success.

The Hammond, La., office of the Social Security Administration holds "red beans and rice" luncheons for employees to recognize what the regional commissioner calls "the small changes that add up to big improvements."

NASA's Lewis Research Center sponsors awareness team recognition ceremonies to celebrate project success. Team members receive a memento folder with a team photograph and a letter of thanks from the center's director. Contractors also participate in the programs.

At the Ogden IRS Service Center, managers identify "quality champions" at the branch and division levels. Bimonthly award ceremonies honor the winners. "Being selected as a quality champion has been the greatest accomplishment of my career," one employee explains. "It was overwhelming to receive this honor, and it pleases me to see that someone recognizes the conscientious efforts of employees!"

The Defense Industrial Supply Center sponsors a TQM Awards Banquet, which annually honors almost 10 percent of its 2,200 employees. "We want to create a win-win environment," the quality coordinator says. "Almost 50 percent of our workforce won a formal award in 1988, and many more participated in informal celebrations. Personalizing quality is an important way to promote buy-in."

> There are many other ways of rewarding behavior, but these are the basic rules: know the behavior you want to encourage, and make the award meaningful.

ACTION STEP 9: Using Communication Tools To Reinforce TQM Principles

"Success breeds success," the quality coordinator at the Ogden IRS Service Center states, "but first you have to get the word out. We have an in-house quality newsletter. We sponsor a yearly 'Quality Month,' in which we run programs and set up audiovisual displays that exhibit quality team achievements. We even have large-screen televisions that show videos of different teams in action."

Every agency has its own way of making quality a "top of mind" concern. For example, laminated "value statement" cards appear in the pockets, wallets, and desk drawers of employees at the Naval Avionics Center. They feature the operating principles of the center, such as "Customers are the reason for the Center's existence; therefore, customer satisfaction is our highest priority," and "The Center will establish an environment that fosters mutual respect, cooperation, and the recognition of the importance of individual contributions to create a strong effective team." Visual cues such as these help shape new attitudes and priorities.

Do not take the "slogans and banners" approach

Take care, though, that your communication tools do not carry empty propaganda. Resist putting up a lot of TQM banners and slogans. Most traditional productivity or efficiency campaigns begin this way, and you do not want people to confuse your TQM effort with them. Should some of your leaders push for this, you might tell them that most experts suggest putting all the banners and slogans in executive meeting rooms — but nowhere else.

Let employees do the promoting

Giving employees the resources to communicate about quality puts a much needed regulator on your promotion effort. When you let them develop materials, what is promoted is that which has happened. This approach prevents overselling the TQM initiative, and makes your promotion convincing.

You also may find that your employees' promotion approach is very different from management's. Employees tend to celebrate the struggles of gaining improvement, not just the results. They will let people know about the emotional side of quality. This signals the type of attitudinal acceptance you want to promote.

Letting Employees Do Their Own Promotion

Given the resources and authority, employees will come up with the most creative and powerful ways to promote quality. At the 3,000-employee AT&T Atlanta Works, a self-managed team in one shop wanted a plant-wide quality celebration. Management gave permission and resources. Originally, this team thought about having a band and a small parade for a "Buy-In Day," when everyone would commit to TQM. Soon hundreds of people started working on floats, costumes, and bands. Yet productivity increased while they were doing this.

The parade itself took place at each of three shifts. It started at two ends of the plant, with the plant manager leading one contingent and the union president the other. They met in the middle of the factory on a specially constructed "Bridge of Hope," and the two leaders embraced each other.

On that day, productivity hit its highest point ever — despite the time spent parading. People had tears of joy in their eyes. Could management ever even conceive of such an event, much less pull it off?

SUSTAINING CHANGE IN CORPORATE CULTURE

Cultural change is difficult to effect because it reaches people on an emotional as well as a rational level. Yet most people can be won over to TQM concepts by action steps such as those discussed in this chapter.

Even so, even the most committed executives, managers, and employees can slip back into the old ways. Also, TQM teamwork and participative management can degenerate into ritualistic behavior — all form, no substance. *TQM is not self-sustaining.* It must be revitalized constantly.

The quality coordinator at the Cincinnati IRS Service Center compares the social change needed to create a TQM environment with the behavior change needed for weight loss. "People make enormous changes, they beat the difficulties, and they lose weight. But unless they work just as hard at keeping the weight off, normal human backsliding puts them right back where they started."

This requires constant monitoring of the corporate culture. Top management must review the numbers and types of TQM team meetings held, conduct periodic surveys, talk to employees and managers, and otherwise keep a finger on the cultural pulse of the organization. Based on this information, management can take positive action to sustain (and continuously improve) a quality culture.

Chapter

11

IMPLEMENTING TQM IN AN ORGANIZATION

■ The magnitude of changes needed to implement TQM requires careful planning and a comprehensive approach

■ The approach must balance long-term changes with short-term results that cover the initial costs and sustain the momentum of introducing TQM

■ Coopers & Lybrand's Twin Track approach consists of four phases:

- Assessment
- Planning
- Implementation
  - Short-term track: pilot projects on critical issues and processes
  - Long-term track: deployment of TQM throughout an organization
- Institutionalization

■ Twin Track is a cycle that needs to be repeated over time to institute TQM fully

In our research, Coopers & Lybrand identified five different ways in which governments are introducing TQM at the agency level.

• *Slow cascading pattern:* Top leaders learn and use TQM methods and teamwork and teach them to their subordinate managers. These managers form management teams and start practicing TQM. They pass what they have learned down to subordinates, and so on, until every manager and worker participates; hence the term "cascading."

This is a comprehensive approach. The benefit is that it ensures top-down understanding and support, and allows the organization to adjust gradually to a new way of doing business.

The downside is that this is a slow process. If you need teams of employees to start working immediately on critical issues in key processes, this strategy will not deliver.

• *All-at-once pattern:* Everyone is trained in TQM within a few months, teams form quickly throughout the organization, and the action starts right away — often because this TQM has the hard-driving support of the top executive.

The benefit to this approach is that it can jar a complacent organization into action and, possibly, deliver quick results.

The downside is that this method usually fails. Managers do not have time to become skilled in TQM methods before the workers do, and so cannot give them guidance and direction. Performance measurement and feedback systems cannot be developed quickly enough, leaving major gaps in the information needed for decision making. Often, training is not "just in time," so that people forget their new skills before they can use them. A change in leadership during all-at-once implementation is usually the end of the effort.

• *Spotty pattern:* Some people get a little training on teamwork and a few TQM tools. Alternatively, only employees participate, as in the old model of quality circles in the United States.

There are no benefits to this approach. It delivers few results, and always dies.

• *"We're doing it already" pattern:* The organization simply labels all its current improvement programs "TQM." This is a common practice right now in both industry and government. Look for it especially among your vendors and distributors.

Only one of these patterns, the "Slow Cascading" approach, has real merit. Yet even it has a downside: it can take so long that you may be overtaken by events such as those described at the end of Chapter 9. For example, you may get a new administrator who is not sold on TQM, or you may have to protect your TQM initiative against budget cuts by showing short-term results. Although it takes three to five years to fully introduce TQM to an organization, you need to start showing results far sooner.

THE TWIN TRACK APPROACH

The Twin Track approach is based on the change management strategies discussed in Chapter 9, and on combining the "Slow Cascading" method with pilot projects at the early stage of implementation.

On the following page, figure 11-1 shows the framework of the Twin Track. The four phases in the approach are:

• *Assessment:* Identify the opportunities for quality improvement.

• *Planning:* Develop a structured program of improvement projects and changes leading to TQM implementation.

• *Implementation:* Introduce quality practices and their support systems.

• *Institutionalization:* Develop internal capacity to perpetuate TQM.

Figure 11-1
Implementing
Total Quality
Management

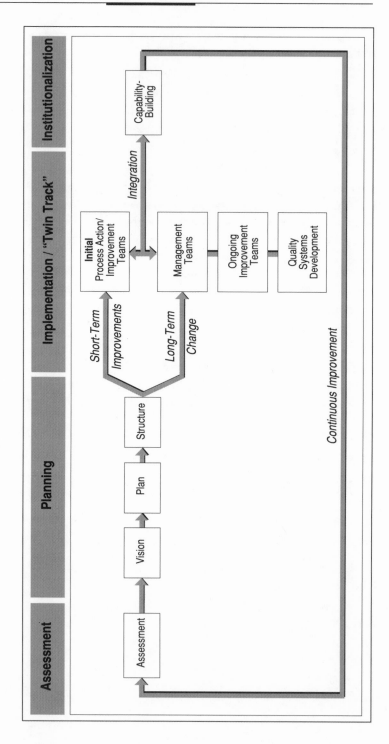

The success and speed of each of phase depend on your organization's size, resources devoted to the effort, leader commitment, and corporate culture. Most of our clients move through all four phases for the first time in two to three years, following a schedule roughly like that shown in Figure 11-2, on the following page. Going through the cycle once does not mean that you have completely transformed your organization. You must repeat the phases as you expand TQM in your organization, to maintain the dynamism of this management philosophy.

ASSESSMENT

"I have become a fanatic about quantifying — but a new sort of quantifying. I insist upon quantifying the 'soft stuff' — quality, service, customer linkups, innovation, organizational structure, people involvement..."

— Tom Peters, *Thriving on Chaos*

The objectives of TQM assessment are to learn the "as-is" quality status of your organization and to identify opportunities for improvement. This includes "hard" data about performance: dollars, costs of quality, adherence to schedule, and so on. It also means the 'soft stuff' Tom Peters talks about. Both are vital to planning how you will introduce TQM. Assessment is also a wedge tactic for planned change: it helps convince people that the "as-is" state is no longer acceptable.

We are going to discuss four ways to assess the "as-is" quality state of your organization:

• *Quality management:* What are your current methods of ensuring quality, compared to what they might be?

• *Organizational culture:* Does your organization's corporate culture support the change to quality?

• *Cost of quality:* What are you spending on prevention, inspection, waste, and failure?

• *Performance in critical areas:* How good are your most critical processes?

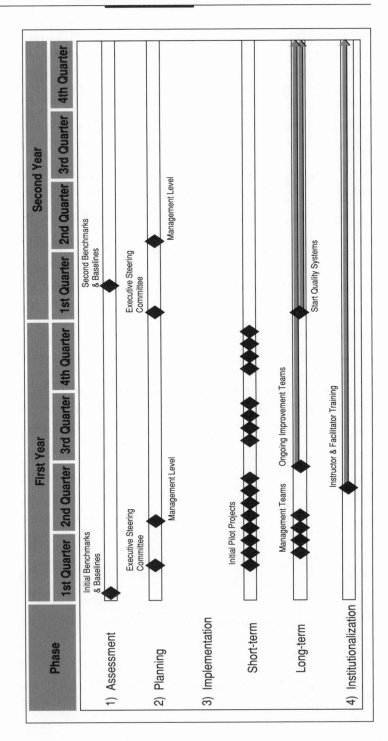

Figure 11-2
Twin Track
Timeline

Each method overlaps the others somewhat. You need to select among them according to your resources, time available, and the information leaders want to see. Do not use all four at once; this is too expensive, and unnecessary. Over time, though, try all the methods, because each reveals a different dimension of your organization. Figure 11-2 shows where you might repeat an assessment during the first two years, to let you see results of your actions and to keep your initiative on track.

Assessment is a team exercise. You want to involve the people most important to the change process: your leaders, and managers of key work processes. This general procedure for all assessments will ensure involvement:

• Have top leaders select the method, and brief them on the procedures, who will be involved, and how results can be used.

• Brief all managers. They frequently will need to help collect the data. Also, often managers are frightened by assessments — they need to have the big picture of how the data will be used.

• Assessment of organizational culture means surveying employees. Make sure they know why you are conducting the survey and how you will use the results. If you have a union, brief its leaders.

• Managers and employees should play active roles in collecting and analyzing data. This gives them a sense of ownership.

• Leaders must use the results in the planning phase.

Quality Management

Leaders often ask, "How do we manage quality now?" and "How does this compare with other organizations?" Quality maturity indices and award programs answer those questions.

Quality maturity indices

Quality maturity indices come from books by quality experts, or are sold as packaged assessments by private consultants. Using a matrix format, they list several areas of quality

Figure 11-3
Quality Maturity
Index

Characteristics	Innocence	Awareness	Understanding	Competence	Excellence
Approach to Assuring Quality	Reactive; fire fighting	Quality improvement	Prevention	Designed-in quality	Continuous improvement
Role of Top Management in Quality	Not involved	Assumes responsibility	Supports process focus	Measures total performance	Stimulates creative response to market evolution
Quality Responsibility	Quality department	Management	Knowledge transfer to operators	Quality at the source	Shared company-wide
Process Quality	Inspect and correct	Try new procedures	Process control	Real-time market feedback	Innovative improvement
Customer Relations	React to worst complaints	Internal customer recognized	Plan to meet requirements of main customers	Improvement plans linked to customer	Customers aid innovation for future benefit
Supplier Relations	React to worst defects	Education; reduce incoming inspection	Joint quality activities	Long-term strategic partnerships	Mutual work to prepare for market evolution
Quality Cost (% of Sales)	Over 20%	15-20%	8-14%	3-7%	Under 3%

management and then provide examples of higher and lower levels of quality maturity in each area. Each level has a score; the sum of all areas gives you an "index" of your quality maturity (see Figure 11-3).

The method for using a quality maturity index is similar to that of the awards programs described next.

Awards programs

Awards programs take the same basic approach as indices, but are more comprehensive. There is also more background information on the awards, which helps you interpret results and make comparisons with other organizations.

The Malcolm Baldrige National Quality Award, a federal government/private industry program, is the best-known system in the United States. It covers:

Leadership: Creating quality values and building the values into the way the organization operates.

Information and analysis: Collecting and analyzing information for quality improvement and planning.

Strategic quality planning: Integrating customer expectations into long-range plans.

Human resource utilization: Maximizing the workforce's potential for quality.

Quality assurance of products and services: Assuring quality in all operations; integrating quality control with continuous improvement.

Quality results: Improving quality and demonstrating quality excellence based upon quantitative measures.

Customer satisfaction: Determining customer expectations and success in meeting them.

Answering all 133 questions in the Baldrige application form points out specific things you can do to improve.

Selecting the right awards program

The purpose of the awards programs is to help you learn about your organization. Even if you happen to win the award, the greater prize is the improvement you make. Choose your program based on how it will help you improve.

The Malcolm Baldrige Award: The Baldrige Award application form is the most rigorous self-examination of any of the awards programs and takes the broadest view of quality. Most of the questions are about internal quality management, but many address how you manage quality with your enterprise partners (other agencies, vendors, and distributors of your funds). They also ask how you respond to community concerns and contribute to community development.

Only private companies are eligible for the Baldrige Award, but do not let this stop you from using it. A few questions may at first seem unrelated to government service, but if you have read this book you will quickly make the translation.

Government awards programs: The federal Quality Improvement Prototype award and the President's Award for Quality and Productivity Improvement are good examples of government programs. They are geared to TQM and give you examples of different levels of quality maturity and how to score them. There are published profiles of Quality Improvement Prototype winners; talk with them to gather ideas for improvement.

If you apply for these awards, a panel of reviewers will score and comment on your application; this is excellent feedback. Only federal organizations are eligible.

Both programs are based on the Baldrige Award, but their criteria are less detailed and may yield less specific information. They do not address your enterprise partners or your community.

For information on all three awards programs, see Appendix A.

Conducting a quality management assessment

Coopers & Lybrand uses a five-phase approach to quality management assessment based on awards programs. We help clients select the best method, advise on any modifications, and assist in data collection, scoring, and reporting:

- *Preparation:* Brief leaders and help them set the scope of assessment, select the people to be involved, allocate the resources, and set a schedule. Then train data collection and scoring teams and identify data sources. The teams should be managers from the key functions of your organization.

- *Data collection:* Collection teams assemble the information needed: qualitative data (rules, procedures, policies) and quantitative data (budgets, incidence of poor quality).

- *"Benchmarking":* Benchmarking is the process of finding comparison measures of the quality of your processes, products, and services (see box titled "Benchmarks and Baselines"). The teams develop benchmarks during the data collection phase.

- *Scoring:* Most awards programs assign points to general areas of quality management. Your scoring team can use benchmarking information to help to do this. Even without benchmarks, a well-trained scoring team can arrive at a fair rating. The results make an excellent baseline for future comparisons.

- *Analysis:* The teams review the findings and decide what steps they might take to improve quality management.

- *Reporting:* Teams report to leaders on their findings and recommendations.

How long this takes depends mainly on data availability. Estimate about one to three months, using part-time manager assistance, for a small to medium-sized organization (up to 4,000 personnel).

Taking action

This assessment will give you specific information on your current quality practices and their results. During the implementation phase, you will want to change policies and practices that get in the way of quality progress, and add those that encourage it. High numbers of defects and complaints, or a large amount of rework or other numeric indicators, will lead you to targeting improvement efforts to the systems and processes that generate them.

Benchmarks And Baselines

By comparing your quality to that of other organizations, you have a *benchmark* for future action. Benchmarks are the quality status of specific processes, products, services, or quality practices of organizations that lead their industry or field. They also may be professional standards. TQM organizations use these benchmarks as goals.

Where can you find benchmarks? In private and public organizations that do the same type of work that you do, among the winners of awards programs, and in professional journals.

Baselines are the "as-is" state of your organization's quality practices and their results. They may come from the assessment methods listed in this chapter, the number of complaints you receive from customers, the physical performance of your goods and services, and so on. After you create a baseline, year after year you return to it to note your progress. Do not be complacent: your most recent gains are the baselines for future improvement.

Organizational Culture

Culture surveys are a way to give you feedback on the "soft things." As the chief of management analysis at the Johnson Space Center points out: "As engineers, we didn't understand our corporate culture because we didn't have the data. Our surveys helped to give this data, and to point the way for improvements. It identified the parts of our working environment we needed to change."

Selecting a survey

All organizations interviewed for this book acquired their surveys from outside groups and modified them to fit their needs. Never develop an employee questionnaire from scratch. They require careful construction and validation by experienced survey and human resources researchers.

If you already use a survey, make sure that it covers the types of information needed to show areas of potential quality improvement. Surveys that deal only with morale and employee satisfaction issues usually do not do this, but can be modified.

Aggregate figures for your entire organization will not show you where you need to improve; look at individual units and make interunit comparisons. You also need to compare your survey's results with those of previous surveys (baselines) or of similar organizations (benchmarks).

If surveying is new to you, consider this advice from the *Federal Total Quality Management Handbook:*

"Private contractors often provide an entire service, rather than just the survey tool itself. The ability to purchase the data analysis and interpretation is a distinct advantage over public sector surveys. Analyzing hundreds of survey responses is far more labor intensive than many organizations anticipate. An automated results processing system becomes more valuable as the size of the survey increases. Purchasing a service improves interpretation of results as well. Most contractors have staff experts that assist an organization in determining what the responses indicate. These experts also help define a plan for improvement."

The Organizational Assessment Process

Our approach to surveys is the Organizational Assessment Process (OAP). The Air Force Leadership and Management Development Center created the original model for the OAP. It has been validated by experts from Harvard, the Massachusetts Institute of Technology, the University of California-Los Angeles, and industry. About 300,000 employees in 120 government and private organizations have participated in the survey. Their results are stored in a national computer data base and used to make comparisons. To ensure confidentiality, the names of the employees and organizations are not in the data base.

Determining content and administration

The OAP has about 110 questions answered on a Likert

scale of one to seven. You can add or subtract some questions, but core questions remain the same. The survey is given to samples of employees, supervisors, and managers from different work units.

Results are used to answer these questions:

• *Do your workers understand what the organization wants from them now that things have "changed"? Are they getting the kind of training and direction they need? How involved and committed are they? How well do they function as a team?*

• *Are your supervisors giving the right kind of feedback and evaluating performance in a constructive way? Are they promoting a shared sense of responsibility? What bureaucratic obstacles are holding things back?*

• *Are your managers giving only lip service to change? Do they have the skills to lead and direct necessary innovation? How customer-oriented are they?*

Analyzing results

Results analysis begins with external and internal comparisons. You compare your results to selected components from the 300,000-respondent data base: groups whose characteristics are similar to those in your organization. You can compare results from your clerical workers, engineers, senior managers, and others to those of people in the data base with similar job descriptions. Also, you can make comparisons to the organization in the data base that has the highest positive scores in functional areas similar to yours.

When you make comparisons among your internal groups, you often will find that units and groups of managers and employees have different perceptions about your organization's culture, ability to innovate, and other issues important to introducing quality management. This helps you determine where you will focus your attention during the planning and implementation phases of TQM.

Taking action

Taking action on OAP or other survey results is a multi-level procedure. During the planning phase, the data are used to describe organization-wide obstacles and opportunities for introducing new quality practices or other changes. They also may lead leaders to focus attention on specific units or types of managers or employees.

During the implementation phase, different units and groups review their results in a team setting. They form action plans to overcome any obstacles shown. This procedure is repeated at lower levels until the entire organization is actively pursuing changes that will lead to a better quality environment.

Cost Of Quality

The fastest way to save money in an organization is to reduce the cost of quality. Chapter 1 addressed the high cost of

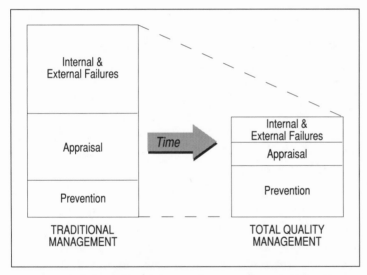

Figure 11-4
Changes in Cost
of Quality

quality in traditional organizations, which is about 20 to 40 percent of sales price in private firms. TQM organizations typically have costs of quality at or below 10 percent of total costs, in the areas shown in Figure 11-4.

The cost of quality consists of:

• *Prevention:* The cost of preventing problems, rejects, scrap, and waste. This may include training, some quality assurance functions, TQM work, pre-award surveys, and other related costs.

• *Appraisal:* The cost of inspecting for errors. Inspection may be of outside supplies received, laboratory tests, reviews, calibration and maintenance of inspection equipment, production audits, and customer acceptance inspections. Quality control falls under this category. If yours is a white collar operation, count the cost of reviewing reports, budgets, estimates, letters, and all other documents for accuracy and fit and of reviewing this material before it goes to higher authority and other "check-off" procedures.

• *Internal failure:* The costs of redoing work, defects discarded, delays for lack of some needed component or information, requests for specification deviations, scrap, and all other forms of waste that occur before a product or service is delivered to an internal or external customer.

• *External failure:* The cost of any repairs or reworking done after you deliver a product or service to a customer. This includes repairs done by the customer, formal investigations by oversight groups as a consequence of failures, answering complaints, and products, reports, and other items returned because they did not perform as intended.

Collecting the data

Ferreting out the hidden costs of quality in any organization is difficult, because data are not routinely collected on all of them. Establishing the costs requires careful review of actual expenditures (not just budget line items) and of how people spend their time, and direct observation of how work is done. Data include financial reports, logs, work record packages, interviews, surveys, designed-for-the-purpose tally sheets, and special studies of key processes.

Analyzing the data

Analysis shows you quality costs for your whole organization and for large subunits. Put these data into pareto charts, and you will see your first improvement targets: the highest costs.

Taking action

During the implementation phase, by focusing on the root causes of the larger costs of quality, you often can reduce them rapidly and substantially. Also, a cost of quality assessment probably will show a need to improve your accounting system so that it captures the right costs. Activity-based costing helps do this (see Chapter 4).

A word of caution: During the first few years that you do cost of quality assessments, the results probably will look progressively worse. This does not mean that you are failing. You are simply becoming better at capturing the hidden information on cost of quality. This is progress, not backsliding.

Performance Of Critical Areas

You have several critical processes that can substantially delay or add costs to operations, or can severely affect other measures of quality. These are often "bottlenecks" through which your most important, or core, products and services pass on their way to final delivery. Bottlenecks also may be support functions to core processes, such as procurement or hiring.

Using a case study approach, teams of managers, employees, and consultants gather relevant facts about a critical process. Information assembly is guided by the case outline, and may include interviews with customers or enterprise partners. The teams can use tools of TQM, such as flow charts, histograms, and run charts, to organize the results. They can note and explain possible contributing factors using cause and effect diagrams and pareto charts. Analysis is descriptive, because the real objective of case studies is to show people that these processes can be improved. Results are used during the planning and implementation phases to form action plans for critical process improvement.

Other Assessment Methods

You also may wish to carry out other assessment activities, such as external customer satisfaction surveys and structured but open-ended interviews with selected managers and employees. You may also want to review oversight agency and inspector general reports, complaint letters, and related material in light of your new quality awareness.

Leader Awareness Training

During this phase your leaders need awareness training on TQM concepts, objectives, practices, and implementation methods. You may want leaders to visit other organizations that have successful TQM initiatives — seeing is believing.

PLANNING

"Plans are nothing. Planning is everything."

> – General Dwight D. Eisenhower,
> Supreme Allied Commander,
> World War II

When leaders plan together, they have to agree on vision, purpose, and goals. This unity permeates an organization and keeps it going in the right direction. The prime objective of planning is, according to the chief of management analysis at the Johnson Space Center, "to enable all people in an organization to make day-to-day decisions about improvement, equipment, work processes, training, and personnel based on tomorrow's needs as well as today's."

Who Does The Planning?

TQM strategic planning begins with leaders; they cannot delegate this responsibility to anyone. This is "top-down" planning. Yet leaders' planning must reflect the input of managers and employees, who know their processes better than anyone else. TQM combines the two to create a future-oriented organization with realistic, comprehensive plans.

The group of leaders who conduct the top-level planning sessions is called the "executive steering committee." As noted in Chapter 6, planning and general monitoring of the TQM initiative are this committee's job. As discussed later in this section, lower-level groups may participate in the planning process in several ways.

The Planning Method

You need a structured planning method such as that shown in Figure 11-5, and you should use professional facilitators. Facilitators help move the meeting along, and help the committee handle group dynamics. We divide the planning process shown in Figure 11-5 into three parts: vision, plan, and structure.

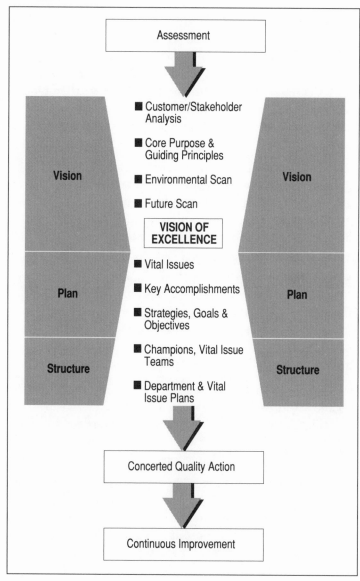

Figure 11-5
TQM Strategic
Planning
Process

Vision

Your leaders need to develop a "vision of excellence" to give your organization direction. This is a description of the desired outcome of the TQM initiative — the "to-be" state. It is "where you want to go." Chapter 8 includes several examples of visions of government agencies.

To do this, your leaders must look at the "as-is" state of your organization, always from the viewpoint of how you meet your customers' expectations. They must first identify your customers, which include all the groups discussed in Chapter 3: your external customers, your enterprise partners, legislators, the community, and your employees. They then rate how well they are meeting customers' expectations, using forms such as the customer exercise worksheet (see Figure 3-5 in Chapter 3).

Next, they review trends and other information to determine factors in future years that will affect their ability to meet customer expectations. These may include changes in technology, customer demography, mission, demand for services, government-wide budgets, and other factors.

With this information, they take a fresh look at the core purpose and guiding principles of your organization. You might assume that your leaders know this already, and the information may actually be written down somewhere; this is a chance to see if it reflects reality. Usually, it does not. Your leaders' next task then is to revise purpose and principles, and agree on them.

Using assessment information, they review the strengths, weaknesses, opportunities, and constraints they face in meeting customer expectations, if your organization does not make any changes. The product is an agreed-on estimate of the factors that influence the direction of the organization.

As pointed out in Chapter 10, even with this information in hand, leaders often find it difficult to arrive at a common vision. This is where "planning as a process" becomes essential. The vision must be the product of consensus among your leaders, because they must each support actions that will help make the vision a reality.

Plan

The assessment phase reveals many issues that *could* be the focus of leader attention and the resources of the TQM initiative. Your leaders must select the "vital few" issues from among the "trivial many." To do this, leaders list all issues, then collapse them into common categories. They rank categories by importance to achieving the vision, and rate how well they are doing on each. The categories with highest importance but lowest performance scores become the vital issues.

The planning participants review each vital issue to decide what your organization has to do to address it successfully. They develop and reach consensus on "mini-visions" of the "to-be" state for each issue, set five to ten years in the future. These are called "key accomplishments." Some examples are:

• *"We have the management and accounting information needed to support sound decisions in improving our processes and services."*

• *"Our personnel use the tools and procedures necessary for continuous improvement."*

• *"We have the right mix of labor skills to do our mission."*

• *"Our organizational structure makes interfunctional cooperation and communication easy and routine."*

Having established where they want to go, the leaders can develop goals, strategies, and objectives for getting there. In this planning model, a strategy is a list of actions that must be taken to achieve the key accomplishment. A goal is a three- to five-year milestone of the strategy; it is time-bound and specific, and its outcome is measurable. Objectives are one- to two-year milestones for gaining a goal. They have the same features as goals, with one addition: they specify the organization unit responsible for their execution.

In some cases the leaders will establish the goals, strategies, and objectives themselves. In others, managers do, because lower echelons may have a better idea of how to proceed toward a key accomplishment. The "quality champions" and issue management team discussed shortly usually do this, or coordinate efforts by departments to "flesh-out" more detailed plans.

The planning dialogue between levels of your organization should be "Here is what we must do," with the response "Here is how to do it." Higher and lower levels are entitled to ask both questions of each other, and obligated to work on the answers together.

Structure

The vision and plan give your organization direction. Now, leaders must structure the transition from the "as-is" to the "to-be" state.

The more stable your organization, the more difficult it will be for your normal management structure to make complex changes. This has more to do with inertia than resistance. Usually you need to create a temporary management system for the first several years of your TQM initiative. This structure is temporary because you do not want to create another permanent management layer. However, eventually some aspects of the temporary structure will probably replace parts of your current system.

Your structure must be aligned with your strategic plans. Most of your initial TQM resources should be put to work on the plan's vital issues. These are your basic survival issues — you have to start working on them immediately. Also, success in these issues is a great motivator for your personnel to adopt TQM.

Champions

Each vital issue needs a *champion*, someone who will take the lead. The champion should be a member of the executive steering committee. If most of the work on a vital issue will be done by one of your major units, that unit's leader is a natural choice to champion the issue.

A champion needs to have these characteristics:

• The power, influence, and resources to get things rolling and maintain momentum;

• The respect of the leaders, and of the groups that will be part of the change; and

• The interpersonal skills needed to persuade people to take action.

In other words, you want your best leaders to be your champions. When issue champions do not have the qualities just listed, their issues go nowhere.

You also want a TQM champion, called the "TQM advocate." Ideally, this will be your chief executive. In reality, the job often goes to the second in command or another leader. The TQM advocate is the "sparkplug": he or she works with the other champions and management teams to promote TQM. The advocate must always have direct access to and meet regularly with the chief executive.

Issue management teams

The champions need small teams of other managers to work on the vital issues. Team members come from the departments, functions, and key processes involved in an issue. This permits cross-functional and interunit teamwork. Depending on the issue, you may want to include representatives from unions or your enterprise partners on these teams.

The teams' job is to manage change. They may continue the strategic planning process for their issue, if the executive steering committee assigns them this task. They also make more specific plans, appoint improvement teams, and monitor progress on the key accomplishment.

The TQM advocate's team oversees the TQM initiative itself. It helps develop and coordinate training, facilitators, and internal consultants. It also monitors how teams are operating and helps design and install quality support systems.

Small organizations often need no more structure than their champions and issue management teams, because all the key players will be on the teams. They may not need the unit management teams discussed later in this chapter. Very large and complex organizations may not need many issue management teams if their key issues fall into line with existing departmental structure. Unit management teams in major departments handle most of the issues instead.

The quality resource group

This group is discussed in more detail in Chapter 8. You

will need a cadre of TQM internal consultants, instructors, and facilitators during the first three to five years of your quality initiative. Outside consultants can do some of this work, but you need your people in there as quickly as possible.

Coopers & Lybrand strongly suggests that all members of the quality resource group serve in these capacities only part time. They should come from many different departments, so that each unit has people who know the ins and outs of TQM.

The one exception may be the quality coordinator and a secretary. During the first several years, the coordinator handles the daily details of training, scheduling, and helping teams. He or she also may develop training materials, teach facilitators, and organize other activities.

All members of the quality support group should be managers, because TQM assistance is a management function in a "quality mature" organization. All your managers should eventually develop the full range of TQM skills. When this happens, you will no longer need a special quality resource group.

Repeating The Planning Cycle

The executive steering committee repeats the planning procedure periodically. Many Coopers & Lybrand TQM clients follow a two-year cycle. Year 1 is a "ground-up" structuring of the plan. Year 2 efforts are less intensive, and focus on validating and updating the Year 1 goals and objectives.

Training During The Planning Phase

Before you begin implementation, your top leaders need more in-depth training in TQM, including TQM and participative management methods. They must use these methods, both to improve how they manage and to model appropriate behavior. The best outcome of this training will be that your leaders teach these skills to their direct subordinates, and lead by example.

Champions and issue management teams need general awareness training followed directly by "just in time" training involving their new work. Your TQM advocate and coordinator will need thorough training in all aspects of the philosophy and its implementation. You may wish to send them to an extended off-site training course for this purpose (just be sure that the course agrees with the approach you take).

Other Activities During The Planning Phase

If you have not yet done so, you will want to select any outside consultants you will use during implementation. As discussed in Chapter 8, these may be private consultants or "borrowed" experts from other agencies. Also, you must obtain training curricula, manuals, and materials (see Chapter 6).

IMPLEMENTATION

"The payback is in implementation."

– Coopers & Lybrand TQM maxim

The objectives of the implementation phase are to start forward momentum, work on critical processes that relate to vital issues, and expand TQM throughout your organization. During this phase, you will work on core activities aimed at improving your processes. You also will develop quality systems to support core activities and achieve cultural transformation. You will use wedge and transition strategies to move people through the adoption process.

Short-Term Track

During the short-term track you will run several pilot projects that employ TQM teamwork and procedures, using management and improvement teams for these projects. As you recall from Chapter 6, management teams manage quality improvement; improvement teams work on specific, time-limited improvement projects.

Pilot projects serve many purposes:

• They help you gain the key accomplishments of the strategic plan.

- They show the rest of the organization that TQM works.

- Managers in the pilots often become the first members of the quality resource group.

- Several well-chosen pilots (and occasionally just one) often will yield cost savings greater than your first- and second-year budgets for introducing TQM.

Pilot projects are part of your wedge strategy for change management. People like to experiment with change, and pilots are experiments. They hold less risk for your leaders and the teams that work on them, because experiments imply that mid-course corrections and even a few failures are acceptable. They give people enough time to evaluate the merits of TQM and to prepare for the changes it brings.

Either the executive steering committee or an issue management team can select pilot projects, but your leaders must always approve them. In making the selection, your leaders and teams must start modeling TQM behavior: they must analyze an issue using the tools and procedures of TQM.

These criteria will help you to select from among possible pilot projects:

- *Return on investment:* Look for high return on investment. This includes cost savings, better products or services, and eliminating critical bottlenecks in a system. If your external customers have been complaining about a product or service, use a pilot to improve it.

- *Meaningful results:* Think about what means the most to your personnel and external customers. Often people care more about faster turnaround time, increased production, or fewer errors than they do about cost savings. Also, if everyone in your organization knows a particular process, they are apt to pay attention to and understand the improvement results.

- *Low-hanging fruit:* If one potential project looks easier than another, choose the easier one. Although results need to be significant, getting them should not be frustrating.

- *Chronic problems:* If you have tried and failed several times to solve a problem, a pilot in this area will be a wonderful demonstration.

- *Good atmosphere:* Projects are more likely to succeed in high-morale units that are open to change. If you conducted a culture survey, use it to find such units.

- *Short time span:* A pilot needs to show results in one to three months. Make sure that resources are available to meet this schedule, and that the project will not be so complex that it requires many months of work.

Keep the scope narrow

Pilot projects need to have narrow scope. If not, teams will spend months working their way down to a more manageable scope. If this happens, you will hear criticism about the time the team is wasting trying to decide where to begin. Much of this criticism will come from the team members, and you want them to be saying positive things about TQM. Chapter 5 shows how a clear, crisp purpose statement narrows project scope.

How many pilot projects?

You can have only as many pilot projects as you have time, money, and skilled quality resource group members; do not outstrip these resources in your zeal to introduce TQM. Also, if your organization is receptive to TQM, you can run more pilots.

But you must run more than one pilot project at a time — you do not want to put all your eggs in one basket. During the first year of implementation, the best approach is to plan for several in each vital issue area.

What about pilot project team members' bosses?

You will often reach deep down into your hierarchy to recruit pilot project team members. You may be doing this before team members' managers come on board the TQM initiative. Have these managers' bosses brief them, and give them recognition for allowing their workers to participate. If a manager's processes happen to be the improvement target, include the manager on the team or otherwise get him or her involved.

Demonstrating leader attention

Leaders always kick off a pilot project. They meet with the teams, emphasize the importance of the work, and reinforce this by dropping in on meetings. During pilots, leaders need to provide all resources required. This includes time, money, and a clearing away of institutional barriers to improvement.

Examples Of TQM Pilot Projects

The Air Force Development Test Center: Maintaining one major test facility at the center costs $300,000 a day whether or not it is used. A team of lieutenants, sergeants, and civilians worked out a better test scheduling system, which will increase the use and thus the productivity of the facility. Said a senior officer at the center: "We could have put a group of top managers to work on this issue for 30 years, and they would not come up with a better solution. I'm convinced now that TQM teamwork *works!*"

The Central Intelligence Agency: Delays and errors caused problems in the purchase requisition process. A team from line departments and the procurement office streamlined the procedure and recommended eliminating paper forms for some types of purchase orders. The result will be faster buys with less paperwork.

The Michigan Department of Commerce: A team reduced the time needed to generate signed community development block grants from 44 to 28 days after the decision is made to award grants.

Publicizing results

Publicize results of pilot projects internally and to enterprise partners. It is as important to tell how the pilot succeeded as to give the results. The best way to do this is to have pilot team members present and discuss the improvement process with their colleagues.

Building self-managed teams from pilot projects

Many pilot project teams will be composed of employees and a line supervisor responsible for a single process or subprocess. These could be your first self-managed teams. Chapter 6 outlined how such teams have the authority and responsibility to run their processes with little management intervention. They are the basic work units of a TQM organization.

These conditions let you form a self-managed team from a pilot project team: the team was successful, used TQM methods well, is in a unit that will accept the transition, and is willing to take this next step. These new teams will need the training and other support discussed in Chapter 6 and later in this chapter.

Training during the short-term track

Give pilot teams a few hours of TQM overview, then use task-focused, "just in time," on-the-job training. Do not worry about teaching them all the TQM methods. Instead, use good facilitators who can show them the methods they need to deal with the project at hand.

Future internal instructors and facilitators can observe training and team meetings to prepare for their new roles. Debrief pilot teams to learn what types of training and facilitating worked best, and how they think you can improve this support.

Some managers on pilot teams will be good candidates for training and facilitating work. Identify these people and use them.

Repeating the pilot project procedure in other areas

Continue to use pilot projects to introduce TQM to other departments and work units during the long-term track of the implementation phase. The benefits of pilots hold true for each new unit you want to bring on board.

Long-Term Track

The activities of the long-term track are divided into four categories:

- Working on vital issues;

- Introducing TQM to the different units in your organization;

- Developing support systems for quality; and

- Extending TQM to your enterprise partners.

Working on vital issues

You have not yet made the transition to TQM throughout your organization, but this is no reason to stop working on the vital issues. For the first year or two of implementation, you will need to continue using a management structure and procedures similar to those of the pilots to do vital issue work.

Training

You should devote more training time and resources to the vital issue improvement teams you form during this phase than to pilot projects. You may use more classroom time for training these teams, but that time should be "just in time" and task-focused. By now, you should have some in-house instructors and facilitators to work with the teams, and you can supplement them with outside consultants.

Introducing TQM throughout the organization

Approach the introduction of TQM throughout your organization from the team perspective.

Forming unit management teams

You want to start management teams in your major work units during this phase. By the end of the second year, these teams should be active at all appropriate levels of your organization.

As noted in Chapter 6, at the unit level these teams consist of the more senior managers. Their job involves:

- Developing and monitoring   unit performance indicators;

- Finding improvement opportunities;

- Working on system improvement ssues themselves, or assigning tasks to unit improvement teams;

- Using change management strategies and methods to introduce TQM and its resulting innovations to their units;

- Reporting interunit improvement opportunities to higher management;

- Undertaking improvement projects assigned by higher management; and

- Forming self-managed teams.

Introducing TQM to unit management teams

Unit management teams are deployed from the top down. This is "cascading": higher level managers brief and train their subordinate managers, with assistance from internal or external consultants if needed. This cascading strategy ensures TQM support up and down the hierarchy.

The guiding rule for cascading is to "make haste slowly." The speed of this process is determined by the creation of a critical mass of managers who accept and use TQM at a particular level before going down to the next (see Chapter 9 for a discussion of critical mass).

Depending on the size of your organization and your resources, you may need two waves of cascading. The first wave is awareness training. Do this as soon as possible after you complete strategic planning, and use it as an opportunity to discuss the plan as well as TQM. Having your chief executive or another leader speak at these awareness sessions is an excellent idea.

The second wave should cover training in TQM tools, procedures, participative management, and managing improvement projects. You may wish to precede this training with team-building exercises such as that discussed in the box entitled "Team Building." Such exercises bring home the internal customer concept to unit managers and clarify intraunit relationships and expectations.

You can use classroom training to teach part of the procedures, tools, and techniques, often with managers from two or more units. When you do this, make sure that the senior managers of each unit join in, and that the participants immediately begin using their new knowledge.

Team Building

Team building takes place in an ongoing series of structured meetings through which members of management-level teams learn each others' needs and expectations, and how to work as a team. They require pre-meeting work by facilitators to gain information on the members and their units; this information is used for group problem-solving exercises during the meetings. The team develops objectives to improve its ability to function as a unit and works on those objectives after the meetings. Periodic team building meetings ensure that the members maintain their common focus and understanding.

Coopers & Lybrand uses team building for management teams, customer/vendor teams, and preparation for strategic planning sessions.

Guiding initial unit management team work

Unit management teams often need initial direction on what they are to do. This can be fleshing out the goals and objectives of the strategic plan, developing indicators for the plan, or working on assignments from higher level teams. This approach ensures that teams' initial work will be important. If you do not do this, they may wonder why you established the teams to begin with.

Initial unit management team meetings use facilitators to guide selection of methods and handle group dynamics. It is not a good idea to have a facilitator who comes from within a unit during the first year or so. Use one from the quality resource group or "borrow" one from another unit. Eventually, though, larger units must start using their own facilitators for all but their top management teams, which may wish to continue using "borrowed" facilitators.

Maintaining momentum

Unit management teams need constant reinforcement from superiors. Missed meetings or meaningless projects should not be tolerated. Your leaders must attend as many unit management team meetings as possible, and thoroughly review the results of these teams' efforts.

From time to time you will want to form other management teams to work on areas of special interest. Use the system for establishing issue management teams to do this.

Creating improvement teams

The composition and function of improvement teams are also covered in Chapter 6. Briefly, these teams:

•   Improve specific processes, functions, or groups of functions;

•   Can comprise managers, employees, and enterprise partners;

•   Operate under a purpose statement from a management team; and

•   Are disbanded once their management teams are satisfied with improvements made.

During the first two years it is better to have fewer well-run improvement teams than many that are poorly run.

Training for improvement teams

These teams receive "just in time" training from managers or first-line supervisors, helped by the quality resource group. The training covers the tools and procedures they will use for improvement. Short classroom sessions followed by on-the-job learning is best for these teams. Some teams will require special training in advanced TQM methods such as vendor partnerships, quality function deployment, and experimental design methods; arrangements for this are discussed in the institutionalization phase of this chapter.

Managing improvement teams in the first few years

Since TQM is new to both improvement team members and their managers, there may be confusion at first. These teams require extra attention during the first year or two of the TQM initiative, and somewhat more time to do their work than they will need in future years. New cross-functional teams may need to work with units that have not yet come on board, which can cause problems. You can prevent these with good advance work.

Also, in later years you will start routine collection of data needed for working on improvement opportunities. Your first teams will have to spend more time gathering these data. This will slow down their progress.

Self-managed teams

These teams are a major transformation in the organizations that use them. They operate best when preceded by all the activities discussed in this chapter. If you try to set up such teams throughout your organization immediately, you will face major disruptions.

Forming self-managed teams

Pilot project improvement teams are good candidates for your first self-managed teams. So are the improvement teams in the long-term track of implementation, and the same conditions and training apply to transforming them into self-managed teams.

Unit management teams must look for other opportunities to form self-managed teams, though. First, you must make sure that these management teams are qualified to handle self-managed teams. This means that they have met regularly, have used TQM tools and procedures well, and are practicing participative management. Second, the management teams need to plan an orderly system for making the transition, which includes change management planning. They must provide the training and support for the self-managed teams.

Restructuring caused by self-managed teams

Very often the forming of self-managed teams means that some lower-level managers and second- and third-level line supervisors will no longer have much responsibility. This is a critical point in the implementation process. It will call for strong leadership commitment to TQM, and for compassion. Your leaders must develop a system to help displaced managers and supervisors find new and meaningful positions, either inside or outside your organization. We discuss this later in the chapter (see "Displaced personnel").

Quality function deployment teams

As you recall from Chapter 5, quality function deployment is TQM's procedure for developing new products or services. QFD teams include representatives from all functions involved in how a product or service will be designed, produced, distributed, and maintained.

You should field some QFD teams during the first year of the initiative. You will be preventing future problems arising from poor product or service design.

Developing Quality Support Systems

The purposes of quality systems are to support:

*   The technical aspects of TQM,
*   The cultural transition, and
*   The alignment of organizational structure with the new management philosophy.

Each of the following activities and systems is designed to meet these purposes.

Performance information systems

Since TQM is a data-driven approach to management, you need quality data systems. These systems must be designed to feed information directly and quickly to those responsible for the day-to-day operation of individual processes. They must be designed to "roll up" this lower-level information into composite indicators for management review.

We discuss performance indicators at length in Chapter 4. During the first year of implementation, you can begin developing indicators at lower levels of your hierarchy as part of your improvement teams' work. Your first higher-level indicators should be for your vital issues. Developing these is a job for issue and unit management teams.

Statistical process control

The main purpose of performance indicators is to keep processes in control, so statistical process control (SPC) should play a heavy part in the system (see Chapter 5 for a discussion of SPC). Data systems should be capable of capturing appropriate data and generating control charts and other reports for employees, managers, and leaders.

At the process level, SPC data are captured and analyzed by employees and first-line supervisors. Very often they can do this with simple checklists and a pocket calculator. Now that personal computers are ubiquitous, you may wish to develop or buy software that will help process-level personnel use SPC.

Most SPC data stay at the process level. Management should be more concerned with ensuring that the data are routinely collected and used by employees than with the content of this raw information.

Therefore, as you deploy SPC among your processes, remember that you must train both employees *and* managers in how to use and interpret this method. Also, you must give employees the authority and means to act on the results of the data.

Development of the system

The degree of detail and the appropriate flows of information within a data system depend on the organization. There are two rules of thumb for determining this. First, the information the system gives to people working in a process must be sufficient for them to control it. Second, they must receive this information quickly enough to spot and solve problems early.

In a large and complex organization with many interrelated processes involving thousands of transactions a month, this may mean a sophisticated computerized system. Smaller organizations with lower transaction volumes may find simpler mini-computer and personal computer systems adequate.

Activity-based costing

Chapter 4 covers activity-based costing (ABC), which permits you to capture cost information at the activity or process level. You can begin to introduce ABC with individual improvement team projects, and gradually spread its use throughout your organization. Comptroller and accounting offices can contribute much to developing and managing an ABC system by beginning to work with managers to identify and control specific cost areas.

Cultural and structural effects of performance information

When people readily see how their processes perform, they shift their concerns from simply following procedures to investigating how to improve operations. When they can see the performance of adjacent processes, they become more concerned about being good customers and suppliers. Finally, they become more cost-conscious. These are cultural changes.

Good data make it possible for employees and line supervisors to control their processes, solve problems, and make improvements. They also give leaders the information they need to make decisions. This information permits a more decentralized structure, since many specialist and management functions once handled farther up the hierarchy can now take place at the process level.

Planning and design of performance measurement and ABC information systems

Development of TQM data systems should be a cross-functional team effort; it should not be assigned to the information resource management or accounting offices (though these offices can take the lead). This cross-functional approach ensures that the needs of all departments will be met. Outside consultants familiar with such systems can be helpful.

Suggestion programs

To summarize the discussion of suggestion programs in Chapter 8, at any given time most of your employees will not be working in teams. If you can encourage individuals or small groups to give you suggestions outside the formal team framework, you will greatly increase the number of improvements you can make. To give you a benchmark, the Coast Guard's "Idea Express" manual says that the average Japanese worker makes 24 suggestions a year.

During implementation you should revamp your suggestion program so that it starts yielding many times the number of improvement ideas you get now. We offer suggestions for this in Chapter 8, and summarize them here:

- Make the suggestion program proactive.
- Eliminate the paperwork.
- Give employees the resources to make suggestions.
- Break down fear of making suggestions.
- Act quickly on suggestions.
- Use meaningful non-monetary awards.
- Keep continuous improvement top-of-mind.

Personal performance appraisals and reward systems

As indicated in Chapter 10, most employee appraisal systems used in this country are not compatible with TQM. They foster unhealthy competition and poor morale. Also, they do not consider normal variation in performance, systems barriers to individual performance, and other factors. Current systems also do not permit you to make the best division of individual and group rewards.

Should you choose to revise your existing system, you can form a special team to address the issue. This approach has been used by several government organizations interviewed for this book. Team members may include compensation specialists, employees, managers, and union representatives. Very often you can avoid problems with civil service rules by making this a demonstration project.

Training and team support during implementation

During the first year of the initiative you probably will not have the in-house capability to train your personnel. Using outside consultants teamed with future in-house instructors and facilitators will help you develop this internal capacity more rapidly, as discussed later in this chapter.

Communication and promotion

Communicating about quality initiatives was discussed in Chapter 8. Methods range from in-house newsletters to awards ceremonies. As stated in that chapter, if your employees run your communication and promotion program, you will see excellent results. This does not require a special team. Instead, management teams and your TQM advocate and coordinator can solicit employee input and give workers the resources to do their own promotions and celebrations.

Remember, do not use banners and slogans. They are too much like previous quality and productivity campaigns, and they seldom motivate anyone.

Avoid surprises

Your plans for TQM implementation must be shared throughout the organization, so that people know what to expect. Because the support of middle managers is so crucial to TQM, they need to have this information before it reaches employees.

Use briefings, newsletters, and site tours to inform your customers and enterprise partners of your plans and progress. They may be inspired to imitate you.

Extending TQM to enterprise partners

Unless you involve your enterprise partners (other government agencies, distributors, and vendors) in TQM, you will eventually hit obstacles to improvement. Chapter 7 reports several ways in which governments are forging new relationships with their partners. During the implementation phase you will want to start doing this, also.

You need an internal team to explore strategies for extending quality to each category of enterprise partner. Set priorities: With whom will you work first? What will you work on? Most of the answers will be found in your strategic plan.

The first step is to start including partners in training and teamwork. The more you depend on a partner, the sooner you should do this. Start your new relationship with important partners with a team-building exercise such as that discussed earlier in this chapter.

You may wish to refrain for a while from requiring distributors and vendors to adopt TQM, to give you time to understand it first, yourself. You can do no greater harm than to send out a half-trained, inexperienced person or group to "teach" these enterprise partners TQM.

Displaced personnel

As noted earlier, TQM can cause temporary or permanent displacement of some people in your organization. This will happen gradually, but preparing for it will improve how you handle these situations and help minimize fear of unemployment resulting from improvements.

Here are two ways to handle this situation:

• Work with your civil service personnel office to develop a transition staffing system such as that used by the Navy's public works centers. The centers put displaced personnel in a transition staffing pool and assigned them work as needed. People could stay in the pool for up to a year, allowing them time to find new jobs inside or outside the centers. The centers gave them special training for their new work, or outplacement counseling and services. With normal attrition, this procedure ensured that almost all people in the staffing pool had new jobs within the year.

• Establish dual-track career systems for professionals, so that people can advance in pay grade without becoming managers. NASA's Lewis Research Center has been very successful with this approach.

These approaches do more than help displaced personnel. In an increasingly tight labor market, you may find it better to retain and retrain your managers and employees than to try to find replacements for them next year.

Organizational restructuring

As you progress through the implementation phase, it will become obvious that your organization eventually must restructure along different lines. One reason is the decentralization of authority and specialist functions to line divisions and self-managed teams that comes with TQM.

Letting decentralization or other restructuring occur "naturally" is a mistake. It must be accompanied by clear policy and sound business practices set forth by top leaders, and by performance measurement systems such as those discussed earlier.

Since the TQM organization is more horizontal due to decentralizing, it needs tighter linkage among all functions and processes in the organization. Trying to establish this linkage through coordinators or high-level management re-establishes vertical structure, so it is better to enable the different units to handle their own coordination. Using cross-functional teams helps to coordinate units without recourse to higher level control. Good advance design work through quality function deployment aligns processes' goals and objectives with those of customers.

This new structure requires an information system that allows the sharing of information that is now isolated in "information islands" throughout your organization. This includes information on strategic goals and objectives, schedules, supplies, product and service descriptions, the capacity of different processes, costs, and other vital data. To the extent possible, everyone should be able quickly and easily to access this information in a meaningful format. Advanced organizations often include their external customers and suppliers in this information loop.

Radically altering your structure during the first few years of your TQM initiative is a mistake. Wait until you have some experience, but when you do, do not hesitate to start the transformation. The traditional organizational hierarchy was built for many of the wrong reasons — it will get in the way of your progress.

Future Implementation Cycles

The implementation phase never really ends. You repeat it to take your organization to higher levels of excellence. These are some of the other innovations you may introduce, once you have your basic structure in place.

Flexible workforce

Coopers & Lybrand helps TQM clients design cross-training programs to create a more flexible workforce. A flexible workforce lets you respond to changes in labor needs without letting employees go or hiring temporaries. Also, self-managed teams frequently require cross-training so that members can do several types of tasks.

Cross-training is not easy when an organization uses dozens of job classifications negotiated with unions or dictated by civil service rules, but it can be done. One example is the multi-trade maintenance crews at the Navy's Public Works Centers, mentioned in Chapter 4. Other Navy installations have adopted this practice for skilled and semi-skilled workers.

Cycle-time reduction and flexible systems

In its simplest form, cycle-time reduction means reducing the time needed to produce a product or service — one outcome of your TQM process improvements. If you handle high volumes of different documents or manufacture a family of products, formal cycle-time reduction systems are worth investigating.

These are sometimes called "flexible systems" because they can handle a variety of products or documents, using the same equipment and personnel. Figure 11-6 contrasts these systems to traditional production methods.

Organizations that use these systems nearly always introduce them with TQM, because the work centers, or processes, operate best when controlled by the employees who run them.

Traditional Production	Flexible Production
Single-purpose work centers, long production runs	Multi-purpose work centers, short production runs
Single-skill employees	Multi-skilled employees
Long set-up times for changeovers	Short set-up times
Large inventories of input, work-in-progress, and output	Input delivered "just in time," and production and customer delivery done immediately
Coordination among different processes and functions	Alignment and synchronicity of different processes and functions

Figure 11-6
Traditional
Versus Flexible
Production

INSTITUTIONALIZATION

"[The employee] was puzzled when I asked about TQM. So I described teams, empowering workers, SPC, participative management, etc. He said, 'Oh, you're talking about the way we do things around here.'"

– Notes from an interview for
Excellence in Government

The objective of the institutionalization phase is to start making people forget the name "Total Quality Management." You want them to call it "the way we do things around here."

More technically, in this phase you will develop the internal capacity to run your TQM initiative and sustain your momentum.

Training

You will always need training and refresher courses in TQM. There are two steps to building the capacity to do this.

• *Temporarily increase the size of the quality resource group:* For the next several years you may have to continue using a sizable part-time quality resource staff. To do this, you need an internal "train the trainer" program. Combine the instructor and facilitator roles, as discussed in Chapter 6, and have well-rounded internal consultants instead. As noted earlier, these people are the "prototype models" of your future management style.

- *Replace the quality resource group with managers:* Next, begin to put your managers and supervisors through these courses. Add training and exercises in participative management, leadership, and change management. Eventually, most of the need for a quality resource group will fade as your managers routinely perform the group's functions. Monitor how your managers train and work with people, help them if they need it, and in every other way make this part of management's routine work.

Specialized training and refreshers

Some TQM topics require special training, such as experimental design and advanced statistical process control. If many of your personnel need this training, develop internal coursework for it. If not, arrange courses through a community college, send people to outside training, or use a private consultant.

Periodic refresher courses for managers and employees are a good idea. These may be as simple as "brown bag" lunches or as formal as structured courses. You also can hold refresher courses at an annual event such as the "QualityFest" used in Volusia County, Fla. (see Chapter 10).

Install a strong evaluation component in your training, and you will get the feedback necessary to improve it. Send selected managers to off-site seminars and conferences, and you will get new ideas for training.

Sustaining Momentum

You must build capacity to sustain the momentum of TQM; without momentum, it will die. You can use transition and magnet strategies to do this:

- Develop a "yes bias" for team improvement suggestions.

- Continue to emphasize the importance of the strategic plan, which drives the TQM initiative. This focuses people on the future and starts them to thinking about how they will achieve the plan's goals.

- Use symbolic decisions. A decision by your top leader to distribute all bonuses equally, or to throw out a set of unnecessary rules, reaffirms TQM (and will become part of your corporate culture in the form of "folk tales").

- Continue your communication effort. Share as much information about TQM as possible.

- Involve people in planning, carrying out, and evaluating improvements to the way you use TQM.

- Allow people to ventilate their feelings. Not everyone will respond to TQM positively. Chapter 9 shows a creative way to channel negative feelings into positive discussion.

- Reward people for participating in TQM teams and modeling TQM behavior. Start promoting managers who use TQM; others will get the message fast. Reward continuous improvement, not fire fighting.

- Give people what they need to do the job: training, resources, and the power to make changes.

Monitoring TQM

You need an excellent monitoring system to ensure that you are maintaining momentum in the right direction. For the next several years, this will be the job of your TQM advocate and, if you have formed one, the TQM issue team. The advocate needs to collect information on team meetings, progress in introducing support systems, complaints about the initiative, and other feedback. This must be done continuously; feedback on TQM should be on the agenda of every meeting of the executive steering committee.

WHERE DO YOU GO FROM HERE?

Go back to assessment and planning, introduce higher levels of TQM, and continue to build your capabilities. Never stop doing this, and you will always succeed: *quality is a journey, not a destination.*

Chapter

12

GOVERNMENT-WIDE APPROACHES TO PROMOTING QUALITY

■ The elements of successful TQM development for all units in a government are:

- Leadership by top elected and appointed officials
- Policies and broad guidelines that give units direction on developing their TQM initiatives
- A system of reporting agency progress to top elected or appointed officials
- Central support services for information sharing and technical assistance
- In large governments, allowing department and agency level units to develop their own TQM approach, subject to broad central guidelines

■ Government's role extends beyond introducing TQM to public services. It can help promote quality in industry and education.

"Continual improvement in government service would earn appreciation of the American public and would hold jobs in the service, and help industry to create more jobs."

— W. Edwards Deming, *Out of the Crisis*

So far this book has focused mostly on TQM at agencies or smaller units of government. This chapter looks at how entire governments at the local, state, and federal levels approach TQM development.

This is not confined to public service operations. As will be shown, they are promoting quality in all sectors of the economy. When they do, they enhance America's position in global competition and, as Deming says, help industry create more jobs.

THE EXISTING PATTERN OF GOVERNMENT-WIDE TQM DEVELOPMENT

At the start of the last chapter, Coopers & Lybrand identified five patterns of introducing TQM at the agency level. A larger pattern, that of an entire government, has also emerged: unit-by-unit development.

This pattern begins within one or a few cabinet-level departments, starting with an agency, bureau, or smaller unit. In the federal government, development may first occur at a large field site, independent of headquarters. This is usually not the planned expansion of TQM among different units, which is discussed in Chapter 11. Instead, each unit pursues a different approach to quality management. When a government recognizes the need for TQM throughout its units, it faces both benefits and problems from the unit-by-unit approach.

Benefit Of The Unit-By-Unit Approach

The benefit of this pattern is that it allows each large unit to develop an approach suitable for its needs. It also increases acceptance by unit managers and employees, who may like a "tailored" system that considers their perceived unique characteristics.

Problems With The Unit-By-Unit Approach

The downside of unit-by-unit development is that it leads to inconsistencies within a larger department, and within the government itself. Some units may practice TQM while others do not. If those that do lack a common "quality language" and style, this lack limits cross-functional and interagency teamwork.

The other problem is the quality of the quality initiatives themselves. Here, too, there are inconsistencies and unevenness that largely go unaddressed (or simply unnoticed) by higher authority.

In this situation, the failure rate for TQM initiatives can be high. One only has to look back on the failure of most quality circles and applications of statistical process control between 1980 and 1985 to see the evidence. Research for this book found several instances in which organizations were taking the same route to failure.

Solutions For Government-Wide Approaches

The solutions to the problems of inconsistency and unevenness include common approaches, reporting guidelines, and leadership by top elected and appointed officials.

Common approach

The government system of allowing units to develop independent approaches to TQM differs markedly from private industry. When a private corporation decides to adopt TQM, it does so with uniform policies and procedures. This is true for companies such as Corning, Xerox, Motorola, Boeing, and Ford, which have workforces comparable in size to all but the largest governments.

Most local governments, small state governments, and medium-sized departments probably should opt for a single approach to implementing TQM. This is a more easily managed system that should be suitable for all, if some modifications are allowed at the unit level. Larger governments may find it better to allow more flexibility, since their agencies tend to be more autonomous and independent; for them, guidelines can be a controlling mechanism in development.

Guidelines

A common set of policy guidelines or criteria would give direction to all of a government's TQM initiatives. These need to cover both the basic principles of TQM, and the way they are to be implemented. The guidelines should be broad enough to allow sound independent approaches. However, they also should have reporting requirements that will give higher authority an indication of progress and results.

Models for these guidelines include the Malcolm Baldrige National Quality Award, the federal Quality Improvement Prototype, or the President's Award for Quality and Productivity Improvement (see Chapter 11). Coopers & Lybrand leans toward the Baldrige award, because it is more comprehensive, but any good set of criteria will do. The key is that the criteria must be dynamic, because our nation's — indeed, the world's — understanding of quality management continues to grow.

The reporting aspect of this approach was rejected by the federal government early in 1990, based on recommendations by a panel of government and industry representatives. One reason was that the panel thought that agencies would treat the reporting as a paper exercise. Coopers & Lybrand respectfully differs with the opinion of the panel.

Yes, there is potential for reporting to become a paper exercise, and ample precedent for it in all governments and in industry, too. But without some form of reporting that measures progress, it is too easy for government units to sidestep their responsibilities. *What gets measured gets attention.*

The only way to make such a reporting system work is for elected and appointed officials to pay attention to the results and take action based on them. This brings up the issue of leadership.

Leadership

When a private company introduces TQM, the chief executive officer takes the lead. The CEO sets policy, participates in its enactment, and calls people to account for their progress and results. *This is usually not so in government.* Very few elected or appointed officials have come forward to champion quality management in their governments.

This lack of interest and commitment is distressing. Without top leadership, TQM will never succeed, because elected and appointed officials are the only people who can make the changes to government policy needed to clear away obstacles to quality progress.

What leaders can do to advance the cause of quality in government is the subject of the next chapter. Right now, let us look at what governments are doing to promote quality inside and outside government. Reviewing this information should be both informative and inspiring; it shows the critical role government can play in improving public service, education, and industry.

HOW FEDERAL, STATE AND LOCAL GOVERNMENTS INTRODUCE TQM

Federal Government

TQM is now being established as a successful way to run a federal organization. In Coopers & Lybrand's 1989 survey of federal executives, 66 percent report that their organizations have taken the first step toward introducing the new quality philosophy, and about 12 percent report taking all the steps needed in a comprehensive approach (see Appendix B).

The federal approach to promoting TQM includes policy, an information and technical assistance support structure, and awards for achievements.

Policy

The current federal mandate for TQM is Executive Order 12637, which establishes "...a government-wide program to improve the quality, timeliness, and efficiency of services provided by the federal government." By 1991, the order says, all executive branch agencies will have programs that improve quality and productivity. By early 1990, the Office of Management and Budget (OMB) reported 235 such initiatives, covering 830,000 of the federal government's 3,000,000 civilian employees, and many uniformed military personnel.

Support structure

The OMB is charged with providing central leadership, coordination, and technical assistance for the federal quality effort. The President's Council on Management Improvement (PCMI), composed of top administrative officials of the executive branch agencies, shares the lead responsibility with the OMB. The council makes recommendations, undertakes projects to define and promote effective methods, and co-sponsors other programs discussed below. The Office of Personnel Management participates by recommending changes to personnel policy to remove barriers to and promote quality practices.

The Federal Quality Institute (FQI) is at the information hub of the federal quality campaign. The FQI conducts TQM seminars to introduce federal executives to the philosophy and how to initiate it. The FQI maintains an information resource center and publishes handbooks on TQM (see Appendix A). FQI staff are forming networks of agency quality coordinators engaged in similar functions to promote communication on common issues and problems.

The OMB and PCMI also sponsor an annual conference on quality and productivity improvement, open only to federal employees. In 1990, a thousand government representatives attended.

Through a Federal Supply Schedule contract coordinated by the FQI, agencies can, with a simple purchase order, obtain the services of qualified private sector experts to help them implement TQM. State and local governments also can use the schedule.

Awards

The OMB and PCMI offer an annual Quality Improvement Prototype award for federal agencies. The winners prepare case studies and videotapes distributed through the FQI, and hold seminars for other agencies. The top prize is the President's Award for Quality and Productivity Improvement.

Where the federal program differs from traditional awards is the feedback loop on agency applications. As noted in the last chapter, each application is reviewed and returned to its agency with helpful suggestions on improving management practices. Just filling out the information needed to apply for the Quality Improvement Prototype or the President's Award is a good exercise in assessing an organization's "quality maturity."

Assessment of the federal approach

The federal system for promoting TQM is a good approach, in that it alleviates many problems faced by organizations just getting started with TQM. These include lack of information, initial guidance on implementation, examples of success, networks and feedback, and finding expert assistance. The progress of the federal TQM initiative is evidence that overcoming these obstacles should be a key goal of any government that wants to see success.

Where the federal effort is less than optimal is in its lack of strong support among elected and appointed officials. None of the highest elected leaders have emerged as TQM advocates (see Chapter 11) for the nation's government, and few top appointed officials in large departments are visibly active in supporting TQM. Only a handful of legislators know about the federal quality initiative, although Congress has held hearings on the subject.

This lack of leadership is reflected in Coopers & Lybrand's 1989 survey of federal executives. Half the civilian agency and one-third of the Defense Department survey respondents said their superiors (agency directors and cabinet-level appointees) did not communicate strong commitment to quality management. Until there is stronger top support, the federal initiative will not progress as quickly as it could, and it will be vulnerable to cutbacks or closure.

State Government

Leadership is not a problem in Wisconsin. The initiative started in 1986 as a grassroots effort among isolated state bureaus, then grew to include several large cabinet-level departments. Some early results were impressive. Using TQM, the Department of Revenue in 1989 was able to send refunds to 1.2 million taxpayers in two weeks rather than eight, which was usual before then.

Impressed by this and other successes, in 1989 Governor Tommy Thompson decided to make Wisconsin's commitment to quality formal. He set up an executive steering committee of five cabinet secretaries to promote and oversee development of TQM in state agencies; the committee started strategic planning in 1990. He also appointed a quality coordinator for the state government, and held a retreat to discuss TQM with his executives. He attends quality conferences and seminars, and promotes quality management for both the public and private sectors.

Elected officials' interest in quality is not limited to the governor. Wisconsin's state legislators voted to require government supervisors to receive TQM training, and they have shown bipartisan support for the quality initiative.

Support structure

Before 1989 support for the Wisconsin quality initiative came mainly from within each unit that was working to introduce TQM. The quality coordinators of these units developed an informal network to share information and engage in joint training. In 1990 the Department of Employee Relations set up an office to coordinate TQM training and technical assistance in the agencies. The network and the office work together to standardize training and materials. Like the federal government, this office is working on pre-qualifying outside TQM consultants.

Assessment of the Wisconsin approach

The state's quality coordinator makes this assessment: "We are still feeling our way toward a more common approach to TQM implementation in the state. We do not want to be rigid, though, and departments will continue to control how they develop their quality initiatives.

"I feel very good about the future, because what we've got here in Wisconsin is the ideal environment. The governor, the cabinet, key elements in both parties of the legislature, and the business community all support TQM. If we can keep this up for another four years or so, we will be at the point where quality management is a permanent part of state government."

Development in other states

Most of the action in other states is still confined to individual departments. One example is the Florida Department of Transportation, which began its journey to quality in the mid-1980s. As noted in Chapter 1, the FDOT estimates that its quality initiative saved the state about $28 million in 1989, and that the gains are growing.

The FDOT has top-level commitment from agency executives, and a headquarters quality office that helps its districts with training, communications, and technical assistance. A quality coordinator in each of seven districts provides local training and assistance to departments and improvement teams.

Teams are found in every function of the FDOT, from top-level policy makers to road crews. The department extends its teamwork to include outside organizations such as utility companies, whose cooperation is needed for maintenance. All units in the FDOT use the same basic TQM methods.

The Michigan Department of Commerce is typical of government agencies just starting out on the journey to quality. It has completed four pilot projects that demonstrate the benefits of TQM, and now is ready to expand the initiative. The pilots helped reduce time needed to process block grants and improved telephone services.

Other states whose departments are getting involved in TQM include Arizona, Arkansas, California, and Pennsylvania.

Local Government

The best estimate is that there are about 50 county and municipal quality initiatives in the United States. Many are among the most advanced TQM organizations in the country and have received national recognition. These include Ft. Collins, Colo., Madison, Wis., Phoenix, Ariz., Rocky Mount, N.C., and Volusia County, Fla.

Wilmington, N.C., is a model for this level of government. The city's initiative had its roots in an earlier quality circles program, which met with limited success. The city renewed the effort with a more comprehensive approach, which included a top leadership vision of excellence. That vision was translated into administrative policy for city government.

Wilmington's city executives, who oversee the initiative through a quality council, wrote a detailed implementation plan fleshed out by each department. Wilmington uses a quality coordinator to help departments in training and facilitating teams, and each department has its own team structure. The city applies TQM methods to both simple and complex issues, from selecting employee uniforms to planning ways to revitalize neighborhoods.

Assessment of local initiatives

Well-run local TQM efforts are probably the "hidden jewels" of the renaissance of American quality. They have managed to introduce TQM to nearly the full spectrum of public service functions. Few private companies face such a complex challenge, which comes very close to that of federal and state governments.

Because local governments have fewer resources, they have to work harder to acquire information, technical assistance, and basic support funds. The critical ingredient in their success is commitment from their elected mayors and top appointed executives. Although elected town or county council members support the quality initiatives, they appear to be less involved. Stronger participation by council members might speed progress and avoid potential cutbacks in funding for quality initiatives.

COOPERATION AMONG GOVERNMENT, INDUSTRY, AND EDUCATION

The most exciting aspect of TQM is the degree of interaction and cooperation among government, industry, and education. At first, this was confined to successful business leaders sharing their TQM experiences with government, and to research by academia. Now, all three sectors of the economy find they have a lot to learn from each other, and government is fast becoming a major influence on national quality.

Government As Catalyst For Quality

Americans require their governments to lead the way in promoting the welfare of the country. TQM is another opportunity to do so.

Promoting quality among vendors and distributors

The effect of government mandates that vendors and distributors use quality management (see Chapter 7) extends far beyond the immediate benefit of less costly, higher quality goods and services paid for with tax dollars. Most of the vendors also sell goods and services to the public. The distributors, which include other government agencies, education institutions, and non-profits, offer services not covered under the distribution arrangement. There is clear evidence that these vendors and distributors have started to apply quality management to all their goods and services. Citizens benefit, and America becomes that much stronger in global competition.

Rewarding excellence

Recognition of quality is another activity for governments. The Malcolm Baldrige National Quality Award is a good example of this. Authorized by President Reagan in 1987 and administered by the National Institute of Standards and Technology (a government agency), the award is part of a national campaign to improve the quality of goods and services in the private sector.

Chapter 11 gives an overview of the Baldrige award criteria, which cover all aspects of an organization's quality management. For private industry, these criteria represent a national consensus of what it takes to be both a world-class company and a good corporate citizen.

Says a Coopers & Lybrand consultant who recently sat on the board of examiners for the award, "The value to America of this award cannot be overestimated. Hundreds of companies go through the tough exercise of conducting a Baldrige self-assessment, where they review every aspect of how they work and decide what they must do to become a winner. And what is a winner? A company that will make more money and more jobs for Americans."

Many state and local governments have introduced similar awards for private companies, again with an emphasis on the application process, not on the prizes themselves. They recognize that their success in global competition requires promoting top-quality organizations at home.

Training industry in quality

California takes direct action to promote quality in its industries. The state channels a portion of unemployment taxes back to employers through employee training grants, including grants for TQM. Coopers & Lybrand provided TQM assistance to Aerojet, an aerospace company in the state, through such a grant.

Announcing an expansion of the program for 1991, Governor George Deukmejian said, "While California leads the nation in aerospace manufacturing, we cannot afford to lose any business to overseas firms, especially in the face of defense budget reductions." Translation: *TQM means that jobs stay in the state.*

California has allocated $2 million for this in 1991 for TQM and related methods of improving productivity. The state projects spending $20 million a year for the program in the future. If successful, this assistance will be extended to industries other than aerospace.

Educational Institutions

A few publicly supported colleges and universities have started adding courses on TQM and some TQM methods to their curricula. Several state universities and community colleges have set up centers that sponsor seminars and offer consulting services on TQM. California's TQM program for industry will operate through community colleges.

These early efforts are promising, but much more is needed from America's educators. An executive at the Air Force Electronic Systems Division says, "The TQM movement in the U.S. would spread faster and more effectively if academia will make it part of the business, engineering, public administration, and other appropriate school curricula. We have to catch people much earlier in their careers, and prepare them to be quality managers. Retraining them in quality is expensive for an organization."

Community colleges and adult education programs can be major training centers for area organizations. As America gears up its quality effort, the demand for workers and managers trained in TQM principles and methods will increase exponentially. Even high schools can join in; many do in Japan, where technical high schools produce entry-level workers already trained in quality practices.

Quality Coalitions

Perhaps the most promising development in the quality field is the local and state quality coalitions. Formed by government, industry, and education agencies, the coalitions provide forums for discussion of quality issues, networks for informal consultation, a method of sharing training costs, and, most of all, promotion of quality in all parts of the community. For example, in Erie, Pa., the chamber of commerce has 23 committees working on different aspects of community excellence, from health promotion and care to government. Other coalitions include the Philadelphia Area Council for Excellence, the Madison and Northeastern Wisconsin Area Quality Improvement Networks, several community coalitions in Arkansas, and state coalitions in Arizona, Ohio, and Wisconsin. Government membership is not confined to the state and local levels; many federal agencies belong to their local coalitions.

The coalition concept recognizes that success in world-class competition and in serving citizens at home requires cooperation among all sectors of the economy. Coalition members are quick to point out that their motives are selfish, not altruistic. Being a "total quality community" is *the* competitive advantage in keeping citizens employed, and in attracting more and better jobs.

LOOKING TOWARD THE FUTURE

The future of the quality movement in American government will be determined by three factors:

- *Leadership:* Stronger leadership by government officials will mean more and better progress.

- *Comprehensive development:* Success will require governments to implement comprehensive quality management. This means including all parts of TQM in development, and taking a planned approach to introducing TQM.

- *Partnership:* Government, industry, and education must form a quality partnership, both to accomplish their own missions and to extend quality management throughout all sectors of the economy.

The final chapter of this book outlines the high-level policy changes required to ensure America's success in achieving excellence in government.

Chapter

13

A QUALITY AGENDA FOR THE 1990s

■ Lack of leadership by elected and appointed officials is the major obstacle to progress in achieving excellence in government

■ These officials must take the following policy actions:

- Include indicators of customer satisfaction and cost of quality in agency performance measurement
- Introduce activity-based costing to agencies
- Decentralize authority to the lowest level, in keeping with sound business practice
- Retain and retrain civil servants displaced by progress
- Develop and enforce firm policy guidelines for quality among agencies, distributors, and vendors
- Provide for technical support of agency quality initiatives
- Promote partnership of government, industry, and education

Most of this book is addressed to the people in the trenches. Now, we want to talk to their bosses: elected and appointed officials. Governors, mayors, county managers, cabinet secretaries, and Mr. President — this chapter is for *you*.

Frankly, those of your employees who are struggling to introduce quality to government products and services are irritated with you. Few of you know anything about quality. Very few of you have stepped forward to champion this cause. Generally, you just pay lip service to it.

Oh, sure, you show up for awards ceremonies. Occasionally you make a speech or sign a proclamation about quality. But where are you when your employees, the public servants, struggle to improve? Have you made it easier for them to do this? Have you inspired them by example? Probably not.

Meanwhile, most governments face fiscal crises. Civil service morale is at an all-time low. Most citizens do not think the government organizations for which you are responsible do a competent job. Less than 10 percent of those citizens express great satisfaction with the products and services you are supposed to be delivering.

This is not your fault. You are saddled with decades of poor government management. You know that you are in a system that needs help — but this help has to come from you.

LEADERSHIP: THE MISSING INGREDIENT IN GOVERNMENT EXCELLENCE

Right now, excellence in government is missing the most important ingredient: leadership. Consider these points:

• 85 percent of senior business executives say that an actively involved top leadership is highly important to improving quality, according to a 1989 poll by the American Society for Quality Control and the Gallup organization.

• A 1989 study of 30 federal TQM initiatives showed that top management started or championed 83 percent of them.

• Every recognized expert in quality management says the same: top leadership commitment and support are essential to modern quality management.

You have two ways to show your leadership: policy and example. This chapter describes what you *must* do to ensure good policy and good leadership for excellence in government.

POLICIES THAT SUPPORT QUALITY

In the 1990s you can help ensure the success of the renaissance of American quality by enacting several policies that are the underpinnings of sound quality management. These include new policies on measurement and accounting, decentralization, cost cutting, and displaced government employees.

Measurement And Accounting

Existing government performance measurement and management/financial information systems are inadequate for the strong fact-based decision making needed in TQM.

Performance reporting

The most frequent measures of government performance (productivity and sticking to budgets and schedules) do not show how well services are delivered. They also do a poor job of evaluating efficiency.

You need two more measures of performance to guide agencies toward improvement and to keep informed of the agencies' progress:

Customer satisfaction

Government personnel cannot be the judges of how well their agencies are performing; their customers must do the measuring. External customers include taxpayers, service recipients, other organizations, and you. Right now, you often depend on individual complaints from citizens, lobbyists, or some scandal to keep you informed about quality.

Simply polling customers with general questions is not enough. Your government organizations need to determine customer expectations in advance — most do not do this. Making customer satisfaction a comparative measure requires agencies to think through what their customers want very carefully. Reporting against these expectations provides you with adequate information to judge performance.

Cost of quality

Cost of quality is the closest thing most public sector agencies have to industry's "bottom line" (see Chapter 1). An honest appraisal of the costs of prevention, inspection, internal and external failures, and waste gives you the best index of efficiency. Detailed back-up information will point precisely to areas of improvement. "Benchmarking" cost of quality indices against those of the best organizations gives needed comparison information. At the least, you should demand that your organizations compare their progress to initial baseline measures of their performance. By focusing on cost of quality and continuous improvement, your agencies will cut waste, not just jobs.

The absence of adequate reporting systems right now should not stop you from starting TQM in government. Developing these soon should be a key objective (see Chapter 4). Remember, what gets measured gets attention. *If you insist on customer satisfaction and cost of quality data, customers and the causes of poor quality will get attention.*

Management accounting

Ask yourself this: "Does the financial information from my agencies show me the true cost of products and services? Can I use it to guide quality improvement?" This is what your agencies say: "Our accounting system does not measure that sort of thing."

Traditional financial accounting and government fund accounting methods do not support making sound decisions about improvement, productivity, or efficiency. Activity-based costing, described in Chapter 4, does.

Why is this so critical? Increased automation has shifted costs from direct categories (where they are more easily traced) to indirect or overhead categories (where they are often lost). Overreliance on standard labor rates and other general guides has masked the true costs of doing government business.

Finally, the cost accounting function of government has become the reporter of yesterday's news instead of tomorrow's challenges and solutions.

During the 1990s, you must shift government accounting away from simply tracking appropriations and expenditures. The new focus must be on financial analysis systems that help line and staff managers identify the best mix of resources to do a task. You also must align accounting with the strategic goals of your agencies and your own goals for public service. Finally, accounting must be capable of delivering cost of quality information.

Decentralize Authority

A true TQM organization is decentralized. Decentralization gives people the power they need to improve processes, and it eliminates layers of bureaucracy.

Some may argue that centralization brings tighter control and economies of scale. In reality, planning and control from afar are root causes of the problems of traditional management. Any slight loss in productivity from farming out staff functions to the line, and headquarters work to the field, will be far outweighed by greater flexibility and increased line and field efficiency.

In the 1990s, decentralization argues for broad budget guidelines and management policy to agencies, programs, and field offices, instead of restrictive line item budgets and detailed instructions and rules. You need to lower authority levels to where they are commensurate with the responsibility for executing tasks.

The success of TQM in doing this will be directly measurable in the flattening of government hierarchical structure. It also will be measured in cubic feet: the mountains of rules and regulations you and your agency administrators use to micro-manage operations — *you will not need these any more.* Finally, success will be measured by savings and better services when local operations have charge of their improvement.

You will need modern management information systems and good performance measures to oversee and control local operations to the extent needed — after all, you are the boss. The systems discussed earlier in this chapter will give you that control.

Take Care Of Displaced Employees

The 1990s will be the decade of displacement. The reasons include changes in technology, the world situation, and effective use of quality management. Given a tightening market for labor, it is penny-wise and pound-foolish — not to mention disloyal — for you to dismiss dedicated public servants during short-term readjustments of the workforce.

To prevent waste of these human resources, you must develop transition staffing systems to shift workers into jobs where they are needed, without seniority "bumping" and other disruptions. Because this means more retraining, do not be so eager to cut sound training programs. You also must increase funding of job counseling and lengthen the time allowed for temporary assignments. Doing so will improve morale and preserve the most valuable resource you have: dedicated employees.

POLICIES FOR INTRODUCING TQM

Government needs to give its agencies clear direction. *This is your job.*

Officials Must Learn TQM

To start, you must first learn about quality management. This is no idle recommendation. You must be able to understand the quality revolution in this country, because it is how America will prosper in the 21st century. Ignorance means you will fail in your leadership role.

So read this book, or any of the others we list in Appendix A. Visit private and public organizations that practice quality management. Attend TQM awareness seminars offered by the Federal Quality Institute, your agencies, or other organizations. Have lunch with a quality expert. Learn to understand what your agencies mean when they talk about control charts, teamwork, and continuous improvement. And learn to lead by example.

Policy Guidelines

You need policies that show your agencies what you expect them to do, and you must demand that they report on their progress. Coopers & Lybrand suggests modeling these on the Malcolm Baldrige Award (see Chapters 11 and 12). The award's criteria are updated annually, and a great deal of background information on this program is available.

And think about this: more than 100,000 people and businesses have ordered Baldrige Award applications. When industry and government march to the beat of the same drummer, the effect on the nation will be tremendous.

Firm Leadership

You must be firm in your resolve to make quality first among equals in other issues. Your budget drafting and hearings must consider quality improvement as both method and goal. The single best practice you can adopt is to put quality on the agenda of nearly every meeting you call. The chief executive officers of Baldrige Award-winning companies do this; so do the directors of government organizations that practice TQM. Can you imagine the effect this would have on your agencies? When the bosses want to work on quality issues, so does everyone else.

Extending TQM Outside Government

No amount of internal improvement will fully compensate for poor quality among vendors and distributors. Government has the power to make sure these outside organizations join the journey to quality (see Chapter 7).

Vendor partnerships

Everyone agrees that procurement reform is a major government agenda item for the 1990s. TQM vendor partnership is a successful model for this kind of reform. It requires that vendors adopt TQM as a way of doing business, which saves money and increases the quality of their goods and services. In return, vendor partnership offers suppliers more security and lower costs of acquiring new business.

Vendor partnership will require changes in government procurement policy. These include a change from lowest price to best value consideration, longer-term contracts, and a shift from arms-length vendor relationships to partnerships. You must lead the way to these reforms, and back them firmly, because second-rate vendors will yell "unfair."

Vendor partnership works. Ask any of the major manufacturers that now use it. They will tell you that it is better to have a few good vendors than many that cannot guarantee quality.

Distributor partnerships

Major portions of government budgets go to distributors. These may be other governments or organizations such as charities, universities, and others that dispense or depend on public grants.

Governments already attach reporting, financial management, and other requirements to these funds. In the 1990s, it also must become standard operating procedure to require a distributor to adopt modern quality practices. This requirement will save taxpayer dollars and increase the quality of services to citizens.

Providing Technical Support For TQM

At this time there are few people in the United States who know how to introduce TQM and use its tools. As a result, many improvement efforts have started down the wrong road and seen limited success or failure.

You will need to support the development of effective training and technical assistance programs on introducing TQM (see Chapter 12). You can do this in several ways: help establish "TQM academies" for public managers, set up courses on TQM at area colleges, borrow experts from other governments through interagency transfer agreements, and use private consultants.

You also can create resource centers such as the Federal Quality Institute. These centers can develop materials, orientation, training, and technical assistance programs to agencies. They also give you more control over the content of information and assistance provided to agencies, vendors, and distributors; a clearinghouse for inquiries; and a technical focal point for agency quality resource groups.

Promoting Partnership Among Government, Industry, And Education

When government, industry, and education unite through quality coalitions (see Chapter 12), they accomplish two great things. First, the coalitions provide the nucleus of quality improvement in an area. Second, they send a clear message that quality is the way to success in all parts of the American economy. They are also a way to share the costs of training, materials, and technical assistance.

In the 1990s, federal, state, and local governments must support the formation of quality coalitions. Appendix A lists contact information for coalitions.

Avoiding Dollar-For-Dollar Budget Cuts

One difficulty in writing this book was that agencies interviewed were often reluctant to reveal how much money they have saved or will save as a result of improvements. They know that the mere mention of savings will cause top officials to cut their budgets — even before the savings occur.

This is no incentive for saving or improvement; the reward is worse than the punishment for not doing so. Punishment is often merely a matter of being lectured by irritated leaders and accepting the cost overrun money they reluctantly provide.

There have to be monetary rewards for quality. Foremost among these is a share in the benefits. You will be surprised by the enthusiasm of agency administrators if they can apply some of their savings to improvement or distribute at least part to employees through organization-wide bonuses or salary increases.

GET STARTED NOW

America stands at a crossroads. One road leads to second-class status in world leadership, cutting back valued government services, and mounting public debt. That is the "business as usual" road. The other leads to world pre-eminence, better service for citizens, and sound fiscal management. You have to make fundamental changes to travel that road.

Quality management gives you the framework, tools, and procedures to do this. But TQM takes at least three to five years to take hold in an organization, and that is only the first part of the never-ending journey to quality. If even one out of ten elected and appointed officials puts quality on the policy agenda this year, by the year 2000 we can have quality in all governments.

Why? Because those of you who take the lead will inspire your colleagues to imitate you. When leaders demand quality, it starts. When they support quality actions in their governments, quality happens. When they constantly pay attention to quality, they see continuous improvement.

Appendix A

TQM RESOURCES

READINGS IN QUALITY IMPROVEMENT

Books

The Deming Management Method, by Mary Walton. New York: Perigee, 1986. Excellent and highly readable overview of Deming's approach to quality. A good introduction to quality management. 262 pages. ISBN 0-399-55001-1.

The Deming Route to Quality and Productivity: Road Maps and Roadblocks, by William Scherkenbach. Washington, D.C.: CeePress (George Washington University), 1986. A shorter read than the Walton book, but not as rich in background. 156 pages. ISBN 0-941893-00-6

Juran on Leadership for Quality: An Executive Handbook, by J.M. Juran. New York: Free Press, 1989. This book covers the basic concepts of quality management from the perspective of top executives. Dr. Juran provides a fair amount of detail on the structure of quality management in an organization, and how top managers introduce and control quality improvement. 376 pages. ISBN 0-02-916681-0.

Juran's Quality Control Handbook, fourth edition, J.M. Juran, editor. New York: McGraw-Hill, 1988. Everything you could possibly want to know about quality is covered in this three-inch-thick handbook. Despite being more than 1,500 pages long, it abbreviates some information and refers readers to other sources (this goes to show that quality is a complex subject). This is a *reference* tool, good for a quality coordinator or TQM advocate. 1,536 pages. ISBN 0-07-033176-6.

Kaizen: The Key to Japan's Competitive Success, by Masaaki Imai. New York: Random House, 1986. This is the definitive work on continuous improvement. Examples in the book are from both Japanese and American companies. 259 pages. ISBN 0-394-55186-9

Quality by Design: Taguchi Methods and U.S. Industry, by Lance A. Ealey. Dearborn, Mich.: ASI Press, 1988. Ealey presents experimental design in the context of comprehensive quality management. Most of the technical information is in appendices. This is for the more advanced TQM organization. 333 pages. ISBN 0-941243-05-2.

Guide to Quality Control, second revised edition, by Kaoru Ishikawa. Tokyo: Asian Productivity Organization, 1986. Available through Quality Resources, One Water Street, White Plains, N.Y. 10601 (toll-free phone (800) 247-8519). Ishikawa wrote this book for quality circles and improvement teams. It is a how-to book that covers the basic tools of Total Quality Management: histograms, cause and effect diagrams, checksheets, pareto diagrams, control charts, etc. 226 pages. ISBN 92-833-1036-5.

Beyond the Bottom Line: Measuring World Class Performance, by Carol J. McNair, William Mosconi, and Thomas F. Norris. Homewood, Ill.: Dow Jones-Irwin, 1989. Part of the Coopers & Lybrand Performance Solutions Series, this book describes the role of accounting and financial analysis in increasing quality and productivity. 212 pages. ISBN 1-55623-194-6

Federal Total Quality Management Handbook, by the President's Council on Management Improvement in collaboration with the U.S. Office of Personnel Management, the Federal Quality Institute, and the Office of Management and Budget. As of May 1990, Parts 1 and 1A on getting started and Part 2 on criteria and scoring guidelines for the President's Award for Quality and Productivity Improvement were available. Future topics planned include: involving employees and unions; education and training; overview for the federal executive; assessing customer needs and measuring organizational performance; analytical tools and techniques; and overcoming barriers and maintaining TQM efforts. Available from the Federal Quality Institute, address listed below under "Resource Groups."

Quality Improvement Prototype Awards. These are case studies of 13 federal activities that received this award from 1988 through 1990. Available from the Federal Quality Institute.

Note: The Federal Quality Institute gives priority to federal requests for its materials, but is pleased to share single copies with state and local governments, subject to availability.

Malcolm Baldrige National Quality Award. To obtain a copy of the award criteria, write to Malcolm Baldrige Award, National Institute of Standards and Technology, Administration Building, Room A-537, Gaithersburg, Md. 20899, or call (301) 975-2036.

Periodicals

We have seen several new quality periodicals lately, but none has matched the usefulness of those listed below. Beware of the rash of high-priced quality newsletters on the market. We saw one 12-page monthly priced at $128 a year, and it was just a rehash of the information you found in this book — dribbled out very slowly.

Quality Progress, monthly publication of the American Society for Quality Control (ASQC), see address below under "Resource Groups." 12 issues/$40; free with membership in the society. Delivers good TQM information, with a few articles on government (mostly Department of Defense). Annual software issue lists programs useful in several TQM methodologies. All issues contain book reviews and listings of special-topic books.

Journal of Quality Technology, monthly publication of the American Society for Quality Control. 12 issues/$13. Strictly technical and statistical information; excellent for a statistician or an internal quantitative measures specialist.

Quality, monthly controlled circulation, from Hitchcock Publishing, 191 S. Gary Avenue, Carol Stream, Ill. 60188. 12 issues/$65, but free to subscribers who are actively involved in quality management. About 60 percent of the articles are about technical aspects of industrial quality control, but the magazine is making a transition to TQM coverage.

Resource Groups

The Federal Quality Institute
P.O. Box 99
441 F Street, NW
Washington, D.C. 20001
Phone: (202) 376-3747

The FQI is the information hub of the federal quality campaign. It provides the materials listed earlier in this appendix. As well, it maintains an information center and lists of other materials, films, and videotapes. The FQI conducts awareness training for senior federal executives and has set up networks of federal personnel working on TQM in specific functional areas. It coordinates a Federal Supply Schedule agreement that enables agencies to obtain materials and technical assistance from qualified private contractors. Agencies that use the Schedule can obtain these services without going through the full request for proposal process.

The American Society for Quality Control
310 West Wisconsin Avenue
Milwaukee, Wisc. 53203
Phone: (414) 272-8575

With about 75,000 members, the ASQC is the nation's largest organization devoted solely to quality, and is the leading promoter of modern quality management. The society has local chapters in all states and most large cities, and special sections that focus on particular industries or technical aspects of quality management and quality control; joining these groups is good networking. The $58 annual membership fee includes the monthly *Quality Progress* and discounts on the society's many books, reports, conferences, seminars, and courses. ASQC also offers certification in various specialty areas of quality management and control.

The Association for Quality and Participation
801-B West Eighth Street, Suite 501
Cincinnati, Ohio 45203
Phone: (513) 381-1959

Formerly the International Association of Quality Circles, this organization has always promoted a comprehensive approach to quality circle implementation. With a membership of 7,000, the association has state and local chapters in many places in the country. The $75 annual membership includes the periodical *Journal for Quality and Participation* and discounts on books, training material and aids, conferences, meetings, and courses.

National Public Sector Network
c/o Michael L. Williamson
97 Bascom
500 Lincoln Drive
University of Wisconsin
Madison, Wisc. 53706
Phone: (608) 263-5510 (M. Williamson)
    (608) 266-9037 (Tom Mosgaller)

Still in the early formative stage, this network is intended to help those in the public and non-profit sectors to have a ready resource for information about quality management efforts taking place anywhere in the nation. Federal organizations can link into this network through the Federal Quality Institute.

Community Quality Coalition
c/o Transformation of American Industry Project
Jackson Community College
2111 Emmons Road
Jackson, Mich. 49201
Phone: (517) 789-1627
FAX: (517) 789-1631

The Community Quality Coalition promotes the development and networking of state and local quality coalitions. It publishes a national directory of quality coalitions, information on forming these groups, and a newsletter entitled *Community Link*.

Appendix B

QUALITY IN THE FEDERAL GOVERNMENT: A SURVEY OF FEDERAL EXECUTIVES

A survey of federal executives shows widespread government acceptance for modern quality management, and plenty of action. Yet responses to the survey's questions warn of problems and missed opportunities for quality in government.

ABOUT THE SURVEY

In 1989 Coopers & Lybrand decided to find out what federal executives know and think about quality management; their current and planned actions; and the obstacles they foresee for its introduction in government. C&L commissioned Louis Harris and Associates to survey members of the Senior Executive Service, generals, and admirals about this. The survey was carried out by telephone from July 15 through October 11, 1989. The sample of 602 respondents can be projected at the 95% confidence level to the combined population of all Senior Executive Service members and to uniformed senior officers at the O7 level or higher.

The survey participants are senior managers and major program directors. As such, they are knowledgeable about high-level policy, but not so far removed from the "troops" to be unaware of day-to-day realities. Their responses are about the organizations they lead, which may range from small units of 50 or less to thousands of employees.

SURVEY RESULTS

Executive's Opinions On Federal Quality

Figure B-1 shows that most federal executives think their organizations do a good job satisfying internal and external customers. They feel they do best at ensuring the quality and reliability of their products and services, and worst in internal operational efficiency and reducing cost and waste.

However, the right-most column in Figure B-1 indicates that barely half measure customer satisfaction; about one-third (32%) have no plans to do this in the future, or are not sure. Those who measured customer satisfaction more often rated themselves excellent at it than those that did not (43% vs. 27%).

Figure B-1
What Executives Think of Their Organizations' Performance

Factor	Percent rating performance:				Percent that track or measure factor:
	Excellent	Pretty Good	Fair	Poor	
Quality and reliability of products & services	39	52	7	1	68
Satisfying internal & external customers	35	52	11	1	52
Internal efficiency & waste/cost reduction	26	55	17	2	68

Comment: What gets measured gets attention. Governments tend to measure productivity, but this in only part of the quality equation. To increase customer satisfaction, they must measure it.

Executives are somewhat familiar with quality management...

Three out of four (76%) executives said they are at least somewhat familiar with quality management, but 46% of defense and 69% of civilian agency executives feel they could know more. Most (59%) believed quality management is simply a new way of packaging tried-and-true management techniques.

Comment: The level of understanding of the executives should not be disturbing at this point, since the federal quality campaign is still in its infancy. A 1989 study of 30 of the more advanced federal quality initiatives showed they were, on average, 2.6 years old, versus 6.3 years for a comparison group of private industry.* What is encouraging is that the executives feel they need to know more.

...see support for the initiative by most others...

Nine out of 10 executives feel that quality management will be acceptable to their employees. As shown in Figure B-2, they believe almost all their superiors and their subordinate middle managers are at least somewhat supportive of the concept. But half (51%) of the civilian agency and one-third (36%) of the defense executives say their superiors (agency directors and cabinet-level appointees) are not communicating strong commitment.

Comment: The lower rating given to commitment by subordinate managers is realistic at this stage of federal quality campaign. Many middle managers in both government and industry initially see TQM as additional work at best, and a threat at worst. Training and leadership by example help to convert them. Yet all too many executives in the survey reported a lack of strong top leadership by their superiors. This is troubling.

Percent responding:	Very	Somewhat	Not Too/Not At All	Not Sure
Acceptable to employees	54	38	6	3
Commitment by managers	46	40	9	5
Commitment by superiors	54	33	10	3

Figure B-2
Perceived
Acceptance and
Support By
Others

...see moderate benefits of quality management...

Four out of five (80%) think quality management will be at least somewhat useful to their organizations, primarily in raising the quality of goods and services. Many say they already

* Johnson, Larry W., "The TQM coordinator as change agent in introducing Total Quality Management," Master's thesis, Naval Post Graduate School, San Diego, Ca., June, 1989.

have individual quality management policies in place (see Figure B-3). However, they expect only moderate benefits from these policies, particularly in managing costs. Reflecting a traditional view that technology is the best route to improvement, they feel automating labor-intensive operations will be more effective.

Figure B-3
Perceived
Benefits of
Quality
Management
Versus
Automation

Management Policy	Percent who have the policy	Percent of those who have such policies who think they will be "very successful" in:	
		Raising Quality	Managing Costs
Automating labor-intensive operations	87	56	44
Teamwork/participative management	81	48	28
Continuous improvement	69	34	23
Rationalizing/simplifying operations	68	34	37
Top management commitment to quality	66	36	26
Identifying customers and their expectations	64	37	21

Comment: The feeling that quality management will not be as effective in managing costs as in raising quality shows some confusion both as to the new definition of quality, and of the power of TQM to save money.

...and see some obstacles.

Half of the executives (49%) said that lack of dependable ways to measure quality is a major obstacle to implementing quality management. Other perceived obstacles include: a deeply ingrained sense of the way things have always been done (26%), cost of implementing quality management (23%), and lack of enthusiasm by employees for taking on new responsibilities (16%).

Comment: Like traditionally managed private industry, when government programs measure quality, they tend to focus on the goods and services produced. Shifting this focus to indicators of how processes are performing and how they meet customer expectations will help overcome the measurement obstacle. Careful and comprehensive implementation of quality management will solve the other problems.

Many formal quality initiatives are underway or planned...

Most comprehensive approaches to making quality management an organization-wide philosophy include the steps listed in Figure B-4. Two-thirds of executives reported having taken the initial step by fall 1989, which is to send individual managers to outside training. About one-third said they had started to implement fully the philosophy as a way of doing business in all functions; by 1991 many more plan to do this, bringing the total to 62%.

Step	Percent reporting step:		Percent of those who had completed a step that said it was at least somewhat successful
	Was Done By 1989	Will Be Done By 1991	
1) Outside training for individual managers	66	14	74
2) Top management vision of excellence	44	24	77
3) Quality council	38	17	75
4) Internal training programs for managers	50	21	79
5) Pilot projects	34	20	76
6) Full implementation	36	26	84

Figure B-4
Steps Taken
and Planned in
Implementing
Quality
Management

...have been successful...

The right-most column in Figure B-4 also shows that the great majority of executives whose organizations have taken these steps report the results to be at least "somewhat successful." In general, they were more likely to rate the advanced steps "very successful" than the initial steps.

...though many organizations are skipping steps along the way.

However, only one-third of the executives who said their organizations have started full implementation reported having done the previous five steps. This is also reflected in future plans, when 40% of "fully implemented" quality management efforts will have skipped previous steps.

Comment: Many federal organizations would do well to re-examine how they are introducing quality management. A well-orchestrated and comprehensive approach is best; leaving out important steps leads to failure.

About The Authors

David K. Carr, a partner in Coopers & Lybrand's Washington, DC Management Consulting Services office, has 15 years experience in working with federal, state, and local governments to improve quality and productivity. He is a former employee of a federal intelligence agency, and holds a bachelors degree and a masters degree in public administration from Pennsylvania State University. Mr. Carr lives in Herndon, Virginia.

Ian D. Littman, director of Coopers & Lybrand's federal TQM services, manages over 50 TQM projects in 30 public organizations. A former state and federal employee, he also has 14 years management consulting experience with governments at all levels. He holds a bachelors degree from Syracuse University and a masters degree in public administration from George Washington University. Mr. Littman lives in Kensington, Maryland.

About Coopers & Lybrand

Coopers & Lybrand is the largest provider of TQM implementation services to American government. One of the world's leading accounting, tax, and management consulting firms, Coopers & Lybrand provides solutions for business in a wide range of industries and federal, state, and local agencies. The firm offers its clients the expertise of more than 16,000 professionals in 98 U.S. cities and 50,000 people in 102 countries worldwide.

Index